INTRODUCTION TO CHRISTIANITY

INTRODUCTION TO CHRISTIANITY

by

JOSEPH RATZINGER

Translated by J. R. Foster

HERDER AND HERDER

1970
HERDER AND HERDER NEW YORK
232 Madison Avenue, New York, N.Y. 10016

This is a translation of Einführung in das Christentum
(*Kösel-Verlag, Munich, 1968*)

Nihil obstat: JOHN M. T. BARTON, S.T.D., L.S.S., Censor
Imprimatur: ✠ PATRICK CASEY, Vicar General
Westminster: 31 July 1969

Library of Congress Catalog Card Number: 71–105403
English translation © 1969 by Burns & Oates Ltd.
Manufactured in the United States

TO MY AUDIENCES
IN FREISING, BONN, MÜNSTER
AND TÜBINGEN

CONTENTS

7

PART TWO: JESUS CHRIST

PREFACE

THE question of the real content and meaning of the Christian faith is enveloped today in a greater fog of uncertainty than at almost any earlier period in history. Anyone who has watched the theological movement of the last decade and who is not one of those thoughtless people who always uncritically accept what is new as necessarily better might well feel reminded of the old story of "Lucky Jack". The lump of gold which was too heavy and troublesome for him he exchanged successively, so as to be more comfortable, for a horse, a cow, a goose, and a whetstone, which he finally threw into the water without losing much more; on the contrary, what he now gained in exchange, so he thought, was the precious gift of complete freedom. How long his intoxication lasted, how sombre the moment of awakening from the illusion of his supposed liberation, is left by the story, as is well known, to the imagination of the reader. The worried Christian of today is often bothered by questions like these: has our theology in the last few years not taken in many ways a similar path? Has it not gradually watered down the demands of faith, which had been found all too demanding, always only so little that nothing important seemed to be lost, yet always so much that it was soon possible to venture on the next step? And will poor Jack, the Christian who trustfully let himself be led from exchange to exchange, from interpretation to interpretation, not really soon hold in his hand, instead of the gold with which he began, only a whetstone which he can be confidently recommended to throw away?

To be sure, such questions are unfair if they are posed in too general terms. It is simply not correct to assert that "modern theology:" as a whole has taken a path of this sort. But it is just as undeniable that there is widespread support for a trend which does indeed lead from gold to whetstone. This trend cannot be countered, it is true, by merely sticking to the precious metal of the fixed formulas of days gone by, for then it remains just a lump of metal, a burden instead of something offering by virtue of its value the possibility of true freedom. This is where the present book comes in: its aim is to help understand faith afresh as something which makes possible true humanity in the world of today, to expound faith without changing it into the small coin of empty talk painfully labouring to hide a complete spiritual vacuum.

The book arose out of lectures which I gave at Tübingen in the summer term of 1967 for students from all faculties. It is an attempt to repeat, in the changed circumstances of our generation, what Karl Adam accomplished almost half a century ago at the same university in such a masterly fashion with his "Spirit of Catholicism". The language has been modified to suit publication in book form, but the structure and scope of the lectures have not been altered, and notes on sources have only been added in so far as it was desirable to name the tools which served directly in the preparation of the lectures.

The dedication of the book to my audiences at the various stages of my academic career is intended to express my gratitude for their questions and intellectual co-operation, which were certainly among the factors from which the enterprise grew. I should also like to thank in particular the publisher, Dr Heinrich Wild, but for whose patient yet unyielding insistence I would scarcely have plucked up the courage to venture on such a bold undertaking as any book of this sort is bound to be. Finally, I must thank all those who have taken so much trouble to help bring the work into existence.

Tübingen, Summer 1968   JOSEPH RATZINGER

INTRODUCTION

"I BELIEVE — AMEN"

Chapter I

BELIEF IN THE WORLD OF TODAY

1. DOUBT AND BELIEF – MAN'S SITUATION
BEFORE THE QUESTION OF GOD

ANYONE who tries today to talk about the question of Christian faith in the presence of people who are not thoroughly at home with ecclesiastical language and thought by calling or convention soon comes to sense the alien – and alienating – nature of such an enterprise. He will probably soon have the feeling that his position is only too well summed up in Kierkegaard's famous story of the clown and the burning village, a simile taken up again recently by Harvey Cox in his book *The Secular City*.[1] According to this story a travelling circus in Denmark had caught fire. The manager thereupon sent the clown, who was already dressed and made-up for the performance, into the neighbouring village to fetch help, especially as there was a danger that the fire would spread across the fields of dry stubble and engulf the village itself. The clown hurried into the village and requested the inhabitants to come as quickly as possible to the blazing circus and help to put the fire out. But the villagers took the clown's shouts simply for an excellent piece of advertising, meant to attract as many people as possible to the performance; they applauded the clown and laughed till they cried. The clown felt more like weeping than laughing; he tried in vain to get people to be serious, to make it clear to them that it was no trick but bitter earnest, that there really was a fire. His supplications only increased the laughter; people thought

[1] H. Cox, *The Secular City*, New York, 1965; London, Pelican Books, 1968, p. 256.

15

he was playing his part splendidly – until finally the fire did engulf the village, it was too late for help and both circus and village were burned to the ground.

Cox cites this story as an analogy of the theologian's position today and sees the theologian as the clown who cannot make people really listen to his message. In his medieval, or at any rate old-fashioned, clown's costume he is simply not taken seriously. Whatever he says, he is ticketed and classified, so to speak, by his role. Whatever he does in his attempts to demonstrate the seriousness of the position, people always know in advance that he is in fact just – a clown. They are already familiar with what he is talking about and know that he is just giving a performance which has little or nothing to do with reality. So they can listen to him quite happily without having to worry too seriously about what he is saying. This picture indubitably contains an element of truth in it; it reflects the oppressive reality in which theology and theological discussion are imprisoned today and their frustrating inability to break through accepted patterns of thought and speech and make people recognize the subject-matter of theology as a serious aspect of human life.

But perhaps our examination of conscience should go still deeper. Perhaps we should admit that this disturbing analogy, for all the thought-provoking truth contained in it, is still a simplification. For after all it makes it seem as if the clown, or in other words the theologian, is a man possessed of full knowledge who arrives with a perfectly clear message. The villagers to whom he hastens, in other words those outside the faith, are conversely the completely ignorant, who only have to be told something of which they are completely unaware; the clown then needs only to take off his costume and his make-up, and everything will be all right. But is it really quite such a simple matter as that? Need we only call on the *aggiornamento*, take off our make-up and don the mufti of a secular vocabulary or a demythologized Christianity in order to make everything all right? Is a change of intellectual costume sufficient to make people run cheerfully up and help to put out the fire which according to theology exists and is a danger to all of us? I may say that in fact the plain and unadorned theology in modern dress appearing in many places today makes this hope look rather naïve. It is certainly true that anyone who tries to preach the faith amid people involved in modern life and thought can really feel like a clown, or rather perhaps like someone who, rising from an ancient sarcophagus, walks into the midst of the world of today dressed and thinking in the ancient fashion and can neither understand nor be understood by this world of ours. Nevertheless, if he who seeks to preach the faith is sufficiently self-critical, he will soon notice that it is not only a question of form, of the kind of dress in which theology enters upon the scene. In the strangeness of theology's aims to the men of our time, he who takes his calling seriously will clearly recognize not only the difficulty of the task of interpretation but also the insecurity of his own faith, the oppressive power of unbelief in the midst of his own will to believe. Thus anyone today who makes an honest effort to give an account of the Christian faith to himself and to others must learn to see that he is not just someone in fancy dress who needs only to change his clothes in order to be able to impart his teaching successfully. Rather will he have to understand that his own situation is by no means so different from that of others as he may have thought at the start. He will become aware that on both sides the same forces are at work, if in different ways.

First of all, the believer is always threatened with the uncertainty which in moments of temptation can suddenly and unexpectedly cast a piercing light on the fragility of the whole that usually seems so self-evident to him. A few examples will help to make this clear. That lovable saint Teresa of Lisieux, who looks so naïve and unproblematical, had grown up in an atmosphere of complete religious security; her whole existence from beginning to end, and down to the smallest detail, was so completely moulded by the faith of the Church that the invisible world had become not just a part of her everyday life, but that life itself. It seemed to be an almost tangible reality that could not be removed by any amount of thinking. To her, "religion" really was a self-evident presupposition of her daily existence; she dealt with it as we deal with the concrete details of our lives. Yet this very saint, a person apparently cocooned in complete security, left behind her, from the last

weeks of her passion, shattering admissions which her horrified
sisters toned down in her literary remains and which have only
now come to light in the new verbatim editions. She says, for
example, "I am assailed by the worst temptations of atheism".
Everything has become questionable, everything is dark.[2] She
feels tempted to take only the sheer void for granted. In other
words, in what is apparently a flawlessly interlocking world
someone here suddenly catches a glimpse of the abyss lurking
– even for her – under the firm structure of the supporting con-
ventions. In a situation like this, what is in question is not the
sort of thing that one perhaps quarrels about otherwise – the
dogma of the Assumption, the proper use of confession – all
this becomes absolutely secondary. What is at stake is the whole
stucture; it is a question of all or nothing. That is the only
remaining alternative; nowhere does there seem anything to
cling to in this sudden fall. All that can be seen is the bottomless
depths of the void into which one is also staring.

Paul Claudel has depicted this situation in a most convincing
way in the great opening scene of the *Soulier de Satin*. A Jesuit
missionary, brother of Rodrigue, the hero of the play (a world-
ling and adventurer veering uncertainly between God and the
world), is shown as the survivor of a shipwreck. His ship has
been sunk by pirates, he himself has been lashed to a mast from
the sunken ship, and he is now drifting on this piece of wood
through the raging waters of the ocean.[3] The play opens with
his last monologue:

---

[2] Cf. the informative survey provided by *Herder Korrespondenz* 7 (1962/3),
pp. 561–565, under the title, "The genuine texts of St. Teresa of Lisieux"
(the quotations cited here occur there on p. 564). This survey is based
mainly on the article by M. Moére, "La table des pécheurs" in *Dieu vivant*,
No. 24, pp. 13–104. Morée refers particularly to the researches and editions
of A. Combes; cf. especially *Le problème de "l'Histoire d'une âme" et des œuvres
complètes de Ste Thérèse de Lisieux*, Paris 1950. Further literature: A. Combes,
"Theresia von Lisieux," in *Lexikon für Theologie und Kirche* (LThK), X,
pp. 102–104.

[3] This recalls in a striking way the text from Wisdom 10.4 which has become so important for early Christian theology of the cross: "Wisdom
saved the drowning world, steering on a paltry raft one innocent man to
safety". For the interpretation of this text in the theology of the Fathers, see
H. Rahner, *Symbole der Kirche*, Salzburg, 1964, pp. 504–547.

Lord, I thank thee for bending me down like this. It sometimes happened that I found thy commands laborious and my will at a loss and jibbing at thy dispensation. But now I could not be bound to thee more closely than I am, and however violently my limbs move they cannot get one inch away from thee. So I really am fastened to the cross, but the cross on which I hang is not fastened to anything else. It drifts on the sea.[4]

Fastened to the cross – with the cross fastened to nothing, drifting over the abyss. The situation of the contemporary believer could hardly be more accurately and impressively described. Only a loose plank bobbing over the void seems to hold him up, and it looks as if he must eventually sink. Only a loose plank connects him to God, though certainly it connects him inescapably and in the last analysis he knows that this wood is stronger than the void which seethes beneath him and which remains nevertheless the really threatening force in his day-to-day life.

This picture contains in addition yet another dimension, which indeed seems to me the really important thing about it. This shipwrecked Jesuit is not alone; in him there is a sort of advance reflection of the fate of his brother; the destiny of his brother is present in him, that brother who considers himself a non-believer, who has turned his back on God because he sees his business not as waiting, but as "possessing the attainable . . ., as though he could be anywhere else than where Thou art".

We do not need here to follow the intricacies of Claudel's conception, to see how he uses the interweaving lines of these two apparently antithetical destinies as guiding threads, up to the point when finally Rodrigue's fate touches that of his brother, in that the conqueror of the world ends up as a slave on a ship, a slave who must be glad when a ragged old nun with a rusty frying-pan takes him too with her as a worthless chattel. Instead, we can return without any more similes to our own situation and say: If on the one hand the believer can only perfect his faith on the ocean of nihilism, temptation and doubt, if he has been assigned the ocean of uncertainty as the only possible site for his faith, on the other the unbeliever is not to be understood undialectically as a mere man without faith. Just

[4] *Le Soulier de Satin*, Act I, Scene I.

as we have already recognized that the believer does not live immune to doubt but is always threatened by the plunge into the void, so now we can discern the entangled nature of human destinies and say that even the non-believer does not represent a rounded and closed existence. However vigorously he may assert that he is a pure positivist, who has long left behind him supernatural temptations and weaknesses, and now accepts only what is immediately certain, he will never be free of the secret uncertainty whether positivism really has the last word. Just as the believer is choked by the salt water of doubt constantly washed into his mouth by the ocean of uncertainty, so the non-believer is troubled by doubts about his unbelief, about the real totality of the world which he has made up his mind to explain as a self-contained whole. He can never be absolutely certain of the autonomy of what he has seen and interpreted as a whole; he remains threatened by the question whether belief is not after all the reality which it claims to be. Just as the believer knows himself to be constantly threatened by unbelief, which he must experience as a continual temptation, so for the un-believer faith remains a temptation and a threat to his apparently permanently closed world. In short, there is no escape from the dilemma of being a man. Anyone who makes up his mind to evade the uncertainty of belief will have to experience the uncertainty of unbelief, which can never finally eliminate for certain the possibility that belief may after all be the truth. It is not until belief is rejected that its unrejectability becomes evident.

It may be appropriate at this point to cite a Jewish story told by Martin Buber; it presents in concrete form the above-mentioned dilemma of being a man.

> An adherent of the Enlightenment [writes Buber], a very learned man, who had heard of the Rabbi of Berditchev, paid a visit to him in order to argue, as was his custom, with him too and to shatter his old-fashioned proofs of the truth of his faith. When he entered the Rabbi's room he found him walking up and down with a book in his hand, wrapped in thought. The Rabbi paid no attention to the new arrival. Suddenly he stopped, looked at him fleetingly and said, "But perhaps it is true after all". The scholar tried in vain to collect himself – his knees trembled, so terrible

was the Rabbi to behold and so terrible his simple utterance to hear. But Rabbi Levi Jizchak now turned to face him and spoke quite calmly: "My son, the great scholars of the Torah with whom you have argued wasted their words on you; as you departed you laughed at them. They were unable to lay God and his Kingdom on the table before you, and nor can I. But think, my son, perhaps it is true." The exponent of the Enlightenment opposed him with all his strength; but this terrible "perhaps" which echoed back at him time after time broke his resistance.[5]

Here we have, I believe – in however strange a guise – a very precise description of the situation of man confronted with the question of God. No one can lay God and his Kingdom on the table before another man; even the believer cannot do it for himself. But however strongly unbelief may feel itself thereby justified it cannot forget the eerie feeling induced by the words "Yet perhaps it is true". That "perhaps" is the unavoidable temptation which it cannot elude, the temptation in which it too, in the very act of rejection, has to experience the unrejectability of belief. In other words, both the believer and the unbeliever share, each in his own way, doubt *and* belief, if they do not hide away from themselves and from the truth of their being. Neither can quite escape either doubt or belief; for the one, faith is present *against* doubt, for the other *through* doubt and in the *form* of doubt. It is the basic pattern of man's destiny only to be allowed to find the finality of his existence in this unceasing rivalry between doubt and belief, temptation and certainty. Perhaps in precisely this way doubt, which saves both sides from being shut up in their own worlds, could become the avenue of communication. It prevents both from enjoying complete self-satisfaction; it opens up the believer to the doubter and the doubter to the believer; for one it is his share in the fate of the unbeliever, for the other the form in which belief remains nevertheless a challenge to him.

2. THE ORIGIN OF BELIEF – PROVISIONAL ATTEMPT AT A DEFINITION OF BELIEF

Even though what has been said has shown that the image of the incomprehensible clown and the unsuspecting villagers is

[5] M. Buber, *Works*, Vol. III, Munich–Heidelberg, 1963, p. 348.

inadequate to represent the interplay of belief and unbelief in the world of today, it cannot be denied that it does express one specific aspect of the problem of belief today. For the basic question in an Introduction to Christianity, which must try to elucidate what it means when a person says "I believe", poses itself to us in a quite definite temporal context. In view of our historical consciousness, which has become a part of our self-consciousness, of our basic understanding of the human situation, it can only be posed in the form, "What is the meaning and significance of the Christian profession 'I believe' *today*, in the context of our present existence and our present attitude to reality as a whole?"

And this brings us immediately to an analysis of the text which will provide the guiding thread of our whole investigation, namely the Apostles' Creed, which in origin is intended to be an "Introduction to Christianity" and a summary of its essential contents. This text begins symptomatically with the words "I believe". We shall not attempt at this point to expound this phrase by reference to its context, nor shall we ask what is signified by the fact that this basic assertion, "I believe", occurs in a well-stamped formula, in connection with a clearly-defined content and conditioned by a ritual context. It is true, of course, that both kinds of context, that of the ritual form and that of the defined context, help to mould the meaning of this little word *"Credo"*, just as *vice versa* the word *"Credo"* supports and moulds everything that follows and also the ritual framework. Nevertheless for the moment we must put aside both considerations in order to ask a more radical question and to ponder quite deeply what kind of attitude is implied if Christian existence expresses itself first and foremost in the word *"Credo"*, thus determining – what is by no means self-evident – that the kernel of Christianity shall be that it is a "belief". We generally assume rather unthinkingly that "religion"' and "belief" are always the same thing and that every religion can therefore just as well be described as a "belief". But this is true only to a limited extent; many of the other religions have other names for themselves and thus establish different centres of gravity. The Old Testament as a whole classified itself not as "belief" but as "law". It is primarily a way of life, in which, to be sure, the act of belief acquires by degrees more and more importance. Again, by *"religio"* Roman religious feeling understood in practice mainly the observance of certain ritual forms and customs. It was not crucial that there should be an act of faith in the supernatural; even the complete absence of such faith did not imply any disloyalty to this religion. As it was essentially a system of rites the crucial factor was the careful observance of these. We could go on like this through the whole history of religions, but enough has been said to make clear that it is by no means self-evident that the central expression of Christianity should be the word *"Credo"*, that the Christian should describe this attitude to reality as being that of "belief". But this only makes our question all the more urgent: what attitude is really signified by this word? And, further, how is it that it is becoming so difficult for our individual, personal "I" to enter into this "I believe"? How is it that again and again it seems almost impossible to us to identify our present-day egos – each of them inalterably separated from everyone else's – with that traditionally predetermined, ready coined "I believe"?

Let us have no illusions; entering into that "I" of the creed-formula, transforming that schematic "I" of the formula into the flesh and blood of the personal "I", was always an agitating affair, something that seemed plain impossible; often, instead of the scheme's being filled with flesh and blood, the "I" itself was transformed into a schema. And when today as believers in our age we hear it said, a little enviously perhaps, that in the Middle Ages everyone without exception in our lands was a believer, it is a good thing to cast a glance behind the scenes, as we can today, thanks to historical research. This will tell us that even in those days there was the great mass of fellow-travellers and a relatively small number of people who had really entered into the inner movement of belief. It will show us that for many belief was only a ready-made mode of life, by which for them the exciting adventure really signified by the word *"Credo"* was at least as much concealed as disclosed. This is simply because there is an infinite gulf between God and man; because man is so made that his eyes are only capable of seeing what is not God, and thus for man God is and always will be the essentially invisible, something lying outside his field of vision. God is essentially invisible – this fundamental assertion of biblical faith in God in its opposition to the visibility of the gods (in the plural) is at the same time, indeed primarily, an assertion about man: man is a seeing creature, whose living area seems to be marked off by the range of what he can see and grasp. But in this area of things that can be seen and grasped, the area which determines the living space of man, God does not occur and will never occur, however much the area may be extended. I believe it is important that in principle the Old Testament contains this assertion: God is not just he who at present lies in fact outside the field of vision but could be seen if it were possible to go further; no, he is the being who stands *essentially* outside it, however far our field of vision may be extended.

We now begin to discern a first vague outline of the attitude signified by the word *"Credo"*. It means that man does not regard seeing, hearing and touching as the totality of what concerns him, that he does not see the area of his world as marked off by what he can see and touch, but seeks a second mode of access to reality, a mode which he calls in fact belief, and in such a way that he finds in it the decisive enlargement of his whole view of the world. If this is so, then the little word *"Credo"* contains a basic option *vis-à-vis* reality as such; is signifies not the observation of this or that fact but a fundamental mode of behaviour towards being, towards existence, towards one's own sector of reality and towards reality as a whole. It signifies the deliberate view that what cannot be seen, what can in no wise move into the field of vision, is not unreal; that on the contrary what cannot be seen in fact represents true reality, the element that supports and makes possible all the rest of reality. And it signifies the view that this element which makes reality as a whole possible is also what grants man a truly human existence, what makes him possible as a human being existing in a human way. In other words, belief signifies the decision that at the very core of human existence there is a point which cannot be nourished and supported on the visible and tangible, which encounters and comes into contact with what cannot be seen and finds that it is a necessity for its own existence.

Such an attitude is certainly to be attained only by what the language of the Bible calls "reversal", "con-version". Man's natural centre of gravity draws him to the visible, to what he can take in his hand and hold as his own. He has to turn round inwardly in order to see how badly he is neglecting his own interests by letting himself be drawn along in this way by his natural centre of gravity. He must turn round to recognize how blind he is if he trusts only what he sees with his eyes. Without this change of direction, without this resistance to the natural centre of gravity, there can be no belief. Indeed belief *is* the con-version in which man discovers that he is following an illusion if he devotes himself only to the tangible. This is at the same time the fundamental reason why belief is not demonstrable: it is an about-turn; only he who turns about is receptive to it; and because our centre of gravity does not cease to incline us in another direction it remains a turn that is new every day; only in a life-long conversion can we become aware of what it means to say "I believe".

From this we can see that it is not just today, in the specific conditions of our modern situation, that belief or faith is problematical, indeed almost something that seems impossible, but that it has always meant a leap, a somewhat less obvious and less easily recognizable one perhaps, across an infinite gulf, a leap namely out of the tangible world that presses on man from every side. Belief has always had something of an adventurous break or leap about it, because in every age it represents the risky enterprise of accepting what plainly cannot be seen as the truly real and fundamental. Belief was never simply the attitude obviously corresponding to the whole slant of human life; it has always been a decision calling on the depths of existence, a decision that in every age demanded a turnabout by man that can only be achieved by an effort of will.

3. THE DILEMMA OF BELIEF IN THE WORLD OF TODAY

Once one has perceived the adventure essentially implicit in the whole attitude of belief, it is impossible to avoid a second consideration, namely that of the particular difficulty of believing which affects us today. On top of the gulf between "visible" and "invisible" there comes, to make things harder for us, the gulf between "then" and "now". The basic paradox already present in belief as such is rendered even more profound by the fact that belief appears on the scene in the garb of days gone by and indeed seems itself to be something old-fashioned, the mode of life and existence current a long time ago. All attempts at modernization, whether intellectual, academic "demythologization" or ecclesiastical, pragmatic "*aggiornamento*", do not alter this fact; on the contrary, they strengthen the suspicion that a convulsive effort is being made to proclaim as contemporary something that is really in fact a relic of days gone by. It is these attempts at modernization which first make us fully aware just how old-fashioned what we are being offered really is. Belief appears no longer as the bold but challenging leap out of the apparent all of our visible world and into the apparent void of the invisible and intangible, it looks much more like a demand to bind oneself to yesterday and to accept it as eternally valid. And who wants to do that in an age when the idea of "tradition" has been replaced by the idea of "progress"?

We touch here on a specific element in our present situation which is of some importance to our question. For intellectual circles in the past the concept "tradition" embraced a firm programme; it appeared as something protective on which man can rely; he could think himself safe and on the right lines if he could appeal to tradition. Today precisely the opposite feeling prevails: tradition appears as what has been laid aside, the merely out-of-date, whereas progress is regarded as the real promise of life, so that man feels at home not in the realm of tradition, of the past, but in the realm of progress and the future.[6] From this point of view, too, a belief that comes to

---

[6] A newspaper advertisement that I read recently seems to me to typify this attitude: "You do not want to buy tradition but rational progress." In this connection it is worth drawing attention to the curious fact that in its reflections on the concept of tradition Catholic theology has been tending more and more strongly for about a century quietly to equate tradition with progress and to re-interpret the idea of tradition into the idea of pro-

him under the label "tradition" must appear as something already superseded, which cannot disclose the proper sphere of his existence to a man who has recognized the future as his real obligation and opportunity. All this means that the primary stumbling-block to belief, the distance between the visible and the invisible, between God and Not-God, is concealed and barred off by the secondary stumbling-block of Then and Now, by the antithesis between tradition and progress, by the loyalty to yesterday which belief seems to include.

That neither the profound intellectualism of demythologization nor the pragmatism of the *aggiornamento* can supply a convincing solution certainly makes it clear that this distortion of the basic scandal of Christian belief is itself a very far-reaching affair which cannot be easily settled either by theories or action. Indeed in one sense it is only here that the peculiarity of the specifically *Christian* scandal becomes visible; I refer to what might be termed Christian positivism, the ineradicable positivity of Christianity. What I mean is this: Christian belief is not merely concerned, as one might at first suspect from all the talk of belief or faith, with the eternal, which as the "quite other" would remain completely outside the human world and time; on the contrary it is much more concerned with God *in* history, with God as man. By thus seeming to bridge the gulf between eternal and temporal, between visible and invisible, by making us meet God as a man, the eternal as the temporal, as one of us, it knows itself as revelation. Its claim to be revelation is indeed based on the fact that it has, so to speak, introduced the eternal into our world: "No one has ever seen God; the only Son, who is in the bosom of the Father, he has made him known" (John 1.18) – one could almost say, in reference to the Greek word, that it has become the "exegesis" of God for us.[7] But let us stick to the English word; the

---

gress, by understanding tradition not as the firmly fixed legacy of the earliest days but as the forward-striving force of the sense of faith. Cf. J. Ratzinger, "Tradition", in LThK, X, pp. 293–299; *Id.*, "Kommentar zur Offenbarungskonstitution", in LThK, Supplementary Vol. II, pp. 498ff. and 515–528.

[7] Θεὸν οὐδεὶς ἑώρακεν πώποτε· μονογενὴς θεὸς . . . ἐξηγήσατο.

original empowers us to take it quite literally: Jesus has really made God known, drawn him out of himself or, as the First Epistle of St John puts it even more drastically, made him manifest for us to look upon and touch, so that he whom no one has ever seen now stands open to our historical touch.[8]

At first glance this really seems to be the maximum degree of revelation, of the disclosure of God. The leap which previously led into the infinite seems to have been reduced to something on a human scale, in that we now need only take the few steps, as it were, to that person in Galilee in whom God himself comes to meet us. But things are curiously double-sided: what at first seems to be the most radical revelation and to a certain degree does indeed always remain revelation, *the* revelation, is at the same moment the cause of the most extreme obscurity and concealment. The very thing which at first seems to bring God quite close to us, so that we can touch him as a fellow man, follow his footsteps and measure them precisely, also became in a very profound sense the precondition for the "death of God" which henceforth puts an ineradicable stamp on the course of history and the human relationship with God. God has come so near to us that we can kill him and that he thereby, so it seems, ceases to be God for us. Thus today we stand somewhat baffled before this Christian "revelation" and wonder, especially when we compare it with the religiosity of Asia, whether it would not have been much simpler to believe in the Mysterious Eternal, entrusting ourselves to it in longing thought; whether God would not have done better, so to speak, to leave us at an infinite distance; whether it would not really be easier to ascend out of the world and hear the eternally unfathomable secret in quiet contemplation than to give oneself up to the positivism of belief in one single figure and to set the salvation of man and of the world on the pin-point, so to speak, of this one chance moment in history. Surely a God thus narrowed down to one point is bound to die definitively in a view of the world which remorselessly reduces man and his history to a tiny grain of dust in the cosmos, which can see itself as the centre of the universe only in the naïve years of its childhood and now, grown out of child-

[8] 1 John 1.1–3.

hood, ought finally to have the courage to awake from sleep,
rub its eyes, shake off that beautiful but foolish dream and
take its place unquestioningly in the huge context in which
our tiny lives have their proper function, lives which should
find new meaning precisely by accepting their diminutiveness?

It is only by putting the question in a pointed form like this
and so coming to see that behind the apparently secondary
stumbling-block of "then" and "now" lies the much deeper
difficulty of Christian "positivism", the "limitation" of God
to one point in history, that we can plumb the full depths of
the question of Christian belief as it must be answered today.
Can we still believe at all? Or rather – for the question must be
posed in a more radical fashion – is it still permissible to believe?
Have we not a duty to break with the dream and to face reality?
The Christian of today must ask himself this question; he is
not at liberty to remain satisfied with finding out that by all
kinds of twists and turns an interpretation of Christianity can
still be found which no longer offends anybody. When some
theologian explains that "the resurrection of the dead" simply
means that one must cheerfully set about the work of the future
afresh every day, offence is certainly avoided. But are we then
really still being honest? Is there not serious dishonesty in
seeking to maintain Christianity as a viable proposition by
such artifices of interpretation? Have we not much rather the
duty, when we feel forced to take refuge in solutions of this
sort, to admit that we have reached the end of the road? Are
we not then bound to emerge from the fog and to face straightforwardly the abiding reality? Let us be quite plain about it:
an "interpreted" Christianity of this kind that has lost all
contact with reality implies a lack of sincerity in dealing with
the questions of the non-Christian, whose "perhaps not"
should worry us as seriously as we want the Christian "perhaps"
to worry him.

If we try like this to accept the interrogation of the other
side as the everlasting self-questioning of our own being, which
cannot be reduced to a treatise and afterwards laid aside, then
on the other hand we shall have the right to observe that here a
counter-question arises. We are inclined today as a matter of
course to suppose that only what is palpably present, what is

"demonstrable", is truly real. But is it really permissible to do this? Should we not ask rather more carefully what "the real" actually is? Is it only the ascertained and ascertainable, or is ascertaining perhaps only one particular method of making contact with reality, one that can by no means comprehend the whole of reality and that even leads to falsification of the truth and of human existence if we assume that it is the only definitive method? By asking this question we are brought back once again to the dilemma of "then" and "now" and at any rate confronted with the specific problem of our "now". Let us try to discern its essential elements somewhat more clearly.

4. THE BOUNDARY OF THE MODERN UNDERSTANDING OF REALITY AND THE PLACE OF BELIEF

If by means of the historical knowledge we enjoy today we survey the road taken by the human spirit so far as it is visible to us, we shall observe that in the various periods of this spirit's development there are various different basic attitudes to reality – the magic, the metaphysical and finally today the scientific ("scientific" here being used in the sense in which we speak of the natural sciences). Each of these basic human orientations has to do in its own way with belief. None of them is equivalent to it, but none of them is simply neutral towards it either; each of them can help it and each of them can hinder it. Characteristic of our contemporary scientific attitude, which moulds, whether we like it or not, every single individual's feeling for life and shows us our place in reality, is the limitation to "phenomena", to what is evident and can be grasped. We have given up seeking the hidden "in-itselfness" of things and sounding the nature of being itself; such activities seem to us to be a fruitless enterprise; we have come to regard the depths of being as in the last analysis unfathomable. We have limited ourselves to our own perspective, to the visible in the widest sense, to what can be seized in our measuring grasp. The methodology of natural science is based on this restriction to phenomena. It suffices us. We can deal with it and thus create for ourselves a world in which we can live as men. As a result a new concept of truth and reality has gradually developed in modern thinking and living, a concept which holds sway, for the most part unconsciously, as the assumption on which we think and speak, and which can only be overcome if it too is exposed to the test of consciousness. At this point the function of non-scientific thinking becomes perceptible, that of considering the unconsidered and bringing the problems it raises before the gaze of consciousness.

(a) The first stage: The birth of the historical approach

If we try to understand how the attitude just described arose, we shall be able to distinguish, unless I am mistaken, two stages in the intellectual revolution. The first, for which the way was prepared by Descartes, attained its full development in Kant, and even before that, in a somewhat different intellectual context, in the Italian philosopher Giambattista Vico (1668–1744), who was almost certainly the first to formulate a completely new idea of truth and knowledge and who, in a piece of bold anticipation, coined the typical formula of the modern spirit when it comes to dealing with the question of truth and reality. Against the scholastic equation *"Verum est ens"* ("Being is truth") he advances his own formula, *"Verum quia factum"*. That is to say, all that we can truly know is what we have made ourselves. It seems to me that this formula denotes the real end of the old metaphysics and the beginning of the specifically modern attitude of mind. The revolutionary character of modern thinking in comparison with all that preceded it is here expressed with absolutely inimitable precision. For the ancient world and the Middle Ages, being itself is true, in other words apprehensible, because God, pure intellect, made it, and he made it by thinking it. To the creative original spirit, the Creator Spiritus, thinking and making are one and the same thing. His thinking is a creative process. Things are, because they are thought. In the ancient and medieval view all being is therefore what has been thought, the thought of the absolute spirit. Conversely, this means that since all being is thought, all being is meaningful, *"logos"*, truth.[9] It follows from this

---

[9] This statement is of course only fully true of Christian thinking, which with the idea of the *creatio ex nihilo* attributes to God the material too; for

traditional view that human thinking is the re-thinking of being itself, re-thinking of the thought which is being itself. Man can re-think the *logos*, the meaning of being, because his own *logos*, his own reason, is *logos* of the one *logos*, thought of the original thought, of the creative spirit that permeates and governs his being.

In contrast to this, from the point of view of the ancient world and the Middle Ages the work of man seems contingent and transitory. Being is thought and therefore thinkable, the object of thought and of knowledge, which strives after truth. The work of man on the other hand is a mixture of *logos* and the a-logical, something moreover that with the passage of time sinks away into the past. It does not admit of full comprehension for it is lacking in presence, the prerequisite for being looked at, and it is lacking in *logos*, in thoroughgoing meaningfulness. For this reason ancient and medieval philosophy took the view that knowledge of human things could only be *"techne"*, manual skill, but never real perception and hence never real knowledge. Therefore in the medieval university the *artes*, the arts, remained only the first step to real knowledge, which reflects on being itself. This standpoint is still clearly evident at the beginning of the modern era in Descartes, who expressly disputes history's claim to be knowledge. The historian, he says, who claims to be familiar with Roman history knows in the last analysis less about it than a cook in Rome did, and to understand Latin means no more than possessing the same ability as Cicero's maid. About a hundred years later Vico was to turn the Middle Ages' criterion of truth, redefined once again here in Descartes, on its head, thus giving expression to the fundamental revolution which marks the arrival of the modern spirit. This was the start of the attitude that introduces the "scientific" age, in which we are still living.[10]

Let us try to think about this a little further, since it is

the ancient world this remained the a-logical element, the universal matter alien to the divine, thus also marking the limit to which reality could be comprehended.

[10] For the historical background see the survey in K. Löwith, *Weltgeschichte und Heilsgeschehen*, 3rd ed., Stuttgart, 1953, pp. 109–128, and also N. Schiffer's book, *Anfragen der Physik an die Theologie*, Düsseldorf, 1968.

fundamental to our question. To Descartes the only thing that seems an absolute certainty is the purely formal intellectual certainty purged of the uncertainties of the factual. Nevertheless there are signs of the approach of the modern period in the fact that he models this intellectual certainty on mathematical certainty and elevates mathematics to the position of prototype of all rational thinking.[11] But whereas here the facts still have to be excluded if one desires certainty, Vico advances the diametrically opposite thesis. Following formally in Aristotle's footsteps, he asserts that real knowledge is the knowledge of causes. I am familiar with a thing if I know the cause of it; I understand something that has been proved if I know the proof. But from this old thought something completely new is deduced: if part of real knowledge is the knowledge of causes, then we can truly know only what we have made ourselves, for it is only ourselves that we are familiar with. This means that the old equation of truth and being is replaced by the new one of truth and factuality; all that can be known is the *"factum"*, that which we have made ourselves. It is not the task of the human mind– nor is it within its capacity – to think about being, but about the *factum*, what has been made, man's own particular world, for this is all we can truly understand. Man did not produce the cosmos and its bottommost depths remain opaque to him. Complete, demonstrable knowledge is attainable only within the bounds of mathematics and in the field of history, which is the realm of man's own activities and can therefore be known by him. In the midst of the sea of doubt which threatened to engulf man at the beginning of the modern period after the collapse of the old metaphysics, the *factum* was here discovered as the dry land on which man could try to build a new existence for himself. The dominance of the fact began, that is, man's complete devotion to his own work as the only certainty.

With this is connected that revaluation of all values which makes subsequent history really a "new" age as compared with the old one. History, previously despised and not regarded as a part of knowledge, now remained, alongside mathematics, the only true knowledge left. That which alone had hitherto seemed worthy of the free mind, thinking about the meaning of being

[11] N. Schiffers, *loc. cit.*

now seemed an idle and aimless enterprise offering no hope of attaining genuine knowledge. Thus mathematics and history now became the dominant disciplines; indeed, history devoured, so to speak, the whole world of learning and transformed it all fundamentally. Through Hegel, and in a different way through Comte, philosophy became a historical question, in which being itself is to be understood as a historical process. With F. C. Baur, theology turned into history and its path became that of rigorous historical research, which asks what happened in the past and thereby hopes to reach the bottom of the matter. With Marx, economics was given a historical slant. Indeed, even the natural sciences were affected by this general tendency towards history: with Darwin, the classification of living beings was understood as a history of life; the constancy of what stays as it was created was replaced by a line of descent in which all things came from one another and could be traced back to one another.[12] Thus the world finally appeared no longer as the firm housing of being but as a process whose continual expansion is the movement of being itself. This meant that henceforth the world was only knowable in so far as it was something made by man. In the last analysis man was no longer in a position to look out at himself except on the level of the fact, where he had to recognize himself as the chance product of age-old developments. This now produced a very curious situation. At the very moment when radical anthropocentrism set in and man could only know his own work, he had to learn to accept himself as merely a chance occurrence, just another "fact". Here too the heaven from which he seemed to come was torn down, so to speak, and he was left with just the earth and its facts in his hands – the earth in which he now sought with the spade to decipher the laborious history of his development.

(b) *The second stage: The turn towards technical thinking*

"*Verum quia factum*": this programme which directs man to history as the receptacle of truth could not suffice, it is true, in

[12] K. Löwith, *op. cit.*, p. 38. On the complete change in the middle of the nineteenth century, see also the informative investigation by J. Dormann, "War J. J. Bachofen Evolutionist?" in *Anthropos*, 60 (1965), pp. 1–48.

itself. It only became fully effective when it was allied to a second principle which, again a good hundred years later, Karl Marx formulated in his classical statement: "So far philosophers have contemplated the world; now they must set about changing it." With this the task of philosophy was once again fundamentally redefined. Translated into the language of the philosophical tradition this maxim meant that "*verum quia factum*" – what is knowable, tending towards truth, is what man has made and what he can now contemplate – was replaced by the new programme "*verum quia faciendum*" – the truth with which we are now concerned is feasibility. To put it again in another way: the truth with which man is concerned is neither the truth of being, nor even in the last resort that of his accomplished deeds, but the truth of changing the world, moulding the world – a truth centred on future and action.

"*Verum quia faciendum*" – this means that the dominance of the fact since the middle of the nineteenth century is being succeeded to an increasing degree by the dominance of the *faciendum*, of what can and must be done, and that consequently the dominance of history is being supplanted by that of "*techne*". For the further man advances along the new way of concentrating on the fact and seeking certainty in it, the more he also has to recognize that even the fact, his own work, largely eludes him. The verifiability for which the historian strives, and which appeared at first in the nineteenth century to be the great triumph of history as opposed to speculation, always retains something disputable about it, an element of reconstruction, of interpretation and ambiguity, so that as early as the beginning of this century history reached a crisis and the historical approach with its proud claim to knowledge became open to question. It grew clearer and clearer that there is no such thing as the pure fact and its unshakable certainty, that even the fact is subject to interpretation and the ambiguity which this implies. It became less and less possible for people not to admit to themselves that once again they did not hold in their hands the certainty that they had at first promised themselves when they turned away from speculation to investigation of the facts.

So the conviction was bound to spread more and more that

in the final analysis all that man could really know was what was repeatable, what he could put before his eyes at any time in an experiment. Everything that he can see only at second hand remains the past and, whatever proofs may be adduced, is not completely knowable. Thus the scientific method, which consists of a combination of mathematics (Descartes!) and devotion to the facts in the form of the repeatable experiment, appears to be the one real vehicle of reliable certainty. The combination of mathematical thinking and factual thinking has produced the science-orientated intellectual standpoint of modern man, which signifies devotion to reality in so far as it is capable of being shaped.[13] The fact has set free the *faciendum*, the "made" has set free the "makable", the repeatable, the provable, and only exists for the sake of the latter. It comes to the primacy of the "makable" over the "made", for in fact what can man do with what has merely existed in the past? He cannot find his real purpose in making himself into the museum attendant of his own past if he wants to master his own contemporary situation.

Like history before it, *techne* now ceases to be a subordinate, preliminary stage in the intellectual development of man, even if to a decidedly arts-oriented mentality it still retains a certain hint of barbarity. The structure of the general intellectual situation has been fundamentally altered: *techne* is no longer banished to the Lower Chamber of learning, or, to be more accurate, here too the Lower Chamber has become the decisive element in the constitution; in comparison with it the "Upper Chamber" now seems only a collection of aristocratic pensioners. *Techne* has become the real strength and obligation of man. What was previously at the bottom is now on top. Simultaneously the perspective is changing once again: at first, in ancient and medieval times, man had concentrated on the eternal, then, during the short-lived predominance of the historical approach, of the past; but now the *faciendum*, the "makable" aspect of things, directs his attention to the future of what he himself can create. If before, perhaps through the conclusions implicit in the doctrine of the origin of species, he

---

[13] Cf. H. Freyer, *Theorie des gegenwärtigen Zeitalters*, Stuttgart, 1958, especially pp. 15–78.

might have resignedly noted that so far as his past was concerned he was just earth, a mere chance development, if he was
disillusioned by such knowledge and felt degraded, he does not
need to be disturbed by this any longer, for now, wherever he
comes from, he can look his future in the eye with the determi-
nation to make himself into whatever he wishes; he does not need
to regard it as impossible to make himself into the God who now
stands at the end as *faciendum*, as something makable, not at the
beginning, as *logos*, meaning. This is already working itself out
concretely today in the form of the anthropological approach.
What already seems more important than the theory of evolution, which for practical purposes already lies behind us as
something self-evident, is cybernetics, the "planability" of the
newly to be created man, so that theologically, too, the manipulation of man by his own planning is beginning to represent a
more important problem than the question of man's past –
although the two questions cannot be separated from each other
and in their general tendency largely govern each other reciprocally: the reduction of man to a "fact" is the precondition
for understanding him as a *faciendum*, which is to be led out of
its own resources into a new future.

(c) The question of the place of belief

When the modern spirit took this second step, when it turned
to the idea of "makability", it simultaneously wrecked theology's
first attempt to come to terms with the new situation. For
theology had sought to meet the problem of the historical
approach, its reduction of truth to facts, by presenting belief
itself as history. At first sight it could be perfectly content with
this turn of events. After all, so far as its content is concerned
Christian belief is essentially centred on history; the statements
of the Bible are not metaphysical but factual in character. So
on the face of it, when the hour of metaphysics was succeeded
by that of history, theology could only agree; for this seemed
to mean at the same time that its own hour had at last struck.
Perhaps indeed it might even be permissible to put down this
whole new development as a product of its own point of
departure.

The progressive dethronement of history by *techne* has swiftly killed these hopes again. Instead another idea is now in the air – people feel tempted to shift belief away from the plane of the fact on to that of the *faciendum* and to expound it by means of a "political theology" as a medium for changing the world.[14] I think myself that this is only doing again in the present situation what "history of salvation" thinking attempted one-sidedly to do in the situation created by the historical approach. People see that the world of today is governed by the notion of the "makable" and respond by transposing belief itself to this plane. Now I should not want to dismiss these two attempts as senseless. That would certainly not be just to them. On the contrary, both bring to light essential factors that in other contexts had been more or less overlooked. Christian belief really is concerned with the *factum;* it lives in a specific way on the plane of history and it is no accident that history and the historical approach grew up precisely in the atmosphere of Christian belief. And indubitably belief also has something to do with changing the world, with shaping the world, with the protest against the lethargy of human institutions and of those who profit from them. Again, it is hardly an accident that the comprehension of the world as something to be "made" grew up in the atmosphere of the Christian-Jewish tradition and was conceived and formulated precisely in Marx out of the inspiration provided by it, if as an antithesis to it. To this extent it is indisputable that both approaches brought to light aspects of the real meaning of Christian belief that had previously remained only too well hidden. Christian belief has a decisive connection with the motivational forces of the modern age. It is in fact the great opportunity of our historical age that we can gain from it a completely new understanding of the position of faith between fact and *faciendum;* it is the task of theology to accept this challenge, to make use of this possibility, and to find and fill the blind spots of past periods.

[14] Symptomatic of this attitude is the book by H. Cox mentioned in footnote 1, and also the "theology of revolution" that has been coming into fashion recently; cf. T. Rendtorff – H. E. Tödt, *Theologie der Revolution, Analysen und Materialen*, Frankfurt, 1968. There is also a tendency in this direction in J. Moltmann, *Theologie der Hoffnung*, Munich, 1964, 5th ed., 1966, and in J. B. Metz, *Zur Theologie der Welt*, Mainz–Munich, 1968.

But it is just as wrong here to jump to conclusions as it is to pass swift judgment. When either of the two approaches described above is adopted exclusively and belief is consigned lock, stock and barrel to the plane of the fact or of "makability", in the end this only conceals what it really means when a man says *"Credo"* – "I believe". For when he says this he is not primarily enunciating a programme for changing the world nor simply attaching himself to a chain of historical events. By way of an attempt to shed some light on what really is involved I should like to suggest that the act of believing does not belong to the relationship "know-make", which is typical of the intellectual context of "makability" thinking, but is much better expressed in the quite different relationship "stand-understand". It seems to me that here we can discern two general conceptions and possibilities of human existence which, though not unconnected with each other, must nevertheless be distinguished from each other.

5. FAITH AS STANDING FIRM AND UNDERSTANDING

In contrasting the two pairs of concepts stand–understand and know–make I am playing on the meaning of a basic biblical statement – untranslatable in the last resort – about belief. Luther tried to capture the profundity of this statement's play on words when he coined the formula, "If you do not believe, then you do not abide". A more literal translation would be, "If you do not believe (if you do not *hold* firm to Yahweh), then you will have no *hold*" (Isaiah 7.9). The *one* root 'mn (Amen) embraces a variety of meanings whose interplay and differentiation go to make up the subtle grandeur of this sentence. It includes the meanings truth, firmness, firm ground, ground, and furthermore the meanings loyalty, to trust, entrust oneself, take one's stand on something, believe in something; thus faith in God appears as a holding on to God through which man gains a firm hold for his life. Faith is thereby defined as taking up a position, as taking a stand trustfully on the ground of the word of God. The Greek translation of the Old Testament (the so-called Septuagint) transferred the above-

mentioned sentence on to Greek soil not only linguistically but
also conceptually by formulating it as "If you do not believe,
then you do not understand either". It has often been said
that this translation is in itself a typical example of the process
of Hellenization, of the way in which the Septuagint is less
"biblical" than the Hebrew text. Belief, so it is said, became
intellectualized; instead of expressing the notion of standing on
the firm ground of the reliable word of God it is now linked
with understanding and reason and thus removed to a quite
different and completely inappropriate plane. There may be
some truth in this. Nevertheless, I think that on the whole the
essential meaning is preserved, even if the imagery is different.
Standing, as presented in the Hebrew as the content of belief,
certainly has something to do with understanding. We shall
have to think further about this in a moment. For the time being
we can simply take up the thread of our earlier reflections and
say that belief operates on a completely different plane from
that of making and "makability". Essentially, it is entrusting
oneself to that which has not been made by oneself and never
could be made, and which precisely in this way supports and
makes possible all our making. But this also means that on the
plane of practical knowledge, on the plane of *"verum quia
factum seu faciendum"*, it neither occurs nor ever could occur and
be discovered, and that any attempt to "lay it on the table",
to demonstrate it as one would a piece of practical knowledge,
is doomed to failure. It is not to be met in the context of this
kind of knowledge and anyone who nevertheless "lays it on the
table" has laid something false on the table. The penetrating
"perhaps" which belief whispers in man's ear in every place
and in every age does not point to any uncertainty *within* the
realm of practical knowledge; it simply queries the absoluteness
of this realm and relativizes it, reminding man that it is only
one plane of human existence and of existence in general, a
plane that can only have the character of something less than
final. In other words, we have now reached a point in our
reflections where it becomes evident that there are *two* basic
forms of human attitude or reaction to reality, one of which
cannot be traced back to the other because both operate on
completely different planes.

It is perhaps permissible here to draw attention to a distinction made by Martin Heidegger, who speaks of the duality of calculating and reflective thought. Both modes of thought are legitimate and necessary, but for this very reason neither can be absorbed in the other. There must therefore be both: calculating thought, which is concerned with "makability", and reflective thought, which is concerned with meaning. And one cannot deny that the Freiburg philosopher has a good deal of justification for expressing the fear that in an age in which calculating thought is celebrating the most amazing triumphs man is nevertheless threatened, perhaps more than ever before, by thoughtlessness, by the flight from thought. By thinking only of the practicable, of what can be made, he is in danger of forgetting to reflect on himself and on the meaning of his existence. Of course, this temptation is present in every age. Thus in the thirteenth century the great Franciscan theologian Bonaventure felt obliged to reproach his colleagues of the theological faculty at Paris with having learned how to measure the world but having forgotten how to measure themselves. Let us repeat the same thing once again in another form: belief in the sense intended by the Creed is not an incomplete kind of knowledge, an opinion that subsequently can or should be converted into practical knowledge. It is much rather an essentially different kind of intellectual attitude, which stands alongside practical knowledge as something independent and particular, and cannot be traced back to it or deduced from it. Belief does not belong to the realm of what can be, or has been made, but to the realm of basic questions which man cannot avoid answering and the answer to which can by its nature occur only in *one* form. This form we call belief. It seems to me essential that this should be seen quite clearly: every man must adopt some kind of attitude to the basic questions, and no man can do this in any other way but that of entertaining belief. There is a realm which allows no other answer but that of entertaining a belief, and no man can completely avoid this realm. Every man is bound to have some kind of "belief".

The most impressive attempt so far to incorporate the attitude of "belief" into the attitude of practical knowledge is to be found in Marxism. For here the *faciendum*, the self-created

future, simultaneously represents the purpose or meaning of
man, so that the bestowal of meaning, which in itself is accomplished or assumed in belief, seems to be transposed on to the
plane of what can be made. Thereby the logical outcome of
modern thinking is unquestionably reached: it looks as if a
successful effort has been made to absorb the meaning of man
completely into the practicable, to equate one with the other.
However, if one looks more closely it becomes clear that not
even Marxism has succeeded in squaring the circle. For not even
Marxism can turn the idea of the "makable" as the purpose of
life into something that can be known; it can only promise
that such is the case and leave the decision to belief. What makes
this Marxist belief so attractive today and so immediately
accessible is the impression it evokes of harmony with practical
knowledge.

Let us return after this little detour to ask once again and
more comprehensively: what is belief really? We can now reply
like this: it is a way of taking up a stand in the totality of reality,
a way that cannot be reduced to knowledge and is incommen-
surable by knowledge; it is the bestowal of meaning without
which the totality of man would remain homeless, on which
man's calculations and actions are based, and without which
in the last resort he could not calculate and act, because he can
only do this in the context of a meaning that bears him up. For
in fact man does not live on the bread of practicability alone;
he lives as *man* and, precisely in the intrinsically human part
of his being, on the word, on love, on meaning. Meaning is the
bread on which man, in the intrinsically human part of his
being, subsists. Without the word, without meaning, without
love he falls into the situation of no-longer-being-able-to-live,
even when earthly comfort is present in abundance. Everyone
knows how sharply this situation of "not being able to go on any
more" can arise in the midst of outward abundance. But meaning is not derived from knowledge. To try to manufacture it in
this way, that is, out of the provable knowledge of what can
be made, would resemble Baron Münchhausen's absurd attempt
to pull himself up out of the bog by his own hair. I believe that
the absurdity of this story mirrors very accurately the basic
situation of man. No one can pull himself up out of the bog

of uncertainty, of not-being-able-to-live, by his own exertions; nor can we pull ourselves up, as Descartes still thought we could, by a *"cogito ergo sum"*, by a series of intellectual deductions. Meaning that is self-made is in the last analysis no meaning. Meaning, that is, the ground on which our existence as a totality can stand and live, cannot be made but only received.

Thus starting from a completely general analysis of the basic attitude "belief" we have arrived directly at the Christian mode of belief. For to believe as a Christian means in fact entrusting oneself to the meaning which bears up me and the world; taking it as the firm ground on which I can stand fearlessly. Using rather more traditional language, we could say that to believe as a Christian means understanding our existence as answer to the word, the *logos*, that bears up and holds all things. It means affirming that the meaning which we do not make but can only receive is already granted to us, so that we have only to take it and entrust ourselves to it. Correspondingly, Christian belief is the option for the view that the receiving precedes the making – though this does not mean that making is reduced in value or proclaimed to be superfluous. It is only because we have received that we can also "make". And further: Christian belief – as we have already said – means opting for the view that what cannot be seen is more real than what can be seen. It is an avowal of the primacy of the invisible as the truly real, which bears us up and hence enables us to face the visible in a calm and relaxed way – knowing that we are responsible before the invisible as the true ground of all things. To that extent it is undeniable that Christian belief is a double affront to the attitude which the present world situation seems to force us to adopt. In the shape of positivism and phenomenalism it invites us to confine ourselves to the "visible", the "apparent", in the widest sense of the terms; to extend the basic attitude to which natural science is indebted for its successes to the totality of our relationship with reality. Again, in the shape of *techne* it calls upon us to rely on the "makable" and to expect to find in this the ground which bears us up. The primacy of the invisible over the visible and that of receiving over making run directly counter to this basic situation. No doubt that is why it is so difficult for us today to make the leap of entrusting ourselves to what cannot be seen. Yet the freedom of making, like that of enlisting the visible in our service by means of methodical investigation, is in the last analysis only made possible by the provisional character with which Christian belief invests both and by the superiority which it has thus revealed.

6. THE INTELLIGENCE OF FAITH

If one ponders all this, one will note how closely the first and last words of the Creed – "I believe" and "Amen" – chime in with one another, encircling the totality of individual assertions and thus providing the inner space for all that lies between. In the harmony of *"Credo"* and "Amen" the meaning of the whole becomes visible, the intellectual movement which it is all about. We noted earlier that the word "Amen" belongs in Hebrew to the root from which the word "belief" is also derived. Thus "Amen" simply says once again in its own way what belief means: the trustful placing of myself on a ground that bears me up, not because I have made it and checked it by my own calculations but, rather, precisely because I have not made it and cannot check it. It expresses the abandonment of oneself to what we can neither make nor need to make, to the ground of the world as meaning, which first of all discloses to me the freedom to make.

Yet what happens here is not a blind surrender to the irrational. On the contrary, it is a movement towards the *logos*, the *ratio*, towards meaning and so towards truth itself, for in the final analysis the ground on which man takes his stand cannot possibly be anything else but the truth revealing itself. At this point, where we might least expect it, we stumble yet again on one last antithesis between practical knowledge and belief. Practical knowledge must – as we have already seen – by its own intrinsic aim be positivistic; it must be confined to what is given and can be measured. But the consequence of this is that it no longer enquires after truth. It achieves its successes precisely by renouncing the quest for truth itself and by directing its attention to the "rightness", the "soundness" of the system whose hypothetical design must prove itself in the functioning of the experiment. In other words, practical knowledge does not enquire what things are like on their own and *in themselves*, but only whether they will function *for us*. The turn towards practical knowledge was accomplished precisely by no longer contemplating being in itself but only how it functioned with regard to our own work. This means that in the separation of the question of truth from being and in its shifting to the fact and the *faciendum* the very concept of truth was itself fundamentally altered. The notion of the truth of being in itself has been replaced by that of the utility of things for us, which is confirmed by the rightness of the results. What is pertinent and irrevocable about this is that only this rightness is vouchsafed to us as something that can be calculated; the truth of being itself eludes knowledge of the calculating variety.

The Christian attitude of belief is expressed in the little word "Amen", in which the meanings trust, entrust, fidelity, firmness, firm ground, stand, truth all interpenetrate each other; this means that the thing on which man can finally take his stand and which can give him meaning can only be truth itself. Thus the Christian act of faith intrinsically includes the conviction that the meaningful ground, the *logos*, on which we take our stand, precisely because it is meaning, is also truth.[15] Meaning or sense which was not truth would be non-sense. The indivisibility of meaning, ground and truth which is expressed both in the Hebrew word "Amen" and in the Greek *logos* at the same time proclaims a whole view of the world. The way – for us inimitable – in which words such as these embrace the indivisibility of meaning, ground and truth throws into relief the whole network of co-ordinates by which Christian faith surveys the world and takes up its position in relation to it. But this also means that in its original nature belief or faith is no blind collection of incomprehensible paradoxes. It means, furthermore, that it is nonsense to plead the "mystery", as people certainly do only too often, by way of an excuse for the failure of reason. If theology arrives at all kinds of absurdities

[15] The Greek word *logos* displays in its range of meanings a certain correspondence with the Hebrew root 'mn ("Amen"): word, meaning, intelligence, truth are all included in its semantic range.

and tries not only to excuse them, but even where possible to canonize them, by pointing to the mystery, then we are confronted with a misuse of the true idea of the "mystery", the purpose of which is not to destroy reason but rather to render belief possible *as* understanding. In other words, it is certainly true that belief or faith is not knowledge in the sense of practical knowledge and its particular kind of calculability. It can never become that, and in the last analysis it can only make itself ridiculous if it tries to adopt its methods. But the reverse is true too: calculable practical knowledge is limited by its very nature to the apparent, to what functions, and does not represent the way in which to find truth itself, which by its very method it has renounced. The tool with which man is equipped to deal with the truth of being is not *knowledge* but *understanding*: understanding of the meaning to which he has entrusted himself. And we must certainly add that "understanding" only reveals itself in "standing", not apart from it. One cannot occur without the other, for understanding means seizing and grasping as *meaning* the meaning which man has received as *ground*. I think this is the precise significance of what we mean by understanding: that we learn to grasp the ground on which we have taken our stand as meaning and truth; that we learn to perceive that *ground* represents *meaning*.

If this is so, understanding not only implies no contradiction with belief but represents its most intrinsic property. For knowledge of the functional aspect of the world, as procured for us so splendidly by present-day technical and scientific thinking, brings with it no understanding of the world and of being. Understanding grows only out of belief. That is why theology as the understanding, *logos*-like (=rational, understanding-through-reason) discussion of God is a fundamental task of Christian faith. This context is also the basis of the inalienable right of Greek thought to a place in Christianity. I am convinced that at bottom it was no mere accident that the Christian message, in the period when it was taking shape, first entered the Greek world and there merged with the enquiry into understanding, into truth.[16] Believing and under-

[16] In this connection one can point to the significant passage in Acts (16.6–10) in which the Holy Spirit forbids Paul "to speak the word in

standing belong together no less than believing and "standing", simply because standing and understanding are inseparable. To this extent the Greek translation of the sentence in Isaiah about believing and abiding reveals a dimension which is implicit in the biblical attitude itself if it is not to be degraded into fanaticism, sectarianism.

To be sure, it is a characteristic of understanding that it is continually outstripping our capacity to *apprehend* and reaching out to a recognition of the way in which we are comprehended. But if understanding is the apprehension of the way in which we are comprehended, then this means that we cannot yet comprehend the latter; it vouchsafes us meaning precisely because it comprehends *us*. In *this* sense we can rightly speak of the mystery as the ground which precedes us and always and ever outstrips us, which can never be caught up or overtaken. But precisely in being comprehended by the not yet apprehended understanding's responsibility is fulfilled, a responsibility without which belief would be undignified and bound in the end to destroy itself.

7. "I BELIEVE IN THEE"

In all that has been said so far the most fundamental feature of Christian faith or belief has still not been specified; namely, its personal character. Christian faith is more than the option in favour of a spiritual ground to the world; its central formula is not "I believe in something", but "I believe in Thee".[17] It is the encounter with the human being Jesus, and in this encounter it experiences the meaning of the world as a person. In Jesus' life from the Father, in the immediacy and closeness of

Asia" and the Spirit of Jesus does not allow him to go into Bithynia; and there is the vision with the Macedonian saying, "Come over to Macedonia and help us". This mysterious text might well represent something like a first attempt at a "theology of history", intended to underline the crossing of the Gospel to Europe, "to the Greeks", as a divinely arranged necessity. Cf. also on this E. Peterson, "Die Kirche", in *Theologische Traktata*, Munich, 1951, pp. 409–429.

[17] Cf. H. Fries, *Glauben-Wissen*, Berlin, 1960, especially pp. 84–95; J. Mouroux, *Ich glaube an dich*, Einsiedeln, 1951; C. Cirne-Lima, *Der personale Glaube*, Innsbruck, 1959.

his association with him in prayer and indeed face to face, he is God's witness, through whom the intangible has become tangible, the distant has drawn near. And further: he is not simply the witness whose evidence we trust when he tells us what he had seen in an existence which had really made the complete about-turn from a false concentration on the foreground of life to the depths of the whole truth; he is the presence of the eternal itself in this world. In his life, in the unconditional devotion of himself to men, the meaning of the world is present before us; it vouchsafes itself to us as love which loves even me and makes life worth living by this incomprehensible gift of a love free from any threat of fading away or any tinge of egoism. The meaning of the world is the "You", though only the one that is not itself an open question but the ground of all, needing itself no other ground.

Thus faith is the finding of a "You" that bears me up and amid all the unfulfilled – and in the last resort unfulfillable – hope of human encounters gives me the promise of an indestructible love which not only longs for eternity but guarantees it. Christian faith lives on the discovery that not only is there such a thing as objective meaning, but this meaning knows me and loves me, I can entrust myself to it like the child that knows all its questions answered in the "You" of its mother. Thus in the last analysis believing, trusting and loving are one, and all the theses round which belief revolves are only concrete expressions of the all-embracing about-turn, of the assertion "I believe in You" – of the discovery of God in the countenance of the man Jesus of Nazareth.

Of course, this does not do away with the need for reflection, as we have already seen earlier. "Are you really He?" This question was asked anxiously in a dark hour even by John the Baptist, the prophet who had directed his own disciples to the rabbi from Nazareth and recognized him as the greater, for whom he could only prepare the way. Are you really He? The believer will repeatedly experience the darkness in which the negation of unbelief surrounds him like a gloomy prison from which there is no escape, and the indifference of the world, which goes its way unchanged as if nothing had happened, seems only to mock his hope. We have to pose the question, "Are you really He", not only through honesty of thought and because of reason's responsibility but also in accordance with the intrinsic law of love, which wants to know more and more him to whom it has given its "Yes", so as to be able to love him more. Are you really He? In the last resort all the reflections contained in this book are subordinate to this question and thus revolve around the basic form of the confession: "I believe in You, Jesus of Nazareth, as the meaning (*logos*) of the world and of my life."

Chapter II

THE ECCLESIASTICAL FORM OF FAITH

1. INTRODUCTORY REMARKS ON THE HISTORY AND STRUCTURE OF THE APOSTLES' CREED[18]

ALL that we have said so far has done no more than attempt to answer the formal question what belief as such is and whereabouts in the world of modern thought it can find a position for itself and a function to perform. The deeper questions relating to its content thus necessarily remained open – with the whole problem perhaps looking only too pale and ill-defined. The answers can only be found by looking at the concrete shape of Christian belief, and this we now mean to consider, using the so-called Apostles' Creed as a guiding thread. It may be useful to preface the discussion with a few facts about the origin and structure of the Creed; these will at the same time throw some light on the legitimacy of the procedure. The basic form of our profession of faith took shape during the course of the second and third centuries in con-

---

[18] The standard work on this subject remains F. Kattenbusch, *Das Apostolische Symbol*, Vol. I, 1894, Vol. II, 1900 (unchanged reprint, Darmstadt, 1962; henceforth referred to as Kattenbusch). Other important books are: J. de Ghellinck, *Patristique et Moyen-âge*, Vol. I, Paris, 2nd ed., 1949; the survey by J. N. D. Kelly, *Early Christian Creeds*, London, 1950; and W. Trillhaas, *Das apostolische Glaubensbekenntnis, Geschichte, Text, Auslegung*, Witten, 1953. A short summary and further literature are to be found in the patrologies; for example, B. Altaner–A. Stuiber, *Patrologie*, Freiburg, 7th ed., 1966, pp. 85ff.; J. Quasten, *Patrology*, Vol. I, Utrecht, 1962, pp. 23–29; see also J. N. D. Kelly, "Apostolisches Glaubensbekenntnis", in LThK, pp. 760ff.

nection with the ceremony of baptism. So far as its place of origin is concerned, the text comes from the city of Rome; but its internal origin lies in worship; more precisely, in the conferring of baptism. This again was fundamentally based on the words of the risen Christ recorded in Matthew 28.19: "Go therefore and make disciples of all nations, baptizing them in the name of the Father and of the Son and of the Holy Spirit." In accordance with this injunction these questions are put to the person to be baptized: "Do you believe in God the Father Almighty? Do you believe in Jesus Christ, the Son of God . . .? Do you believe in the Holy Spirit . . .?"[19] The person being baptized replies to each of these three questions with the word *"Credo"* – I believe – and is then each time dipped in the water. Thus the oldest form of the confession of faith takes the shape of a tripartite dialogue, of question and answer, and is, moreover, embedded in the ceremony of baptism.

Probably in the course of the second century, and even more in the third, the originally quite simple tripartite formula, which simply uses the written text of Matthew 28, was expanded in the middle section, that is, the question about belief in Christ. Here after all the decisively Christian element was involved and it was felt necessary to give in the framework of this question a brief summary of what Christ means for the Christian; similarly, the third question, the profession of faith in the Holy Spirit, was further clarified and developed as a confession of faith in the present and future of the Christian attitude. Then in the fourth century we meet a continuous text detached from the question-and-answer plan; that it is still in Greek makes it probable that it dates originally from the third century, since by the fourth the final change to Latin even in the liturgy had been made in Rome. A Latin translation also appears very soon afterwards in the fourth century. Because of the special position acquired by the Church of Rome in relation to the whole of the West, the Roman baptismal profession (known as the *"Symbolum"*, symbol)

---

[19] Cf. for example the text of the *Sacramentarium Gelasianum* (ed. Wilson), p. 86, cited in Kattenbusch, II, p. 485, and especially the text in the *Traditio apostolica* of St Hippolytus (ed. Botte), Münster, 2nd ed., 1963, p. 484.

was quickly able to gain currency in the whole Latin-speaking area. It is true that in the process it underwent a series of small textual alterations, until finally Charlemagne secured the recognition of one form of the text throughout his empire, a form which – based on the old Roman text – had received its final shape in Gaul. This unified text was adopted in the city of Rome in the ninth century. From about the fifth century, possibly as early as the fourth, we come across the legend of the apostolic origin of this text. Very soon (probably still in the fifth century) this legend crystallized into the assumption that each of the twelve articles into which the whole was now divided had been contributed by one of the twelve apostles.

In the East this Roman symbol or creed remained unknown; it came as no small surprise to the Roman representatives at the ecumenical Council of Florence in the fifteenth century when they learned from the Greeks that the *Symbolum* presumed to stem from the apostles was not employed by them. The East had never developed a unified symbol of this sort because no individual Church there occupied a position comparable with that of Rome in the West – as the one "apostolic see" in the Western world. The East was always characterized by the variety of its symbols, which also deviate somewhat in theological type from the Roman symbol. The Roman creed (and with it the Western creed in general) is more concerned with the history of salvation and with Christology. It lingers, so to speak, on the positivistic side of the Christian story; it simply accepts the fact that to save us God became man; it does not seek to penetrate beyond this story to its causes and to its connection with the totality of being. The East, on the other hand, has always sought to see the Christian faith in a cosmic and metaphysical perspective, which is mirrored in professions of faith above all by the fact that Christology and belief in creation are related to each other and thus the uniqueness of the Christian story and the everlasting, all-embracing nature of the creation come into close association. We shall return later to discuss how today this enlarged perspective is at last beginning to gain currency in the Western consciousness as well, especially as a result of stimuli from the work of Teilhard de Chardin.

2. LIMITS AND MEANING OF THE TEXT

The rough sketch of the history of the Creed which I have just attempted possibly suggests a brief supplementary reflection. For this swift glance at the growth of the text is sufficient to show that this process of growth mirrors the whole tension of the first millennium of the Church's history, with all its splendour and misery. It seems to me that this too is a statement that has something to do with the question of Christian belief itself and makes its intellectual physiognomy perceptible. First, the Creed cuts right across all cleavages and tensions and expresses the common ground of belief in the Triune God. It is an answer to the challenge that went out from Jesus of Nazareth: "Make disciples of all nations and baptize them." It is a profession of faith in him as the nearness of God, in him as the true future of man. But it also expresses already the beginning of the fateful split between East and West. The special position which Rome acquired in the West as the administrative centre of apostolic tradition and the tension which consequently arose for the Church as a whole become visible in its growth. And finally in its present shape this text also expresses the politically inspired uniformity impressed on the Church in the West and thus the political alienation of belief, its utilization as a means to imperial unity. In using this text, which was promoted as the "Roman" one and in the process forced on Rome in this shape from outside, we find present in it the necessity for belief to break through the prison-bars of political aims and to assert its own independence. Thus the fate of this text demonstrates how the answer to the call from Galilee mingles, at the moment of its entry into history, with all the human circumstances of man: with the special interests of one region, with the estrangement of those called to unity among themselves, with the tricks of the powers of this world. I think it is important to see this, for this too is a part of faith as it exists in the world, namely that the bold leap into the infinite which it signifies can only take place on the petty scale of everything human; that here too, where man makes his greatest venture, so to speak, the leap over his own shadow to the meaning that bears him up, his action is not pure, noble greatness, but instead shows him up as a divided being pitiful in his greatness, yet still great while he is pitiful. Something absolutely central becomes visible here, namely that faith has to do, and must have to do, with forgiving; that it aims at leading man to recognize that he is a being that can only find itself in the reception and transmission of forgiveness, that needs forgiveness itself at its best and purest.

When one follows up in this way the traces left behind in the text of the Creed by man and his human attributes, the doubt may well arise whether it is right to use this text as a peg on which to hang the sort of introduction to the basic content of the Christian faith aimed at in this book. Is it not to be feared that by doing so we are already moving on hotly disputed territory? The question must be posed, but anyone who follows it up will nevertheless be able to confirm that in spite of its checkered history this Creed does represent at all decisive points an accurate echo of the ancient Church's faith, which for its part is, in its kernel, the true echo of the New Testament message. The differences between East and West of which we spoke just now are in fact differences of theological emphasis, not differences of creed. It remains true, of course, that in our attempt at understanding the Creed we must take care to keep referring the whole to the New Testament and to read and interpret it in the light of the aims of the latter.

3. CREED AND DOGMA

Yet another point must also be made. When we concern ourselves here with a text whose original setting was the ceremony of baptism, we meet at the same time the original meaning of "doctrine" and "creed" in Christianity, and with them also the meaning of what was later to be called "dogma". We saw earlier that the Creed is pronounced in the framework of baptism as the triple answer to the triple question, "Do you believe in God – in Christ – in the Holy Spirit?" We can now add that it thereby represents the positive corollary to the triple renunciation that precedes it: "I renounce the devil, his service and his work."[20]

[20] Hippolytus, *loc. cit.*, 46: *Renuntio tibi, Satana, et omni servitio tuo et omnibus operibus tuis.*

This means that faith is located in the act of conversion, in the shift of gravity from worship of the visible and practicable to trust in the invisible. The phrase "I believe" could here be literally translated by "I hand myself over to", "I assent to".[21] In the sense of the Creed, and by origin, faith is not a recitation of doctrines, an acceptance of theories about things of which in themselves one knows nothing and therefore asserts something all the louder; it signifies a movement of the human existence; to use Heidegger's language, one could say that it signifies an "about-turn" by the whole person which from then on constantly structures one's existence. In the procedure of the threefold renunciation and the threefold assent, linked as it is with the thrice-repeated death-symbol of drowning and the thrice-repeated symbolization of resurrection to new life, the true nature of faith or belief is clearly illustrated: it is a conversion, an about-turn, a shift of being.

In this process of turning about, as which faith must consequently be understood, the I and the We, the I and the You interact in a way which expresses a whole image of man. On the one side we have a highly personal process, whose inalienable individuality finds clear expression both in the triple "*I* believe" and in the triple "*I* renounce" which precedes it: it is *my* existence which must turn here, which is to *trans*form itself. But together with this extremely personal element we also find here that the decision of the I is made in answer to a question, in the interplay of "Do you believe?" and "I do believe!" This original form of the symbol, which consisted at first only of the two-in-oneness of question and answer, seems to me to be a very much more accurate expression of the structure of faith than the later simplified, collective "I"-form. If we wish to feel our way towards the fundamental nature of Christian faith it will be right to go back beyond the later, purely teaching texts and to regard this its first dialogue form as the most appropriate one ever created. This form is also more suited to its purpose than the We-type of creed which (unlike our I-creed) was developed in Christian Africa and then at the big Eastern Councils.[22] The latter kind represents a new type

---

[21] Kattenbusch, II, p. 503.

[22] Cf. A. Hahn, *Bibliothek der Symbole und Glaubensregeln der Alten Kirche*, 3rd

of creed, no longer rooted in the sacramental context of the ecclesiastical ceremony of conversion, in the execution of the about-turn, and thus in the real birthplace of faith, but proceeding from the striving of the bishops assembled at the Council for the right doctrine and thus clearly becoming the first step towards the future form of dogma. All the same, it is important that these councils did not get to the point of formulating rules; their striving for the right doctrine still takes the form of striving for a perfect ecclesiastical profession of faith and thus of striving for the true mode of that conversion, that about-turn, which being a Christian implies.

This could be clearly demonstrated from the dramatic struggle over the question, "Who is, who was Christ?" which shook the Church in the fourth and fifth centuries. This striving was not concerned with metaphysical speculations; such things could not have shaken those two centuries down to their very foundations and down to the simplest people living in them. On the contrary, the question at issue was this: What happens when I myself become a Christian, when I enroll myself under the banner of this Christ and thereby accept him as the authoritative man, as the measure of humanity? What kind of shift in being do I thus accomplish, what attitude to the business of being a man do I adopt? How deep does this process go? What estimate of reality as a whole does it involve?

4. THE CREED AS EXPRESSION OF THE STRUCTURE OF FAITH

To conclude these reflections let us finally draw attention to two factors which also emerge from the text and history of the Symbolum.

(a) Faith and word

The Creed is a formula that forms the residue of the original dialogue "Do you believe – I do believe". This dialogue refers for its part to a "We believe" in which the "I" of the "I believe"

---

ed., 1897; new impr., Hildesheim, 1962; G. L. Dosetti, *Il simbolo di Nicea e di Constantinopoli*, Rome, 1967.

is not absorbed but allotted its place. Thus in the prehistory of this confession and in its original form the whole anthropological shape of belief is present as well. It becomes evident that belief is not the result of lonely meditation in which the "I", freed from all ties and reflecting alone on the truth, thinks something out for itself; on the contrary, it is the result of a dialogue, the expression of a hearing, receiving and answering which guides man through the exchanges of "I" and "You" to the "We" of those who all believe in the same way.

"Faith comes from what is heard", says St Paul (Rom. 10.17). This might seem like a very transient factor, which can change; one might be tempted to see in it purely and simply the result of one particular sociological situation, so that one day it would be right to say instead, "Faith comes from reading" or "from reflection". In reality it must be stated that we have here much more than the reflection of a historical period now past. The assertion "faith comes from what is heard" contains an abiding structural truth about what happens here. It illuminates the fundamental differences between faith and mere philosophy, a difference which does not prevent faith, in its core, from setting the philosophical search for truth in motion again. One could say epigrammatically that faith does in fact come from "hearing", not – like philosophy – from "reflection". Its nature lies in the fact that it is not the thinking-out of something which can be thought out and which at the end of the process is then at my disposal as the result of my thought. On the contrary, it is characteristic of faith that it comes from hearing, that it is the reception of something that I have not thought out, so that in the last analysis thinking in the context of faith is always a thinking-over of something previously heard and received.

In other words, in faith the word takes precedence over the thought, a precedence which differentiates it structurally from the architecture of philosophy. In philosophy the thought precedes the word; it is after all a product of the reflection which one *then* tries to put into words; the words always remain secondary to the thought and thus in the last resort can always be replaced by other words. Faith on the other hand comes to man from outside, and this very fact is fundamental to it. It is –

let me repeat – not something thought up by myself; it is something said to me, which hits me as something which has not been thought out and could not be thought out, and lays an obligation on me. This double structure of "Do you believe? – I do believe!", this form of the call from outside and the reply to it, is fundamental to it. It is therefore not at all abnormal if, with very few exceptions, we have to say: I did not come to believe through the private search for truth but through a process of reception that had, so to speak, already forestalled me. Faith cannot and should not be a mere product of reflection. The idea that faith really ought to arise through our thinking it up for ourselves and finding it in the process of a purely private search for truth is basically the expression of a definite ideal, an attitude of mind which fails to recognize the intrinsic quality of belief, which consists precisely in being the reception of what cannot be thought out – responsible reception, it is true, in which what is learnt never becomes entirely my own property, and the lead held by what is received can never be completely wiped out, but in which the goal must be to make what is received more and more by own, by handing myself over to it as the greater.

Because of this, because faith is not something thought up by me but something that comes to me from outside, its word cannot be treated and exchanged as I please; it is always fore-ordained, always ahead of my thinking. The positivity of what comes towards me from outside myself, opening up to me what I cannot give myself, typifies the process of belief or faith. Therefore here the fore-given word takes precedence over the thought, so that it is not the thought that creates its own words but the given word that points the way to the thinking that understands. With this primacy of the word and the "positivity" of belief apparent in it goes the social character of belief, which signifies a second difference from the essentially individualistic structure of philosophical thinking. Philosophy is by its nature the work of the solitary individual, who ponders as an individual on truth. A thought, what has been thought out, is something that at any rate seems to belong to me myself, since it comes from me, although no one's thinking is self-supporting; consciously or unconsciously it is intertwined with many other strands. The place where a thought is perfected is the interior of the mind; thus at first it remains confined to me and has an individualistic structure. It only becomes communicable later, when it is put into words, which usually make it only approximately comprehensible to others. In contrast to this the primary factor for belief is, as we have seen, the proclaimed word. While a thought is interior, purely intellectual, the word represents the element that unites us with others. It is the way in which intellectual communication takes place, the form in which the mind is, as it were, human, that is, corporeal and social. This primacy of the word means that faith is focused on community of mind in a quite different way from philosophical thinking. In philosophy, what comes first is the private search for truth, which then, secondarily, seeks and finds travelling companions. Faith, on the other hand, is first of all a call to community, to unity of mind through the unity of the word. Indeed, its significance is, *a priori*, an essentially social one: it aims at establishing unity of mind through the unity of the word. Only secondarily will it then open the way for each individual's private venture in search of truth.

If in the dialogic structure of faith an image of man is thus defined, we can add that it also brings to light an image of God. Man comes to deal with God in coming to deal with his fellow men. Faith is fundamentally centred on "You" and "We"; only *via* this double clamp does it link man with God. The corollary of this is that by the inner structure of faith our relationship to God and our fellowship with man cannot be separated from each other; the relationship to God, to the "You" and to the "We" are intertwined; they do not stand alongside each other. The same thing could be formulated from a different point of view by saying that God wishes to approach man only through man; he seeks out man in no other way but in his fellow humanity.

Perhaps from this angle it is possible to render comprehensible a state of affairs, at any rate in the inner sanctum of faith, which at first must seem curious and may make the religious attitude of man seem problematical. The phenomenology of religion demonstrates – and we can all test this for ourselves – that there are, or at least appear to be, in religion, as in all other realms of the human spirit, various degrees of endowment. Just as in the field of music we find the creative, the receptive and finally those who are completely unmusical, so it seems to be in religion too. Here too one meets people who are religiously "talented" and others who are "untalented"; here too those capable of direct religious experience and thus of something like religious creativity through a living awareness of the religious world are few and far between. The "mediator" or "founder", the witness, the prophet, or whatever religious history likes to call such men, remains here too the exception. Over against these few, for whom the divine thus becomes undisguised certainty, stand the many whose religious gift is limited to receptivity, who are denied the direct experience of the holy, yet are not so deaf to it as to be unable to appreciate an encounter with it through the medium of the man granted such an experience.

At this point one feels forced to object that every man must surely have direct access to God if "religion" is supposed to be a reality that concerns everyone and if everyone has the same demands made upon him by God. Must there not then necessarily be "equality of opportunity" and must not the same certainty be available to everyone? But it will perhaps be evident from our line of argument that this question is misdirected: God's dialogue with men operates only through men's dialogue with each other. The difference in religious gifts which divides men into "prophets" and hearers forces them into speaking to and for one another. The programme of the early Augustine, "God and the soul – nothing else", is impracticable; and it is also unchristian. In the last analysis there is no religion along the solitary path of the mystic, but only in the community of proclaiming and hearing. Man's conversation with God and men's conversation with one another demand and condition each other. Indeed, perhaps the mystery of God is from the start the most compulsive challenge – one that can never be carried to a final conclusion – ever issued to man to take up the dia-logue which, however much it may be obstructed and disturbed, causes the *logos* to resound, the real word from which all words proceed and which all words are always seeking to express.

No real dialogue yet takes place where men are still only talking about *something*. The conversation between men only comes into its own when they are no longer trying to express something, but to express themselves, when dialogue becomes communication. But when this happens, when man brings himself into the conversation, then God too is involved in some way or other, for he has been the real theme of controversy between men since the beginning of their history. Moreover, only where man brings himself into the conversation does the *logos* of all being enter, along with the *logos* of human being, into the words of human speech. That is why the testimony of God is inaudible where language is no more than a technique for imparting "something". God does not occur in logistic calculations.[23] Perhaps the difficulty we find today in speaking about God arises precisely from the very fact that our language is tending more and more to become pure calculation, that it is becoming more and more a mere means of passing on technical information, less and less a means for our common being to make contact in the *logos*, a process in which consciously or unconsciously contact is also made with the ground of all things.

(b) Belief as "symbol"

Our consideration of the history of the Apostles' Creed has led us to the recognition that here, in the baptismal formulary, Christian doctrine stands before us in its original shape, and thus also, in its primitive form, what we today call "dogma". Originally there was no such thing as a series of doctrinal propositions which could be enumerated one after the other and entered up in a book as a well-defined body of dogmas. Such a notion, which today may be difficult to resist, would have to be described as a misconception of the nature of the Christian assent to the God revealed in Christ. The content of the Christian faith has its inalienable place in the context of the profession of faith which is, as we saw, in the form of assent and dissent

[23] Cf. F. G. Jünger, "Sprache und Kalkül", in *Die Künste im technischen Zeitalter*, published by the Bavarian Academy of Fine Arts, Darmstadt, 1950, pp. 86–104.

or renunciation, a con-version, an about-turn of human being
into a new direction of life. In other words, Christian doctrine
does not exist in the form of analysable propositions but in the
unity of the *symbolum*, as the Ancient Church called the baptismal profession of faith. This is probably the moment to look
rather more closely at the meaning of this word. *"Symbolum"*
comes from *"symballein"*; in English, to fall together, to cast
together. The background to the word's etymology is an ancient
usage: two corresponding halves of a ring, a staff or a tablet
were used as tokens of identity for guests, messengers or partners
to a treaty. Possession of the corresponding piece entitled the
holder to receive a thing or simply to hospitality.[24] A *symbolum*
is something which points to its complementary other half and
thus creates mutual recognition and unity. It is the expression
and means of unity.[25]

Thus in the description of the creed or profession of faith as
the *symbolum* we have at the same time a profound interpretation of its true nature. For in fact this is just what the original
meaning or aim of dogmatic formulations in the Church was:
to facilitate a common profession of faith in God, common
worship of him. As *sym-bolum* it points to the other person, to
the unity of the spirit in the one Word. To this extent, dogma
(or symbol respectively) is also always, as Rahner has rightly
pointed out,[26] essentially an arrangement of words which from
a purely intellectual point of view could have been quite
different, yet precisely as a form of words has its own significance – that of uniting people in the community of the confessing word. It is not a piece of doctrine standing isolated in and
for itself but the form of our worship of God, the form of our

[24] Cf. J. H. Emminghaus, "Symbol III", in LThK, IX, pp. 1208ff.

[25] In *Plato* the idea of the symbol is expanded into an interpretation of
human nature. In the *Symposium* (191d), he describes man himself, in connection with the androgyne myth, as a half which calls for its complementary other half: "Each of us is accordingly only the σύμβολον (symbol, half)
of a human being, because we have been cut, like flat-fish, out of a pair.
Each of us is always looking for the σύμβολον that belongs to him (for his
other half)."

[26] K. Rahner, "Was ist eine dogmatische Aussage?" in *Schriften zur
Theologie* V, Einsiedeln, 1962, pp. 54–81, especially 67–72. This whole
chapter is much indebted to this important article.

conversion, which is not only a turn to God but also a turn to one another in the common glorification of God. It is only in this context that Christian doctrine assumes its proper place. It would be fascinating to attempt one day from this point of view a history of the form of ecclesiastical doctrine, from the baptismal dialogue *via* the conciliar We to the anathema, the Protestant Confessions and finally the dogma as isolated assertion. Such an investigation would almost certainly throw a great deal of light on the problems involved in the expression of faith and the differing degrees of awareness present in the various attempts.

A further point follows from what we have said: it also means that every man holds the faith only as a *"symbolon"*, a broken, incomplete piece that can only attain unity and completeness when it is laid together with the others. Only in *"symballein"*, in fitting together with them, can the *"symballein"*, the fitting together with God, take place. Faith demands unity and calls for the fellow believer; it is by nature related to a Church. A Church is not a secondary organization of ideas, quite out of accordance with them and hence at best a necessary evil; it belongs necessarily to a faith whose significance lies in the interplay of common confession and worship.

This discovery also points, it is true, in another direction: even the Church itself, as a whole, still holds the faith only as a *symbolon*, as a broken half, which signifies truth only in its endless reference to something beyond itself, to the quite other. It is only through the infinitely broken nature of the symbol that faith presses forward as man's continual effort to excel himself and reach up to God.

With this, one last thing becomes clear, something which at the same time leads back to the beginning. Augustine relates in his confessions how it was decisive for his own path when he learnt that the famous philosopher Marius Victorinus had become a Christian. Victorinus had long refused to join the Church because he took the view that he already possessed in his philosophy all the essentials of Christianity, with whose intellectual premises he was in complete agreement.[27] Since

[27] See the account of Marius Victorinus' conversion and the impression which it made on Augustine in *Confessions*, VIII, 2, 3–5; also A. Solignac,

from his philosophical thinking, he said, he could already regard the central Christian ideas as his own, he no longer needed to institutionalize his convictions by belonging to a Church. Like many educated people both then and now, he saw the Church as Platonism for the people, something of which he as a full-blown Platonist had no need. The decisive factor seemed to him to be the idea alone; only those who could not grasp it themselves, as the philosopher could, in its original form needed to be brought into contact with it through the medium of ecclesiastical organization. That Marius Victorinus nevertheless one day joined the Church and turned from Platonist into Christian was an expression of his perception of the fundamental error implicit in this view. The great Platonist had come to understand that a Church is something more and something other than an external institutionalization and organization of ideas. He had understood that Christianity is not a system of knowledge but a way. The believers' "We" is not a secondary addition for small minds; in a certain sense it is the matter itself – the community with one's fellow men is a reality that lies on a different plane from that of the mere "idea". If Platonism provides an *idea* of the truth, Christian belief offers truth as a *way*, and only by becoming a way has it become *man's* truth. Truth as mere perception, as mere idea, remains bereft of force; it only becomes man's truth as a way which makes a claim upon him, which he can and must tread.

Thus belief embraces, as essential parts of itself, the profession of faith, the word and the unity which it effects; it embraces entry into the community's worship of God and so finally the fellowship which we call Church. Christian belief is not an idea but life; it is not mind existing for itself, but incarnation, mind in the body of history and its "We". It is not the mysticism of the self-identification of the mind with God, but obedience and service: the outstripping of oneself, liberation of the self precisely through its being taken into service by something not made or thought out by myself, the liberation of being taken into service for the whole.

"Le cercle milanais", in *Les Confessions* (*Œuvres de St Augustin* 14), Desclée, 1962, pp. 529–536.

PART ONE

GOD

"I BELIEVE IN GOD, THE RULER OF ALL, CREATOR OF HEAVEN AND EARTH"

The *symbolum* begins with the profession of faith in God, who is more precisely described by these predicates: Father – Ruler of All (this is the proper translation of the Greek word "*pantokrator*", which we usually render, following the Latin text, by "almighty") – Creator.[1] Consequently our first task is to consider this question: what does it mean when the believer professes his faith in God? This question embraces the further one, what does it signify when this God is characterized by the titles "Father", "Ruler of All", "Creator".

[1] The word "creator" is missing in the original Roman text; but the notion of creation is included in the concept "ruler of all".

Chapter I

PROLEGOMENA TO THE SUBJECT OF GOD

1. THE SCOPE OF THE QUESTION

WHAT in fact is "God" really? In other ages this question may have seemed quite clear and unproblematical; for us it has become a genuine enquiry again. What can this word "God" signify? What reality does it express, and how does the reality concerned make contact with man? If one wished to pursue the question with the thoroughness really needed today, one would first have to attempt an analysis, from the angle of the philosophy of religion, of the sources of religious experience. Such an enquiry would also have to consider how it is that the theme of God has left its stamp on the whole history of humanity and right up to the present can raise such passionate argument – yes, right up to this very moment when the cry that God is dead resounds on every side and when nevertheless, in fact for this very reason, the question of God casts its shadow overpoweringly over all of us.

Where does this idea of "God" really come from? From what roots does it grow? How is it that what is apparently the most superfluous, and from an earthly point of view, most useless subject in history has at the same time remained the most insistent one? And why does this subject appear in such fundamentally different forms? So far as this point is concerned, it could of course be demonstrated that in spite of a confusing appearance of extreme variety the subject exists in only three forms (which occur in a number of different variations, of course) – monotheism, polytheism and atheism, as one can

67

briefly describe the three great paths taken by human history on the question of God. Moreover, we have already noted that even atheism's dismissal of the subject of God is only apparent, that in reality it represents a form of man's concern with the question of God, a form that can express a particular passion about this question and not infrequently does. If we wanted to pursue the fundamental preliminary questions it would then be necessary to describe the two roots of religious experience to which the manifold forms of this experience can almost certainly be traced back. The peculiar tension existing between them was once defined by van der Leeuw, the well-known Dutch expert on the phenomenology of religion, in the paradoxical assertion that in the history of religion God the Son was there before God the Father.[2] It would be more accurate to say that God the Saviour, God the Redeemer appears earlier than God the Creator, and even this clarification must be qualified by the reminder that the formula is not to be taken in the sense of a temporal succession, for which there is no kind of evidence. As far back as we can see in the history of religion the subject always occurs in both forms. Thus the word "before" can only mean that for concrete religious feeling, for the living existential interest, the Saviour stands in the foreground as compared with the Creator.

Behind this double shape in which humanity saw its God stand those two points of departure of religious experience of which we spoke just now. One is the experience of one's own existence, which again and again oversteps its own bounds and in some form or other, however concealed, points to the quite other. This too is a process with many layers – as many layers as human existence itself. Bonhoeffer thought, as is well known, that it was time to finish with a God whom we insert to fill the gap at the limit of our own powers, whom we call up when we ourselves are at the end of our tether. We ought to find God, he thought, not, so to speak, in our moments of need and failure, but amid the fullness of earthly life; only in this way could it be shown that God is not an escape, constructed by necessity,

[2] G. van der Leeuw, *Phänomenologie der Religion*, Tübingen, 2nd ed., 1956, p. 103.

which becomes more and more superfluous as the limits of our powers expand.[3] In the story of man's striving for God both ways exist, and both seem to me equally legitimate. Both the poverty of human existence and its fullness point to God. Where men have experienced existence in its fullness, its wealth, its beauty and its greatness, they have always become aware that this existence is an existence for which they owe thanks; that precisely in its brightness and greatness it is not the self-evident but the bestowed that comes to meet me, welcomes me with all its goodness before I have done anything, and thus requires of me that I *give* a meaning to such riches and thereby *receive* a meaning. On the other hand, man's poverty has also acted again and again as a pointer to the quite other. The question which human existence not only poses but itself *is*, the inconclusiveness inherent in it, the bounds which it comes up against and which yet yearn for the unbounded (more or less in the sense of Nietzsche's assertion that all pleasure yearns for eternity, yet experiences itself as a moment), this simultaneity of being limited and of yearning for the unbounded and open has always prevented man from resting in himself, made him sense that he is not self-sufficient but only comes to himself by going outside himself and moving towards the quite other and infinitely greater.

The same thing could be demonstrated in the theme of loneliness and security. Loneliness is indubitably one of the basic roots from which man's encounter with God grew up. Where man experiences his solitariness, he experiences at the same time how much his whole existence is a cry for the "You" and how ill-adapted he is to be only an "I" in himself. This loneliness can become apparent to man on various levels. To start with it can be comforted by the discovery of a human "You". But then there is the paradox that, as Claudel says, every "You" found by man finally turns out to be an unfulfilled and unful-

---

[3] Cf. on this point R. Marlé, "Die fordernde Botschaft Dietrich Bonhoeffers", in *Orientierung*, 31 (1967), pp. 42–46, especially the classical passage from *Widerstand und Ergebung* (ed. Bethge), Munich, 12th ed. 1964, p. 182: "I should like to speak of God not at the limits, but in the middle, not in the weaknesses but in the strength, and thus not alongside death and guilt, but in the life and goodness of man."

fillable promise;[4] that every "You" is at bottom another disappointment and that there comes a point when no encounter can surmount the final loneliness: the very process of finding and of having found thus becomes a pointer back to the loneliness, a call to the absolute "You" that really descends into the depths of one's own "I". But even here it remains true that it is not only the need born of loneliness, the experience that no sense of community fills up all our longing, which leads to the experience of God; it can just as well proceed from the joy of security. The very fulfilment of love, of finding one another, can cause man to experience the gift of what he could neither call up nor create and make him recognize that in it he receives more than either of the two could contribute. The brightness and joy of finding one another can point to the proximity of absolute joy and of the simple fact of being found which stands behind every human encounter.

All this is just intended to give some idea how human existence can be the point of departure for the experience of the absolute, which from this angle is seen as "God the Son", as the Saviour or, more simply, as a God related to existence.[5] The other source of religious perception is the confrontation of man with the world, with the sinister forces that he meets in it. Again, it remains true that the cosmos has brought man to the experience of the all-surpassing power that both threatens him and bears him up as much through its beauty and abundance as through its deficiencies, its terrors and its unfathomability. Here the resulting image is the somewhat vaguer and more distant one crystallized in the image of God the Creator, the Father.

If one were to pursue further the questions here adumbrated one would run up of one's own accord against the problem, touched on above, of the three varieties of theism to be found in history – monotheism, polytheism and atheism. Then, so it seems to me, the underlying unity of these three paths would

---

[4] P. Claudel, *Le Soulier de Satin* – the great concluding dialogue between Dona Prouhèze and Rodrigue; see also the whole preceding scene with the double shadow.

[5] Cf. on this point A. Brunner, *Die Religion*, Freiburg, 1956, especially pp. 21–94; R. Guardini, *Religion und Offenbarung* I, Würzburg, 1958.

become apparent, a unity which of course cannot be synony-
mous with identity and cannot imply that, if one only digs deep
enough, everything finally becomes one and foreground differences lose their importance. Such demonstrations of identity,
which philosophical thinking might feel tempted to undertake,
take no note of the seriousness of human decisions and could
certainly not do justice to reality. But even if there can be no
question of identity a deeper look would be able to recognize
that the differences between the three great paths lie elsewhere
than is suggested by their three labels, which declare respectively: "There is one God"; "There are many Gods"; and
"There is no God". Between these three formulas and the professions contained in them there exists an opposition that cannot be swept aside, but there also exists a relationship of which
the mere words contain no hint. For all three – this could be
demonstrated – are in the last analysis convinced of the unity
and oneness of the absolute. It is not only monotheism that
believes in this unity and oneness; even for polytheism the
many gods which it worshipped and in which it placed its
hopes were never the absolute itself; even to the polytheist it
was clear that somewhere or other behind the many powers
there stood the one Being, that in the last resort being was
either one or at any rate the eternal strife of two principles
opposed to each other from the beginning.[6] On the other hand,
although atheism disputes the recognition of the unity of all
being through the idea of God, this does not mean at all that
for the atheist the unity of being itself is abolished. Indeed, the
most influential form of atheism, namely Marxism, asserts in
the strictest form this unity of being in all that is by declaring
all being to be matter; it is true that the one thing which is
being itself is, as matter, completely separated from the earlier
concept of the absolute, which is linked to the idea of God, but
it simultaneously acquires features which make its absoluteness
clear and thus once again recall the idea of God.

---

[6] Cf. J. A. Cuttat, *Begegnung der Religionen*, Einsiedeln, 1956; J. Ratzinger,
"Der Christliche Glaube und die Weltreligionen", in *Gott in Welt* (Festschrift für K. Rahner), II, Freiburg, 1964, pp. 287–305; also the material
in P. Hacker, *Prahlada: Werden und Wandlungen einer Idealgestalt*, I and II,
Mainz, 1958.

Thus all three paths are convinced of the unity and oneness of the absolute; where they differ is only in their notions of the mode and fashion in which man has to deal with the absolute or alternatively the absolute behaves towards him. If – to treat the question very schematically – monotheism starts from the assumption that the absolute is consciousness, which knows man and can speak to him, for materialism the absolute, being matter, is devoid of all personal predicates and can in no way be brought into contact with the concepts of call and answer; the most one could say is that man himself must liberate what is divine from matter, so that he would then no longer have God behind him as something preceding him but only in front of him as something to be creatively effected by him, as his own better future. Finally, polytheism can be closely related to both monotheism and atheism, because the powers of which it speaks imply the oneness of a supporting power, which can be thought of in either way. Thus it would not be difficult to show how in antiquity polytheism went perfectly well with a metaphysical atheism but was also combined with philosophical monotheism.[7]

All these questions are important if one wishes to pursue the subject of God in our present situation today. To deal with them adequately would of course require a great deal of time and patience. It must therefore suffice here to have at any rate mentioned them; we shall meet them again and again if we now go on to consider the fate of the idea of God in the faith of the Bible, an investigation of which is demanded by our subject. While we thus follow up further the problem of God at one quite specific point, we shall remain confronted with humanity's whole struggle for its God and open to the full scope of the question.

[7] One need only point to the fact that ancient philosophy embraced both philosophical atheists (Epicurus, Lucretius, etc.) and philosophical monotheists (Plato, Aristotle, Plotinus), and that both groups were by religion polytheists – a state of affairs that, thanks to the prevailing way of looking at it exclusively from the point of view of the history of philosophy, is seldom given sufficient attention. It is only against this background that one can see clearly the revolutionary nature of the Christian attitude, in which philosophical and religious orientation become identical; cf. on this point J. Ratzinger, *Volk und Haus Gottes in Augustins Lehre von der Kirche*, Munich, 1954, pp. 2–12 and 218–234.

2. THE CONFESSION OF FAITH IN THE ONE GOD

Let us therefore return to our point of departure, to the words of the Creed: I believe in God, the Almighty, the Father, the Creator. This statement, with which Christians have been confessing their faith in God for almost two thousand years, is the product of a still older history. Behind it stands Israel's daily confession of faith, the Christian form of which it represents: "Hear, O Israel, Yahweh, thy God, is an only God".[8] With its first words the Christian creed takes up the creed of Israel and takes up with it Israel's striving, its experience of faith and its struggle for God, which thus becomes an inner dimension of the Christian faith, which would not exist without this struggle. Quite by the way we meet here an important law of the history of religion and belief, which always proceeds by linked steps; there is never complete discontinuity. The faith of Israel is certainly something new in comparison with the faith of the surrounding peoples; nevertheless it is not something that has fallen from heaven; it takes shape in the conflict with this faith of other peoples, in the combative selection and re-interpretation which is both continuation and transformation.

"Yahweh, thy God, is an only God" – this fundamental confession, which forms the background to our creed, making it possible, is in its original sense a renunciation of the surrounding gods. It is a confession in the fullest sense of this word, that is, it is not the registration of one view alongside others but an existential decision. As a renunciation of the gods it also implies the renunciation both of the deification of political powers and of the deification of the cosmic *"Stirb und werde"*.* If one can say that hunger, love and power are the forces which motivate man, then one can point out, as an extension of this observation, that the three main forms of polytheism are the worship of bread, the worship of love and the idolization of

---

[8] Text of the *Sch'ma* (as this prayer is called, after the introductory phrase "Hear, O Israel") in R. R. Geis, *Vom unbekannten Judentum*, Freiburg, 1961, pp. 22f.

* A quotation from Goethe which means literally "die and become" (Trans.).

power. All three paths are aberrations; they make absolutes
out of what is not in itself the absolute and thereby makes
slaves of men. They are also, it is true, aberrations in which
something is sensed of the power that bears up the universe.
Israel's confession is, as we have said, a declaration of war on
this triple worship and thus an event of the greatest importance
in the history of man's liberation. As a declaration of war on
this threefold worship this confession of faith is at the same
time a declaration of war on the multiplication of the divine
in general. It is a renunciation – we shall have to look at this
more closely later on – of gods of one's own or, in other words,
of the deification of one's own possessions, something which is
fundamental to polytheism. In this it is simultaneously a
renunciation of the attempt to keep one's own possessions safe,
a renunciation of the fear which tries to tame the mysterious
by worshipping it, and an assent to the one God of heaven as
the power that guarantees everything; it signifies the courage
to entrust oneself to the power that governs the whole world
without grasping the divine in one's hands. This starting-point,
which stems from the faith of Israel, has not been fundamentally
changed in the early Christian creed. Here too entry into the
Christian community and the acceptance of its "symbol"
signifies an existential decision with serious consequences. For
whoever assented to this creed renounced at the same time the
laws of the world to which he belonged; he renounced the
worship of the ruling political power, on which the late Roman
empire rested, he renounced the worship of pleasure, and the
cult of fear and superstition which ruled the world. It was no
coincidence that the struggle over Christianity flared up in the
field thereby defined and grew into a struggle over the whole
shape of public life in the ancient world.

I believe that it is of decisive importance for a proper understanding of the Creed today that we should see these events in
their proper context. It is only too easy for us to regard the
Christian refusal, even if it meant the loss of one's life, to take
any part in the cult of the emperor as a piece of fanaticism
appropriate to an early period; excusable, perhaps, for this
reason, but certainly not to be imitated today. Christians rejected even the most harmless forms of the cult, such as putting

one's name down on the list of those contributing to the cost of a sacrificial victim, and were ready to risk their lives by such an action. Today in a case like this one would distinguish between the unavoidable act of civic loyalty and the real religious act, in order to find an acceptable way out and at the same time to take account of the fact that heroism cannot be expected of the average man. Perhaps such a distinction is today really possible in certain circumstances as a result of the decision carried out in those days. In any case it is important to realize that this refusal was far from being a piece of narrow-minded fanaticism, and that it changed the world in a way in which it can only be changed by the readiness to suffer. Those events showed that faith is not a matter of playing with ideas but a very serious business: it says no, and must say no, to the absoluteness of political power and to the worship of the might of the mighty in general – "He has put down the mighty from their thrones" (Luke 1.52); and in doing so it has shattered the political principle's claim to totality once and for all. In this sense the confession "There is only one God" is, precisely because it has itself no political aims, a programme of decisive political importance: through the absoluteness which it lends the individual from his God, and through the relativization to which it relegates all political communities in comparison with the unity of the God who embraces them all, it forms the only definitive protection against the power of the collective and at the same time implies the complete abolition of any idea of exclusiveness in humanity as a whole.

Much the same as has been said about the Christian faith as the struggle against the worship of power could be demonstrated in the realm of the striving for the true pattern of human love as against the false worship of sex and Eros, which was and still is responsible for just as great an enslavement of humanity as the misuse of power. More than mere imagery is involved when Israel's fall from faith is depicted again and again in the Prophets by the "image" of adultery; Not only did these alien cults almost always involve cult prostitution, so that they could be literally described as "adultery"; these outward manifestations also revealed their inner tendency. The unity, finality and indivisibility of the love between man and woman can in the last analysis only be made a reality and understood in the light of belief in the unity and indivisibility of the love of God. We are beginning to understand more and more clearly today that this concept of love is by no means a philosophically deducible, self-supporting principle, and that to a large extent it stands or falls with belief in the one God. We are also coming to understand more and more clearly that the apparent liberation of love and its conversion into a matter of impulse mean the delivery of man to the self-styled powers of sex and Eros, to whose merciless slavery he falls a victim just when he is under the illusion that he has freed himself. When he eludes God, the gods put out their hands to grasp him; he can only be liberated by allowing himself to be liberated and by ceasing to try to rely on himself.

No less important than the clarification of the renunciation contained in the Creed is a proper understanding of the assent, the "yes", which it involves; first simply because the "no" can only exist by virtue of the "yes", but also because the renunciation of the first few Christian centuries has turned out to be so effective historically that the gods have disappeared beyond recall. To be sure, the *powers* expressed in them have not disappeared, nor has the temptation to regard them as absolutes. Both facts are part of the basic human situation and express the enduring "truth", so to speak, of polytheism; we are threatened no less than the people of ancient times by the tendency to make absolutes of power, bread and Eros. But even if the gods of those days are still "powers" which try to claim absoluteness, they have irrevocably lost the mask of divinity and must now show themselves unmasked in their true profanity. Here we have a fundamental difference between pre-Christian and post-Christian paganism, which bears the stamp of the Christian rejection of the gods and its power to alter history. This gives all the more urgency to the question which arises in the vacuum in which we now in many respects live: What is the content of the assent which the Christian faith involves?

Chapter II

THE BIBLICAL BELIEF IN GOD

ANYONE who wishes to understand the biblical belief in God must follow its historical development from its origins with the fathers of Israel right up to the last books of the New Testament. The Old Testament, with which we must consequently begin, itself gives us a thread to guide our labours: basically, it formulated its idea of God in two names, Elohim and Yahweh. These two main names for God reflect the parting and the choice that Israel effected in its religious world, and they also throw light on the positive option implicit in this choice and in the progressive reshaping of what had been chosen.

1. THE PROBLEM OF THE STORY OF THE BURNING BUSH

It is probably fair to take as the central text for the Old Testament understanding of God and confession of faith in him the story of the burning bush (Ex. 3), in which, with the revelation of the name of God to Moses, the foundation is laid for the idea of God henceforth to prevail in Israel. The text describes the calling of Moses to be the leader of Israel by the God both concealed and revealed in the burning thorn bush, and the hesitation of Moses, who demands a clear knowledge of his employer and clear proof of his authority. This is the background to the dialogue which has puzzled people ever since:

> Then Moses said to God, "If I come to the people of Israel and say to them, 'The God of your fathers has sent me to you', and they ask me, 'What is his name?' what shall I say to them?" God

said to Moses, "I AM WHO I AM". And he said, "Say this to the people of Israel, 'I AM has sent me to you'". God also said to Moses, "Say this to the people of Israel, 'The LORD, the God of your fathers, the God of Abraham, the God of Isaac, and the God of Jacob, has sent me to you': this is my name for ever, and thus I am to be remembered throughout all generations" (Ex. 3.13–15).

It is clearly the aim of the text to establish the name "Yahweh" as the definitive name of God in Israel, on the one hand by anchoring it historically in the origins of Israel's nationhood and the sealing of the covenant, and on the other by giving it a meaning. The latter is accomplished by tracing back the incomprehensible word "Yahweh" to the root *hayah* = to be. From the point of view of the Hebrew consonant system, this is quite possible; but whether it corresponds philologically with the real origin of the name Yahweh is at least questionable. As so often in the Old Testament, it is a question of a theological rather than a philological etymology. It is not a matter of enquiring into the original linguistic sense but of giving a meaning here and now. Etymology is in reality a means of establishing a meaningful attitude. This illumination of the name "Yahweh" by the little word "Being" (I AM) is accompanied by a second attempt at clarification consisting of the statement that Yahweh is the God of (Israel's) fathers, the God of Abraham, Isaac and Jacob. This means that the concept of "Yahweh" is to be enlarged and deepened by the equation of the God so described with the God of Israel's fathers, a God who had probably been addressed for the most part by the names El and Elohim.

Let us try to visualize clearly what kind of image of God arises in this way. First, what does it mean when the idea of Being is here brought into play as an interpretation of God? To the Fathers of the Church, with their background of Greek philosophy, it seemed a bold and unexpected confirmation of their own intellectual past, for Greek philosophy regarded it as its decisive discovery that it had discovered, behind all the many individual things with which man has to deal daily, the comprehensive idea of Being, which it also considered the most appropriate expression of the divine. Now the Bible too seemed to be saying precisely the same thing in its central text on the image of God. It is not surprising if this seemed an absolutely amazing confirmation of the unity of belief and thought, and in fact the Fathers of the Church believed that they had discovered here the deepest unity between philosophy and faith, Plato and Moses, the Greek mind and the biblical mind. So complete did they find the identity between the quest of the philosophical spirit and the acceptance which had occurred in the faith of Israel that they took the view that Plato could not have advanced so far on his own but had been familiar with the Old Testament and borrowed his idea from it. Thus the central concept of the Platonic philosophy was traced back to revelation; people did not dare to attribute an insight of such profundity to the unaided power of the human mind.

The text of the Greek Old Testament, which the Fathers had before them, could very well suggest such an identity of thought between Plato and Moses, but the dependence is probably the other way round; the scholars who translated the Hebrew Bible into Greek were influenced by Greek philosophical thinking and interpreted the text from this angle; the idea that here the Hellenic spirit and the faith of the Bible overlapped must already have inspired them; they themselves built the bridge, so to speak, from the biblical concept of God over to Greek thought if they translated the "I AM WHO I AM" of verse 14 by "I am He that is". The biblical name for God is here identified with the philosophical concept of God. The scandal of the name, of the God who names himself, is resolved in the wider context of ontological thinking; belief is wedded to ontology. For to the thinker it is a scandal that the biblical God should bear a name. Can this be more than a reminder of the polytheistic world in which the biblical faith had at first to live? In a world swarming with gods Moses could not say, "God sends me", or even "The God of our fathers sends me". He knew that this meant nothing, that he would be asked, "Which god?" But the question is, could one have ever given the Platonic "Being" a name and referred to it by this name as a kind of individual? Or is the fact that one can name this God not a sign of a fundamentally different conception? If one adds that it is an important detail of the text that one can only name God because he has named himself, then one only deepens still further the gulf between this conception and Platonic, absolute Being, the final stage of ontological thinking, which is not named and names itself still less.

Are the Greek translations of the Old Testament, then, and the conclusions which the Fathers drew from it based on a misunderstanding? Today, not only are the exegetical scholars unanimous that they are, but the dogmatic theologians emphasize the point strongly and with all the thoroughness appropriate to a question which exceeds in importance all other individual problems of exegesis. For example, Emil Brunner has stated with the utmost firmness that the insertion here of an "equals" sign between the God of faith and the God of the philosophers means turning the biblical idea of God into its opposite. The name, Brunner says, is here replaced by the concept, and the not-to-be-defined is replaced by a definition.[9] But this means that at this one spot the whole patristic exegesis, the Ancient Church's faith in God, and the image of God and profession of faith in him to be found in the *Symbolum* come under discussion. Are they a decline into Hellenism, a falling away from the God whom the New Testament names as the Father of Jesus Christ, or do they say again in new conditions what must always be said?

Above all else we must try, if as briefly as possible, to look into the actual findings of exegesis. What does this name Yahweh signify and what is the meaning of its explanation by the little word "Being"? The two questions are connected but, as we saw, not identical. Let us try first to get a little closer to the first one. Can we still make out at all what the name Yahweh originally means according to its etymological origin? This is almost impossible because we are completely in the dark about its origin. One thing at any rate can be clearly stated: firm evidence of the name Yahweh before Moses or Israel is lacking; and none of the numerous attempts to clarify the pre-Israelite roots of the name is really convincing. Syllables like *yah, yo, jahw* are known earlier, but so far as we can see today the full form of the name Yahweh first occurs in Israel; its development

[9] E. Brunner, *Die christliche Lehre von Gott. Dogmatik* I, Zürich, 1960, pp 124–135; cf. J. Ratzinger, *Der Gott des Glaubens und der Gott der Philosophen*, Munich, 1960.

seems to be the work of Israel's faith which, not without models but creatively transforming them, here moulded its own name for God and in this name its own figure of God.[10]

Indeed, today there is again a good deal to be said for the view that the formation of this name was in fact the deed of Moses, who with it brought new hope to his enslaved fellow countrymen: the final development of their own name for God and in it of their own image of God seems to have been the starting-point of Israel's nationhood. Even from a purely historical point of view one can say that Israel became a people thanks to God, that it only came to itself through the call of hope signified by the name of God. Of the manifold references to pre-Israelite antecedents of the name Yahweh, which do not need to be discussed here, the best-grounded and most fruitful suggestion seems to me to be the observation made by H. Cazelles, who points out that in the Babylonian kingdom theophorous names occur (that is, personal names containing a reference to God), formed with the word "*yaun*" or containing the syllable *yau* or *ya*, which has more or less the meaning "mine" or "my God". In the tangle of gods with whom people dealt, this word-formation refers to the personal god, that is, the god who is concerned with man and is himself personal and person-centred. It is the God who, as the personal Being, deals with man as man. This indication is noteworthy in that it links up with a central element in Israel's pre-Mosaic faith, with the God-figure whom we are accustomed to describe, following the Bible, as the God of our fathers.[11] The suggested etymology would thus fit in exactly with what the story of the burning bush itself described as the inner assumption of the Yahweh-faith, with the faith of (Israel's) fathers, with the God of Abraham, Isaac and Jacob. Let us therefore turn our attention

[10] That is how it will be expressed from the point of view of the historian. This will not affect the believer's conviction that this "creative transforma-tion" was only possible in the form of a reception of revelation. In any case the creative process is always a process of reception. For the historical aspect cf. H. Cazelles, "Der Gott der Patriarchen", in *Bibel und Leben*, 2 (1961), pp. 39–49; O. Eissfeldt, "Jahwe, der Gott der Väter", in *Theologische Literaturzeitung*, 88 (1963), pp. 481–490; G. von Rad, *Theologie des AT*, I, Munich, 1958, pp. 181–188.

[11] Cazelles, *loc. cit.*

for a moment to this figure, without which the meaning of the
Yahweh-message cannot be understood.

2. THE INTRINSIC ASSUMPTION OF THE BELIEF IN YAHWEH:
THE GOD OF (ISRAEL'S) FATHERS

The linguistic and semantic root of the name Yahweh, a root
which we thought we recognized in the "personal God"
indicated by the syllable *yau*, throws light not only on the
choice and separation effected by Israel in its religious environment but also on the continuity with Israel's own early
history from the time of Abraham. The God of its fathers had
not, it is true, been called Yahweh; when we meet him he bears
the names El and Elohim. The fathers of Israel were thus able
to use as their starting-point the El-religion of the surrounding
peoples, a religion which is characterized chiefly by the social
and personal character of the divinity denoted by the word
"*El*". The God upon whom they decided is characterized by
the fact that, in the language of religious typology, he is a
numen personale (personal god), not a *numen locale* (local god).
What does this mean? Let us try to elucidate briefly what is
meant by each phrase. First we should recall that the religious
experience of the human race has continually been kindled at
holy places, where for some reason or other the "quite other",
the divine, becomes particularly palpable to man; a spring,
a huge tree, a mysterious stone, or even an unusual happening
that occurred at some spot or other, can have this effect. But
then the danger immediately arises that in man's eyes the spot
where he experienced the divine and the divine itself merge
into each other, so that he believes in a special presence of the
divine at that particular spot and thinks he cannot find it in
equal measure elsewhere: consequently, the spot becomes a
holy spot, the dwelling-place of the divine. The local connection
of the divine thus resulting then also leads, however, by a sort
of inner necessity, to its multiplication. Because this experience
of the holy occurs not just in *one* spot but in many, while the
holy is regarded in each case as confined to the spot concerned,
the result is a multitude of local divinities, who thus become at
the same time gods of their own respective areas. A faint echo

of these tendencies can be traced even now in Christianity: to less enlightened believers the Madonnas of Lourdes, Fatima or Altötting sometimes seem to be absolutely different beings and by no means simply the same person. But back to our subject! In contrast to the heathen tendency towards the *numen locale*, the locally defined and limited deity, the "God of our fathers" expresses a completely different approach. He is not the god of a place, but the god of men: the God of Abraham, Isaac and Jacob. He is therefore not bound to one spot, but present and powerful wherever man is. In this fashion one arrives at a completely different way of thinking about God. God is seen on the plane of I and You, not on the plane of the spatial. He thus moves away into the transcendence of the illimitable and by this very fact shows himself to be he who is always (not just at one point) near, whose power is boundless. He is not any-where in particular; he is always to be found where man is and where man lets himself be found by him. By deciding in favour of El, the fathers of Isra-el thus made a choice of the greatest importance: they opted for the *numen personale* as opposed to the *numen locale*, for the personal and person-centred God, who is to be thought of and found on the plane of I and You, not primarily in holy places.[12] This basic characteristic of El remained the one sustaining element not only of the reli-gion of Israel, but also of the New Testament faith: the emana-tion of God's personality, the understanding of God on the plane defined by the I-and-You relationship.

To this aspect, by which the spiritual locality of the El-faith is basically defined, a second must be added: El is regarded not only as the sustainer of personality, as father, creator of creatures, the wise, the king; he is seen also and above all things as the highest God of all, as the greatest power of all, as he who stands above all else. It is unnecessary to emphasize that this second element too put its stamp on the whole biblical experience of God. It is not just some power or other, effective somewhere or other, which is chosen, but that power alone which embraces in itself all power and stands above all indi-vidual powers.

[12] Though it must be pointed out again (as already in Note 10) that this sort of decision embraces gift, reception and, to that extent, revelation.

Finally, attention must be directed to a third element, which likewise persists throughout biblical thinking: this God is the God of the Promise. He is not a force of nature, in whose epiphany the eternal might of nature, the eternal *"Stirb und Werde"*, is demonstrated; he is not a God who orientates man by the recurring pattern of the cosmic cycle; he directs man's attention to the coming events towards which his history marches, to a meaning and goal which have a final validity; he is regarded as the God of hope in the future, in a direction which is irreversible.

Finally, it must be pointed out that the El-faith was accepted in Israel chiefly in its extension to "Elohim", an extension which also hints at the process of transformation which even the El-figure needed. It may seem curious that in this way the singular El was replaced by a word (Elohim) that really indicates a plural. We cannot go into the complex details of this process here; suffice it to say that this very development enabled Israel to give better and better expression to God's uniqueness. He is one, but as the exceeding great, quite other, he himself outsteps the bounds of singular and plural, he lies beyond them. Although in the Old Testament, especially in its early books, there is certainly no kind of revelation of the Trinity, nevertheless in this process there is latent an experience which points towards the Christian concept of the triune God. People realized, if still quite unreflectively, that while God is indeed radically One, he cannot be forced into our categories of singular and plural, but stands above them, so that in the last analysis, even though he is truly one God, he cannot be fitted with complete appropriateness into the category "one". In the early history of Israel (and later on too – for us especially) this means that at the same time the legitimacy of the question implicit in polytheism is admitted.[13] The plural,

---

[13] Cf. Maximus Confessor, *Expositio Orationis Dominicae*, in *Patrologia Graeca* (PG), 90, 892: in his view heathen polytheism and Jewish monotheism are reconciled in the Gospel. "The former is contradictory multiplicity unchecked, the latter is unity without inner riches." Maximus regards them both as equally imperfect and in need of supplementation. But now they reach out beyond themselves to the idea of the tri-une God, which supplements the Jewish concept of unity, "in itself narrow, imperfect and

when it refers to one God, means, so to speak, "He is everything divine".

If one wished to speak appropriately about the "God of our fathers", one would now have to add a reminder of the renunciation implicit in the "yes" which presents itself to us at first in El and Elohim. However, here we must make do with a reference to two catch-words, to two names of gods dominant in the regions round Israel. The Jews rejected the notions of God current in the surrounding areas under the names of Baal, "The Lord", and Melech (or Moloch), "The King". What was renounced here was fertility-worship and the local connection of the divine which it brings with it; and the "no" to the king-god Melech also involved the rejection of a certain social pattern. The God of Israel is not moved away to the aristocratic distance of a king; he is a stranger to the boundless despotism linked in those days with the image of a king – he is the near-at-hand God, who fundamentally can be the God of each and every man. What food for thought this provides! But let us forgo the pleasure of such speculations and return again to our point of departure, to the question of the God of the burning bush.

3. YAHWEH, THE "GOD OF OUR FATHERS" AND THE GOD OF JESUS CHRIST

Since Yahweh, as we have seen, is explained as the "God of our fathers", the Yahweh-faith automatically absorbs the whole context of the faith of Israel's fathers, though this context at the same time acquires a new element and a new look. But what is the specifically new element expressed by the name "Yahweh"? The answers to this question are numerous; the precise meaning of the formulas in Exodus 3 can no longer be ascertained with certainty. Nevertheless, two aspects emerge clearly. We have already established that to our way of think-

---

almost valueless", with the "lively and brilliant plurality of the Greek". Such is Maximus' view according to H. U. von Balthasar, *Kosmische Liturgie. Das Weltbild Maximus des Bekenners*, Einsiedeln, 2nd ed., 1961, p. 312. Cf. also A. Adam, *Lehrbuch der Dogmengeschichte*, Vol. I, Gütersloh, 1965, p. 368.

ing the mere fact that God bears a name, and thereby appears
as a kind of individual, is a scandal. But if we look more closely
at the text which we are considering the question arises, is it,
properly speaking, really a name? This question may at first
seem nonsensical, for it is indisputable that Israel knew the
word Yahweh as a name for God. Yet a careful reading shows
that the thorn-bush scene expounds this name in such a way
that as a name it seems to be absolutely cancelled out; in any
case it moves out of the series of appellations of divinities to
which it at first seems to belong. Let us listen once again carefully. Moses says: "The children of Israel, to whom you send
me, will ask, 'Who is the God who sends you? What is he
called?' What shall I then say to them?" We are next told that
God replied: "I am who I am". The words could also be
translated, "I am what I am". This really looks like a rebuff;
it seems much more like a refusal to give a name than the
announcement of a name. In the whole scene there is a sense
of displeasure at such importunity: I am just who I am. The
idea that here no name is really given and that the question is
rejected acquires additional probability when a comparison is
made with the two passages which could be adduced as the
best parallels to our text: Judges 13.18 and Genesis 32.30. In
Judges 13.18 a certain Manoah asks the God who meets him
for his name. The answer which he is given is: "Why do you
ask my name, seeing it is a secret?" (Another possible translation is "seeing it is wonderful".) A name is not given. In
Genesis 32.30 it is Jacob who, after his nocturnal struggle with
the stranger, asks his name and receives only the discouraging
answer, "Why is it that you ask my name?" Both passages are
linguistically and in general construction very closely related to
our text, so that it is hardly disputable that there is also an
affinity in the thought. Here again we have the gesture of
repulse. The God with whom Moses deals in the burning bush
cannot give his name in the same way as the gods round about,
who are individual gods alongside other similar gods and
therefore need a name. The God of the burning bush will not
put himself on a level with them. In the gesture of rebuff which
we have come upon here there is a hint of a God who is quite
other than "the gods". The explanation of the name Yahweh

by the little word "am" thus serves as a kind of negative theology. It cancels out the significance of the name as a name; it
effects a sort of withdrawal from the only too well known,
which the name seems to be, into the unknown, the hidden.
It dissolves the name into the mystery, so that the familiarity
and unfamiliarity of God, concealment and revelation, are
indicated simultaneously. The name, a sign of acquaintance,
becomes the cipher for the perpetually unknown and unnamed
quality of God. Contrary to the view that God can here be
grasped, so to speak, the persistence of an infinite distance is
in this way made quite clear. To this extent it was in the last
analysis a legitimate development which led people in Israel
more and more to avoid pronouncing this name, to use some
sort of periphrasis, so that in the Greek Bible it no longer occurs
at all but is simply replaced by the word "Lord". This development shows in many ways a more accurate understanding of
the mystery of the burning bush than multifarious learned
philological explanations do.

But so far of course we have only been looking at half the
situation, for Moses was in fact empowered all the same to say
to the questioners: "I AM has sent me to you" (Ex. 3.14). He
has an answer at his disposal, even if it is a riddle. And can we
not, indeed must we not, un-riddle it a bit in a positive sense?
Most contemporary biblical scholars see in the phrase the
expression of helpful proximity; they say that God does not
reveal in it – as philosophical thought tries to – his nature as
it is in itself, he reveals himself as a God for Israel, as a God for
man. "I am" is as much as to say "I am there", "I am there
for you"; God's presence for Israel is emphasized; his Being is
expounded not as Being in itself, but as a Being-for.[14] Eissfeldt,
it is true, considers possible not only the translation "He helps"
but also "He calls into existence, he is the creator", "He is",
and even "He who is". The French scholar Edmond Jacob
thinks that the name El denotes life as power, while Yahweh
expresses endurance and presence. When God here calls
himself "I AM", he is to be explained, according to Jacob, as he
who "is", as Being in contrast to Becoming, as that which

[14] Cf. W. Eichrodt, *Theologie des AT*, Vol. I, 2nd ed., Leipzig, 1939, pp.
92f.; G. von Rad, *op cit.* (see Note 10), p. 184.

abides and persists in all passing away. "All flesh is grass, and
all its beauty is like the flower of the field. . . . The grass withers,
the flower fades; but the word of our God will stand for ever"
(Is. 40.6–8).

The reference to this text indicates a connection which
hitherto has probably been given too little attention. To the
Deutero–Isaiah it was a fundamental part of his message that
the things of this world pass away; that men, however force-
fully they behave, are in the end like flowers, which bloom one
day and are cut off and withering away the next, while in the
midst of this gigantic display of transience the God of Israel
"is" – not "becomes". Amid all the becoming and passing
away he "is". But this "is" of God, who abides above all the
inconstancy of becoming as the constant one, is not proclaimed
as something unconnected with anything else. On the contrary,
God is at the same time he who grants himself; he is there for
us and from his own firm standing he gives us firmness in our
infirmity. The God who "is" is at the same time he who is
with *us;* he is not just God in himself, but our God, the "God
of our fathers".

This brings us back to the question which arose at the
beginning of our reflections on the story of the burning bush:
what is really the relationship between the God of the biblical
faith and the Platonic idea of God? Is the God who names
himself and has a name, the God who helps and is always
there, radically different from the *esse subsistens*, the absolute
Being, which is discovered in the lonely silence of philosophical
speculation, or what? To deal with this question properly and
to grasp the meaning of the Christian notion of God, I think
we must look rather more closely both at the biblical idea of
God and at the significance of philosophical thinking. To deal
first with the Bible, it is important not to isolate the story of
the burning bush. We have already seen that it is to be understood primarily against the background of a world saturated
with gods, in which it makes Israel's faith visible, both in its
continuity and in its efforts to differentiate itself, and at the
same time forwards its development by adding the many-
faceted idea of Being as an intellectual element. The process of
interpretation which we encountered in the story does not end

with it; in the course of the biblical struggle for God this process was continually being taken in hand again and carried further. Ezechiel and especially the Deutero-Isaiah could be described in so many words as the theologians of the name Yahweh; it was not least on this that they based their prophetic preaching. The Deutero-Isaiah is speaking, as is well known, at the end of the Babylonian exile, at a moment when Israel is looking into the future with new hope. The apparently invincible Babylonian power which had enslaved Israel has been broken and Israel, the supposed corpse, is arising out of the ruins. Thus one of the prophets' central ideas is to compare with gods that pass away the God who *is*. "I, Yahweh, the first, and with the last, I am He" (41.4). The last book of the New Testament, the Apocalypse, in a similarly difficult situation, was to repeat this assertion: before all these powers he stands already and after them he still stands (Apoc. 1.4,; 1.17; 2.8; 22.13). But let us listen once again to the Deutero-Isaiah: "I am the first and I am the last; besides me there is no god" (44.6). "I am He, I am the first, and I am the last" (48.12). In this context the prophet has coined a new formula, in which the interpretative thread in the story of the burning bush is taken up and given a different emphasis. The formula which in Hebrew seems mysteriously to run simply "I–He" is rendered in Greek, and certainly with accuracy, as "I am" (ἐγώ εἰμι)[15]. In this simple "I am" the God of Israel confronts the gods and identifies himself as him who *is*, in contrast to those who have been toppled over and pass away. The brief, enigmatic phrase "I am" thus becomes the axis of the prophet's proclamation, expressing his struggle against the gods, his struggle against Israel's despair, and his message of hope and certainty. In face of the worthless pantheon of Babylon and its fallen potentates the might of Yahweh rises simply, needing no commentary, in the expression "I am", which describes its absolute superiority to all the godly and ungodly powers of this world. The

---

[15] On the origin and meaning of this formula, see especially E. Schweizer, *EGO EIMI* . . . , Göttingen, 1939; H. Zimmermann, "Das absolute ἐγώ εἰμι als die neutestamentliche Offenbarungsformel", in *Biblische Zeitschrift*, 4 (1960), pp. 54–69; E. Stauffer, *Jesus. Gestalt und Geschichte*, Berne, 1957, pp. 130–146.

name Yahweh, whose meaning is brought home in such a fashion, thus moves a step further towards the idea of him who "is" in the midst of the ruins of appearance, which has no endurance.

Let us now take one last step which carries us over into the New Testament. The line of thought that puts the idea of God more and more in the light of the idea of Being and explains God by the simple "I am" occurs once again in St John's gospel, that is, in the last retrospective biblical interpretation of the belief in Jesus, an interpretation which for us Christians is at the same time the last step in the self-explanation of the biblical movement in general. John's thinking is directly based on the Wisdom literature and the Deutero–Isaiah, and can only be understood against this background. He makes the "I am" of Isaiah into the central formula of his faith in God, but he does it by making it into the central formula of his Christology; a process as decisive for the idea of God as for the image of Christ. The formula which first occurs in the episode of the burning bush, which at the end of the Exile becomes the expression of hope and certainty in face of the declining gods and depicts Yahweh's lasting victory over all these powers, now finds itself here too at the centre of the faith, but through becoming testimony to Jesus of Nazareth.

The significance of this process becomes fully visible when one also realizes that John takes up again, in a much more striking way than any New Testament author before him, the heart of the burning bush story: the idea of the name of God. The notion that God names himself, that it becomes possible to call on him by name, moves, together with "I am", into the centre of his testimony. In John, Christ is compared with Moses in this respect too; John depicts him as him in whom the story of the burning bush first attains its true meaning. All Chapter 17 – the so-called "high priest's prayer", perhaps the heart of the whole gospel – centres round the idea of "Jesus as the revealer of the name of God" and thus assumes the position of New Testament counterpart to the story of the burning bush. The theme of God's name recurs like a *leitmotiv* in verses 6, 11, 12 and 26. Let us take only the two main verses: "I have manifested thy name to the men whom thou gavest me out

of the world" (v. 6). "I made known to them thy name, and I
will make it known, that the love with which thou hast loved me
may be in them, and I in them" (v. 26). Christ himself, so
to speak, appears as the burning bush from which the name of
God issues to mankind. But since in the view of the fourth
gospel Jesus unites in himself, applies to himself, the "I am" of
Exodus 3 and Isaiah 43, it becomes clear at the same time that
he himself is the name, that is, the "invocability" of God. The
idea of the name here enters a decisive new phase. The name
is no longer merely a word but a person: Jesus himself. Christology, or belief in Jesus, is raised to the level of an exposition of
the name of God and of what it signifies. This brings us to the
point where we must finally deal with an important question
affecting the whole discussion of the name of God.

4. THE IDEA OF THE NAME

After all our reflections we must now finally ask in completely general terms: What is a name really? And what is the
point of speaking of a name of God? I do not want to undertake
a detailed analysis of this question – this is not the place for
such an analysis – but simply to try to indicate in a few lines
what seem to me to be the essential points. First, we can say
that there is a fundamental difference between the purpose of a
concept and that of a name. The concept tries to perceive the
nature of the thing as it is in itself. The name on the other hand
does not ask after the nature of thing as it exists independently
of me; it is concerned to make the thing nameable, that is,
"invocable"; to establish a relation to it. Here too the name
should certainly fit the thing, but to the end that it comes into
relation to me and in this way becomes accessible to me. Let
us take an example: if I know of someone that he falls under the
concept "man", this is still not enough to enable me to establish a relation to him. Only the name makes him nameable;
through the name the other enters into the structure, so to
speak, of my fellow-humanity; through the name I can call
him. Thus the name signifies and effects the social incorporation, the inclusion in the stucture of social relations. Anyone who
is still regarded only as a number is excluded from the structure

of fellow-humanity. But the name establishes the relation of
fellow-humanity. It gives to a being the "invocability" from
which co-existence with the namer arises.

This will probably make clear what Old Testament faith
means when it speaks of a name of God. The aim is different
from that of the philosopher seeking the concept of the highest
Being. The concept is a product of thinking that wants to know
what that highest Being is like in itself. Not so the name. When
God names himself after the self-understanding of faith he is not
so much expressing his inner nature as making himself nameable;
he is handing himself over to men in such a way that he can
be called upon by them. And by doing this he enters into co-
existence with them, he puts himself within their reach, he is
"there" for them.

Here too is the angle from which it would seem to become
clear what it means when John presents the Lord Jesus Christ
as the real, living name of God. In him is fulfilled what a mere
name could never in the end fulfil. In him the meaning of the
discussion of the name of God has reached its goal, and so too
has that which was always meant and intended by the idea of
the name of God. In him – this is what the evangelist means by
this idea – God has really become he who can be invoked. In
him God has entered for ever into co-existence with us. The
name is no longer just a word at which we clutch, it is now
flesh of our flesh, bone of our bone. God is one of us. Thus
what had been meant since the episode of the burning bush
by the idea of the name is really fulfilled in him who as God
is man, and as man is God, God has become one of us and
so the truly nameable, standing in co-existence with us.

5. THE TWO SIDES OF THE BIBLICAL CONCEPT OF GOD

If one tries to survey the question as a whole it becomes
apparent that there are always two components in the biblical
concept of God. One side is the element of the personal, of
proximity, of invocability, of self-bestowal, an element which
is heralded in the idea of the "God of our fathers, of Abraham,
Isaac and Jacob", summed-up comprehensively in the giving
of the name, and concentrated again later in the idea of "the

God of Jesus Christ". It is always a matter of the God of men, the God with a face, the personal God; on him were focused continuity, the choice and the decision of the faith of Israel's fathers, from which a long yet straight road leads to the God of Jesus Christ.

On the other side is the fact that this proximity, this accessibility, is the free gift of what stands above space and time, bound to nothing and binding everything to itself. The element of timeless power is characteristic of this God; it becomes concentrated more and more emphatically in the idea of Being, of the enigmatic and profound "I am". As time went on, Israel visibly tried to interpret something of this second element to the surrounding peoples, to impress on them the special character, the "otherness" of its faith. It placed the "is" of God over against the becoming and passing away of the world and its gods – gods of the earth, of fertility, of one nation. It compared the God of heaven, standing over all, to whom everything belongs and who belongs to no one, with the various particular gods. It insisted emphatically that its God was not a national god of Israel in the way that every people had its own god. Israel insisted that it had no god of its own, but only the God of all people and of the whole universe; it was convinced that precisely for this reason it alone worshipped the real God. One does not have God until one no longer has any god of one's own but only trusts the God who is just as much the next man's God as mine, because we both belong to him.

The paradox of the biblical faith in God consists in the conjunction and unity of the two elements just described, in the fact, therefore, that Being is accepted as a person and the person accepted as Being itself, that only what is hidden is accepted as He who is near, only the inaccessible as He who is accessible, the one as the One who exists for all men and for whom all exist. At this point let us break off our analysis of the biblical faith and take up again on a broader basis the question of the relationship between faith and philosophy, between faith and understanding, which we came up against at the start and which now poses itself to us again at the end.

Chapter III

THE GOD OF FAITH AND THE GOD OF THE PHILOSOPHERS

I. THE DECISION OF THE EARLY CHURCH IN FAVOUR OF PHILOSOPHY

THE choice made in the biblical image of God had to be made once again in the early days of Christianity and the Church; at bottom it has to be made afresh in every spiritual situation, and thus always remains just as much a task as a gift. The early Christian proclamation of the Gospel and the early Christian faith found themselves once again in an environment teeming with gods and thus once again before the problem with which Israel had been confronted in its original situation and in its debate with the great powers of the exilic and post-exilic period. Again it was a question of stating which God the Christian faith really had in mind. It is true that the early Christian decision could base itself on the whole preceding struggle, especially on the last phase of it, on the words of the Deutero-Isaiah and the Wisdom literature, on the step that had been taken in the Greek translation of the Old Testament, and finally on the writings of the New Testament, especially St John's gospel. It was in the wake of this whole series of events that early Christianity boldly and resolutely made its choice and carried out its purification by deciding *for* the God of the philosophers and *against* the gods of the various religions. Wherever the question arose to which god the Christian God corresponded, Zeus perhaps or Hermes or Dionysus or some other god, the answer ran: to none of them. To none of the gods to whom you pray but solely and alone to him to whom you do not pray, to that highest being of whom your philosophers speak. The early Church resolutely put aside the whole cosmos of the ancient religions, regarding the whole of it as deceit and illusion, and explained its faith by saying: When we say God, we do not mean or worship any of this; we mean only Being itself, what the philosophers have exposed as the ground of all being, as the God above all powers – that alone is our God. This proceeding involved a choice, a decision, no less fateful and formative for ages to come than the choice of El and "yah" as opposed to Moloch and Baal had been in its time, with the subsequent development of the two into Elohim and towards Yahweh, the idea of Being. The choice thus made meant opting for the *logos* as against any kind of myth; it meant the definitive demythologization of the world and of religion. Was this decision for the *logos* rather than the myth the right one? To find the answer to this we must keep in view all our previous reflections on the inner development of the biblical concept of God, the last stages of which had in essentials already determined that the position to be taken up by Christianity in the Hellenistic world should be this one. On the other side, it must be noted that the ancient world itself knew the dilemma between the God of faith and the God of the philosophers in a very pronounced form. Between the mythical gods of the religions and the philosophical knowledge of God there had developed in the course of history a stronger and stronger tension, which is apparent in the criticism of the myths by the philosophers from Xenophanes to Plato, who even thought of trying to replace the classical Homeric mythology by a new mythology appropriate to the *logos*. Contemporary scholarship is coming to see more and more clearly that there are quite amazing parallels in chronology and content between the philosophers' criticism of the myths in Greece and the prophets' criticism of the gods in Israel. It is true that the two movements start from completely different assumptions and have completely different aims; but the movement of the *logos* against the myth, as it evolved in the Greek mind in the philosophical enlightenment, so that in the end it was bound to involve the fall of the gods, has an inner parallelism with the enlightenment which the prophetic and Wisdom literature cultivated in its demythologization of the divine

powers in favour of the one and only God. For all the differences between them, both movements coincide in their striving
towards the *logos*. The philosophical enlightenment and its
"physical" view of Being pressed the mythological semblance
further and further back, though certainly without doing away
with the religious form of the worship of the gods. The ancient
religion did eventually break up because of the gulf between
the God of faith and the God of the philosophers, because of
the total dichotomy between reason and piety. That no success
was achieved in uniting the two, that reason and piety moved
further and further apart, and the God of faith and the God of
the philosophers were separated from each other, meant the
inner collapse of the ancient religion. The Christian religion
would have to expect just the same fate if it were to accept a
similar amputation of reason and were to embark on a corresponding withdrawal into the purely religious, as advocated by
Schleiermacher and present, paradoxically enough, in a certain
sense in Schleiermacher's great critic and opponent, Karl
Barth.

The opposing fates of myth and Gospel in the ancient world,
the end of myth and the victory of the Gospel, are fundamentally to be explained, from the point of view of cultural history,
by the opposing relationship established on both occasions
between religion and philosophy, between faith and reason.
The paradox of ancient philosophy consists, from the point of
view of religious history, in the fact that intellectually it destroyed myth but simultaneously tried to legitimize it afresh as
religion; in other words, that from the religious point of view
it was not revolutionary but, at the most, evolutionary, that it
treated religion as a question of the regulation of life, not as a
question of truth. Paul, following the Wisdom literature, has
described this circumstance in his Epistle to the Romans (1.18–
31) in the language of the prophetic sermon (or Old Testament
Wisdom discourse) with perfect accuracy. The reference to this
mortal fate of the ancient religion, and to the paradox implicit
in the separation of truth and piety, occurs in the Book of
Wisdom, Chapters 13–15. Paul recapitulates in a few verses
what is said there in some detail, accounting for the fate of the
ancient religion by the division between *logos* and myth: "For

what can be known about God is plain to them, because God has shown it to them . . . [but] although they knew God they did not honour him as God or give thanks to him . . . [they] exchanged the glory of the immortal God for images resembling mortal man or birds or animals or reptiles" (Rom. 1.19–23).

Religion did not go the way of the *logos* but lingered in myths already seen to be devoid of reality. Consequently its decline was inevitable; this followed from its divorce from the truth, a state of affairs which led to its being regarded as a mere *institutio vitae*, that is, as mere furniture and outward form of life. The Christian position, as opposed to this situation, is put emphatically by Tertullian when he says with splendid boldness: "Christ called himself truth, not custom".[16] In my view this is one of the really great assertions of patristic theology. In it the struggle of the early Church, and the abiding task with which the Christian faith is confronted if it is to remain itself, is summed up with unique conciseness. The idolization of the *consuetudo Romana*, of the "tradition" of the city of Rome, which had made its own customs into a self-sufficient code of behaviour, was challenged by the truth and its claim to uniqueness. Christianity thus put itself resolutely on the side of truth and turned its back on a conception of religion satisfied to be mere outward ceremonial which in the end can be interpreted to mean anything one fancies.

Another observation may help to clarify the point. The ancient world had finally tried to face up to the dilemma of its religion, to its divorce from the truth of the knowledge attained through philosophy, by adopting the idea of three theologies: physical, political and mythical theology. It had justified the separation of myth and *logos* by consideration for the feelings of the people and consideration for the good of the state, in so far as a mythical theology permitted the simultaneous existence of a political theology. In other words, it had in fact weighed truth against custom, usefulness against truth. The exponents of the Neo-Platonic philosophy went a step further, by interpreting myth ontologically, expounding it as symbolic theology and

---

[16] Dominus noster Christus veritatem se, non consuetudinem cognominavit. *De virginibus velandis*, I, 1, in *Corpus Christianorum seu nova Patrum collectio* (CChr), II, p. 1209.

thus trying *via* interpretation to reconcile it with the truth. But what can only go on existing through interpretation has in reality ceased to exist. The human spirit rightly turns to the truth itself, not to what by means of devious interpretation can be shown to be reconcilable with the truth, though no longer containing any truth itself.

Both procedures have something frighteningly contemporary about them. In a situation in which the truth of the Christian approach seems to be disappearing, the struggle for Christianity has brought to the fore again the two very methods which ancient polytheism employed to fight – and lose – its last battle. On one side we have the retreat from the truth of reason into a realm of mere piety, mere faith, mere revelation; a retreat which in reality bears a fatal resemblance, whether by design or accident, and whether the fact is admitted or not, to the ancient religion's retreat before the *logos*, to the flight from truth to beautiful custom, from nature to politics. On the other side we have an approach which I will call for short "interpreted Christianity": the stumbling-blocks in Christianity are removed by the interpretative method and as part of the process of thus rendering it unobjectionable its actual content is written off as dispensable phraseology, as a periphrasis not required to say the simple things now alleged, by complicated modes of exposition, to constitute its real meaning.

In contrast to all this, the original Christian option was something quite different. The Christian faith opted, we have seen, against the gods of the various religions and in favour of the God of the philosophers, that is, against the myth of custom and in favour of the truth of Being itself and nothing else. Hence the accusation made against the early Church that its adherents were atheists; this reproach arose out of the fact that the early Church did indeed reject the whole world of the ancient religion, declaring none of it to be acceptable and sweeping the whole system aside as empty custom that was contrary to the truth. The God of the philosophers, however, who was left over, was not regarded by the ancient world as having any religious significance but as an academic extra-religious reality. To leave only him standing and to profess faith in him alone and in nothing else seemed like lack of religion, as a denial of religion, as atheism. The suspicion of atheism with which early Christianity had to contend makes its intellectual orientation, its decision against *religio* and custom devoid of truth, its option in favour of the truth of Being clearly apparent.

2. THE TRANSFORMATION OF THE GOD OF THE PHILOSOPHERS

Of course, the other side of the picture must not be overlooked. By deciding in favour of the God of the philosophers and logically declaring this God to be the God who speaks to man and to whom one can pray, the Christian faith gave a completely new significance to this God of the philosophers, removing him from the purely academic realm and thus profoundly transforming him. This God who had previously existed as something neutral, as the highest, culminating concept; this God who had been understood as pure Being or pure thought, circling round for ever closed in upon itself without reaching over to man and his little world; this God of the philosophers, whose pure eternity and unchangeability had excluded any relation with the changeable and transitory, now appeared to the eye of faith as the God of men, who is not only thought of all thoughts, the eternal mathematics of the universe, but also *agape*, the power of creative love. In this sense there does exist in the Christian faith what Pascal experienced on the night when he wrote on a slip of paper which he henceforth kept sewn in the lining of his jacket the words: "Fire. 'God of Abraham, God of Isaac, God of Jacob', not 'of the philosophers and scholars'."[17] He had encountered the burning bush experience, as opposed to a God sinking back completely into the realm of mathematics, and had realized that the God who is the eternal geometry of the universe can only be this because he is creative love, because he is the burning bush from which

[17] The text of the "mémorial", as this slip of paper is called, is quoted in R. Guardini, *Christliches Bewusstsein*, 2nd ed., Munich, 1950, pp. 47f.; on p. 23 there is a facsimile, reduced in size, of the original; see also Guardini's analysis, *ibid.*, pp. 27–61. This is supplemented and corrected by H. Vorgrimler, "Marginalien zur Kirchenfrömmigkeit Pascals", in J. Daniélou–H. Vorgrimler, *Sentire ecclesiam*, Freiburg, 1961, pp. 371–406.

a name issues forth, through which he enters the world of man. So in this sense there is the experience that the God of the philosophers is quite different from what the philosophers had thought him to be, though he does not thereby cease to be what they had discovered; that one only comes to know him properly when one realizes that he, the real truth and ground of all Being, is at one and the same time the God of faith, the God of men.

In order to see the transformation undergone by the philosophical concept of God through being equated with the God of faith, one needs only to look at any passage in the Bible which speaks of God. Let us take quite at random Luke 15.1–10, the parables of the lost sheep and the lost drachma. The point of departure is the irritation felt by the Scribes and Pharisees at the fact that Jesus sat down to eat with sinners. In reply comes the story of the man who owns a hundred sheep, loses one of them, goes after it, looks for it and finds it, and rejoices more than over the ninety-nine for which he never needed to search. The story of the lost drachma which, when found again, causes more joy than the one that was never lost tends in the same direction: "Just so, I tell you, there will be more joy in heaven over one sinner who repents than over ninety-nine righteous persons who need no repentance" (15.7). This parable, in which Jesus depicts and justifies his activity and his task as the emissary of God, involves not only the relations between God and man but also the question who God himself is.

If we try to answer the question on the basis of this passage we shall have to say that the God who meets us here appears to be, as in so many passages of the Old Testament, highly anthropomorphic, highly unphilosophical; he has emotions as a man does, he rejoices, he seeks, he waits, he goes to meet. He is not the unfeeling geometry of the universe, neutral justice standing above things undisturbed by a heart and its emotions; he *has* a heart, he stands there like a person who loves, with all the capriciousness of someone who loves. Thus in this passage the transformation of purely philosophical thinking becomes clear, and it becomes apparent how far we still are fundamentally from this identification of the God of faith and the God of the philosophers, how incapable we are of catching up with it, and how badly our basic image of God and our understanding of the Christian reality come to grief *on this very point*.

Most people today still admit in some form or other that there probably is some such thing as a "supreme being". But people find it an absurd idea that this being should concern himself with man; we have the feeling – for it happens again and again even to those who try to believe – that this sort of thing is the expression of a naïve anthropomorphism, of a primitive mode of thought comprehensible in a situation in which man still lived in a small world, in which the earth was the centre of all things and God had nothing else to do but look down on it. But, we think, in an age when we know how infinitely different things are, how unimportant the earth is in the vast universe and consequently how unimportant that little speck of dust, man, is in comparison with the dimensions of the cosmos – in an age like this it seems an absurd idea that this supreme being should concern himself with man, his pitiful little world, his cares, his sins and his non-sins. But although we may think that in this way we are speaking truly appropriately about God, in reality we are in fact thinking of him in a very petty and only too human way, as if his retention of a general view involved making a choice. We thereby imagine him as a consciousness like ours, which has limits, must somewhere or other call a halt, and can never embrace the whole.

In contrast to such limited notions the aphorism with which Hölderlin prefaced his "Hyperion" will serve to recall the Christian image of the true greatness of God: "*Non coerceri maximo, contineri tamen a minimo, divinum est*" ("Not to be encompassed by the greatest, but to let oneself be encompassed by the smallest – that is divine"). The boundless spirit who bears in himself the totality of Being reaches beyond the "greatest", so that to him it is small, and he reaches into the smallest, because to him nothing is too small. Precisely this overstepping of the greatest and reaching down into the smallest is the true nature of absolute spirit. At the same time we see here a reversal in value of maximum and minimum, greatest and smallest, that is typical of the Christian understanding of reality.

To him who as spirit bears up and encompasses the universe, a spirit, a man's heart with its ability to love, is greater than all the milky ways in the universe. Quantitative criteria become irrelevant; other scales become visible, reckoned by which the infinitely small is the truly embracing and truly great.[18]

From this angle yet another prejudice is unmasked as a prejudice. It always seems to us in the last analysis self-evident that the infinitely great, the absolute spirit, cannot be emotion and feeling but only pure cosmic mathematics. We unthinkingly assume that pure thought is greater than love, while the message of the Gospel, and the Christian picture of God contained in it, corrects philosophy and lets us know that love is higher than mere thought. Absolute thought is a kind of love; it is not unfeeling idea, but creative, because it is love.

To sum up, we can say that in the link-up with the God of the philosophers which the Christian faith consciously effected purely philosophical thinking was exceeded on two fundamental points:

(a) *The philosophical God is essentially self-centred*, thought simply contemplating itself. The God of faith is basically defined by the category of relationship. He is creative fullness encompassing the whole. Thereby a completely new picture of the world, a completely new world-order is established: the highest possibility of Being no longer seems to be the detachment of him who exists in himself and needs only himself. On the contrary, the highest mode of Being includes the element of relationship. It is hardly necessary to say what a revolution it must mean for the direction of man's existence when the supreme Being no

[18] The origin of the "epitaph on Loyola" quoted by Hölderlin has been explained by H. Rahner, "Die Grabschrift des Loyola", in *Stimmen der Zeit*, 72nd year, Vol. 139 (February 1947), pp. 321–337: the saying comes from the great work *Imago primi saeculi Societatis Jesu a Provincia Flandro–Belgica eiusdem Societatis repraesentata*, Antwerp, 1640. On pages 280–282 of this work there is an *elogium sepulchrale* on St Ignatius by an unknown young Flemish Jesuit from which the saying is taken; cf. also Hölderlin, *Works*, Vol. III (ed. by F. Beissner, special edition for the Wissenschaftliche Buchgesellschaft, Darmstadt), Stuttgart, 1965, pp. 346f. The same idea occurs in a large number of impressive late Jewish texts; cf. on this aspect P. Kuhn, *Gottes Selbsterniedrigung in der Theologie der Rabbinen*, Munich, 1968, especially pp. 13–22.

longer appears as absolute, enclosed autarchy but turns out to be at the same time involvement, creative power, which creates and bears and loves other things . . .

(b) *The philosophical God is pure thought:* he is based on the notion that thought and thought alone is divine. The God of faith, as thought, is also love. His image is based on the conviction that to love is divine. The *logos* of the whole world, the creative original thought, is at the same time love; in fact this thought is creative because, as thought, it is love and, as love, it is thought. It becomes apparent that truth and love are originally identical; that where they are completely realized they are not two parallel or even opposing realities but one, the one and only absolute. At this point it also becomes possible to glimpse the starting-point of the confession of faith in the tri-une God, to which we shall return later.

3. THE REFLECTION OF THE QUESTION IN THE TEXT OF THE CREED

In the Apostles' Creed, the point of departure of our reflections, the paradoxical unity of the God of faith and the God of the philosophers, on which the Christian image of God rests, is expressed in the juxtaposition of the two attributes "Father" and "Almighty" ("Lord of All"). The second title – "*pantokrator*" in Greek – points back to the Old Testament "Yahweh Zebaoth" (Sabaoth), the meaning of which can no longer be fully elucidated. Literally translated, it means something like "God of hosts", "God of powers"; it is sometimes rendered in the Greek Bible by "Lord of powers". For all the uncertainties about its origin we can at any rate see that this word is intended to describe God as the Lord of heaven and earth; it was probably intended above all to define him, in opposition to the Babylonian religion of the stars, as the Lord to whom the stars too belong, alongside whom the stars cannot exist as independent divine powers: the stars are not gods, but *his* tools, at his disposal like a warlord's armies. Thus the word "*pantokrator*" has at first a cosmic significance; later it also has a political sense, describing God as the Lord of all Lords.[19] By calling God simultaneously "Father" and "Almighty" the Creed has joined together a family concept and the concept of cosmic power in the description of the one God. It thereby expresses accurately the whole point of the Christian image of God: the tension between absolute power and absolute love, absolute distance and absolute proximity, between absolute Being and a direct affinity with the most human side of humanity, the interplay of maximum and minimum of which we spoke just now.

The word "Father", which in its reference-point here still remains quite open, at the same time links the first article of the Creed to the second; it points forward to Christology and thus harnesses the two sections together in such a way that what is said of God only becomes fully comprehensible when one at the same time looks over at the Son. For example, what "almightiness" and "lordship of all" mean only becomes clear from a Christian point of view in the crib and the cross. It is only here, where the God who is recognized as Lord of all has voluntarily chosen the final degree of powerlessness by delivering himself up to his weakest creature, that the Christian concept of the almightiness of God can be truly formulated. At this point simultaneously a new concept of power and a new concept of lordship and dominion is born. The highest power is demonstrated as the calm willingness completely to renounce all power; and we are shown that it is powerful not through force but only through the freedom of love, which, even when it is rejected, is stronger than the exultant powers of earthly violence. Here and only here does that revaluation of criteria and dimensions which made itself heard earlier in the antithesis of maximum and minimum finally come into its own.

---

[19] Kattenbusch, Vol. II, p. 526; P. van Imschoot, "Heerscharen", in H. Haag, *Bibellexikon*, Einsiedeln, 1951, pp. 667–9. In the second edition (1968), p. 684, the article has been drastically shortened.

Chapter IV

FAITH IN GOD TODAY

AFTER all we have said, what does it mean today when a man says, in the words of the Creed, "I believe in God"? Anyone who utters these words makes first and foremost a decision about values and emphasis in this world which is certainly comprehensible as truth (and indeed in a qualified sense must be regarded as a decision for the truth) but in the last analysis can only be called for in the decision and as decision. What thus takes place is also a decision in the sense that a separation is made between various different possibilities. What Israel had to do in the early days of its history, and the Church had to do again at the beginning of its career, must be done afresh in every human life. Just as in those days the verdict had to be delivered against the possibilities symbolized by Moloch and Baal, against custom and in favour of truth, so the Christian statement "I believe in God" is always a process of separation, of acceptance, of purification and of transformation. Only in this way can the Christian confession of faith in the one God be maintained in the passing ages. But in what directions does this process point today?

1. THE PRIMACY OF THE LOGOS

Christian faith in God means first the decision in favour of the primacy of the *logos* as against mere matter. Saying "I believe that God exists" also implies opting for the view that the *logos* – that is, the idea, freedom, love – stands not merely at the end but also at the beginning; that it is the originating and encompassing power of all being. In other words, faith means deciding for the view that thought and meaning do not just form a chance by-product of being; that on the contrary all being is a product of thought and indeed in its innermost structure is itself thought. To that extent faith means in a specific sense deciding for the truth, since, to faith, being itself is truth, comprehensibility, meaning, and all this does not simply represent a secondary product of being which arose at some point or other but could have no structural, authoritative meaning for reality as a whole.

This decision in favour of the intellectual structure of the kind of being which emerges from meaning and understanding includes the belief in creation. This means nothing else than the conviction that the objective mind which we find present in all things, indeed as which we learn increasingly to understand things, is the impression and expression of subjective mind and that the intellectual structure which being possesses and which we can meditate *upon* is the expression of a creative *pre*-meditation, to which they owe their existence.

To put it more precisely, in the old Pythagorean saying about the God who practises geometry there is expressed that insight into the mathematical structure of being which learns to understand being as being-thought, as intellectually structured; there is also expressed the perception that even matter is not simply non-sense which eludes understanding, that it too bears in itself truth and comprehensibility which make intellectual comprehension possible. In our time, through the investigation of the mathematical construction of matter and the way it can be conceived and evaluated in mathematical terms, this insight has gained an amazing solidity. Einstein said once that in the laws of nature "an intelligence so superior is revealed that in comparison all the significance of human thinking and human arrangements is a completely worthless reflection".[20]

This surely means that all our thinking is indeed only a re-thinking of what in reality has already been thought out beforehand. It can only try in a paltry way to trace over that being-thought which things are and to find truth in it. The mathematical understanding of the world has here discovered,

[20] A. Einstein, *Mein Weltbild*, ed. by C. Seelig, Zürich, Stuttgart, Vienna, 1953, p. 21.

through the mathematics of the universe, so to speak, the "God of the philosophers" – with all its problems, as is shown when Einstein over and over again rejects the concept of a personal God as "anthropomorphic", ascribing it to the "religion of fear" and the "religion of morality", with which he contrasts, as the only appropriate attitude, the "cosmic religiosity" which to him expresses itself in "enraptured wonder at the harmony of the laws of nature", in a "deep faith in the intelligence of the structure of the world", and in the "longing for understanding, if only of a pale reflection of the intelligence revealed in this world".[21]

Here we have before us the whole problem of belief in God. On the one side there is the transparence of being, which as being-thought points to a process of thinking; on the other we have the impossibility of bringing this thinking of being into relation with man. It becomes easy to see the barrier to the equating of the "God of faith" and the "God of the philosophers" constituted by a narrow and insufficiently pondered concept of person.

Before we try to make any progress on this point I should like to cite another similar statement by a scientist. James Jeans once said: "We discover that the universe shows traces of a planning and controlling power which has something in common with our own individual minds, not, so far as we have yet discovered, feeling, morality or aesthetic capacity, but the tendency to think in a way which for lack of a better word we have called geometry."[22] This is the same thing all over again: the mathematician discovers the mathematics of the cosmos, the being-thought-ness of things; but no more. He discovers only the God of the philosophers.

But is this really surprising? Can the mathematician who looks at the world mathematically find anything else but mathe-

---

[21] *Op. cit.*, pp. 18–22. In the section entitled "The necessity for an ethical culture" (pp. 22–24) there are signs of a loosening of the previously intimate connection between scientific knowledge and religious wonder; his perception of the specifically religious seems to have been somewhat sharpened by increased tragic experiences.

[22] Quoted in W. von Hartlieb, *Das Christentum und die Gegenwart*, Salzburg, 1953 (Stifterbibliothek, Vol. 21), pp. 18f.

matics in the universe? Should not one rather ask him whether
he has not himself at some time or other looked at the world in
an other than mathematical way? Whether, for example, he
has never seen an apple tree in blossom and wondered why the
process of fertilization by the interplay between bees and tree
is not effected otherwise than through the roundabout way of
the blossom, thus including the completely superfluous wonder
of beauty, which again of course can only be understood by
co-operation, by relying on that which is already beautiful
even without us? When Jeans opines that this kind of thing has
so far not been discovered in the mind of which he speaks, one
can confidently say to him that it will indeed never be discovered by physics and cannot be, because in its investigations
it abstracts, in accordance with its nature, from the aesthetic
feeling and from the moral attitude, questions nature from a
purely mathematical point of view and consequently can also
sight only the mathematical side of nature. The answer depends
quite simply on the question. The man who seeks a view of the
whole will have to say: In the world we find present, without
doubt, objective mathematics; but we also find equally present
in the world unparalleled and unexplained wonders of beauty,
or, to be more accurate, there are events which appear to the
apprehending mind of man in the form of beauty, so that he is
bound to say that the mathematician responsible for these
events has displayed an unparalleled degree of creative imagination.

If we summarize the observations which we have strung
together in a sketchy and fragmentary fashion we can say: The
world is objective mind; it meets us in an intellectual structure,
that is, it offers itself to our mind as something that can be
reflected upon and understood. From this follows the next step.
To say "*Credo in Deum* – I believe in God" expresses the conviction that objective mind is the product of subjective mind and
can only exist at all as the declension of it, that, in other words,
being-thought (as we find it present in the structure of the
world) is not possible without thinking.

It may be useful to clarify and confirm this statement by
inserting it – again only in broad strokes – into a kind of self-
criticism of historical reason. After two and a half thousand

years of philosophical thinking it is no longer possible for us to speak happily of the matter itself as if so many different people had not tried to do the same thing before us and come to grief. Moreover, when we survey the acres of shattered hypotheses, vainly applied ingenuity and empty logic which history shows us, we might well lose all heart in the quest for the real, hidden beyond-the-obvious truth. Yet the situation is not quite so hopeless as it must appear at first sight, for in spite of the almost endless variety of the opposing philosophical paths which man has taken in his attempts to think out being, in the last analysis there are only a few basic ways of explaining the secret of being. The question to which everything finally leads could be formulated like this: In all the variety of individual things what is, so to speak, the common stuff of being – what is the one being behind the many "things", which nevertheless all "exist"? The many answers produced by history can finally be reduced to two basic possibilities. The first and most obvious would run something like this: Everything we encounter is in the last analysis stuff, matter; *this* is the only thing that always remains as demonstrable reality and consequently represents the real being of all that exists – the materialistic solution. The other possibility points in the opposite direction. It says: Whoever looks thoroughly at matter will discover that it is being-thought, objectivized thought. So it cannot be the ultimate. On the contrary, before it comes thinking, the idea; all being is in the last resort being-thought and can be traced back to mind as the original reality; this is the "idealistic" solution.

To reach a verdict we must ask still more precisely: What is matter really? And what is mind? Abbreviating drastically, we could say that we call "matter" a being that does not itself comprehend being, that "is", but does not understand itself. The reduction of all being to matter as the primary form of reality consequently implies that the beginning and ground of all being is constituted by a form of being that does not itself understand being; this also means that the understanding of being only arises as a secondary, chance product during the course of development. This at the same time also gives us the definition of "mind": it can be described as being that understands itself, as being by itself. The idealistic solution to the

problem of being accordingly signifies the idea that all being
is the being-thought by one single consciousness. The unity of
being consists in the identity of the one consciousness, whose
movements constitute the many things that are.

The Christian belief in God is not completely identical with
either of these two solutions. To be sure, it too will say, being is
being-thought. Matter itself points beyond itself to thinking as
the earlier and more original factor. But in opposition to
idealism, which makes all being into moments of an all-
embracing consciousness, the Christian belief in God will say:
Being is being-thought – yet not in such a way that it remains
only thought and that the appearance of independence discloses itself to him who looks more closely as mere appearance.
On the contrary, Christian belief in God means that things are
the being-thought of a creative consciousness, of a creative
freedom, and that the creative consciousness that bears up all
things has released what has been thought into the freedom of
its own, independent existence. In this it goes beyond any mere
idealism. While the latter, as we have just established, explains
everything real as the content of a single consciousness, in the
Christian view what supports it all is a creative freedom that
sets what has been thought in the freedom of its own being, so
that on the one hand it is the being-thought of a consciousness
and yet on the other true self-being.

This also clarifies the root of the conception of creation: the
model from which creation must be understood is not the
craftsman but the creative mind, creative thinking. At the
same time it becomes evident that the idea of freedom is the
characteristic mark of the Christian belief in God as opposed
to any kind of monism. At the beginning of all being it puts
not just some kind of consciousness but a creative freedom
which creates further freedoms. To this extent one could very
well describe Christianity as a philosophy of freedom. For
Christianity, the explanation of reality as a whole is not an
all-embracing consciousness or one single materiality; on the
contrary, at the summit stands a freedom that thinks and,
thinking, creates freedoms, thus making freedom the structural
form of all being.

2. THE PERSONAL GOD

If Christian belief in God is first of all an option in favour of the primacy of the *logos*, faith in the pre-existing, world-supporting reality of the creative meaning, it is at the same time, as belief in the personal nature of that meaning, the belief that the original thought, whose being-thought is represented by the world, is not an anonymous, neutral consciousness but freedom, creative love, a person. Accordingly, if the Christian option for the *logos* means an option for a personal, creative meaning, then it is at the same time an option for the primacy of the particular as against the universal. The highest is not the most universal but, precisely, the particular, and the Christian faith is thus above all also the option for man as the irreducible, infinity-related being. And here once again it is the option for the primacy of freedom as against the primacy of some cosmic necessity or natural law. Thus the specific features of the Christian faith as opposed to other intellectual choices of the human mind now stand out in clear relief. The position occupied by a man who utters the Christian *Credo* becomes unmistakably clear.

Moreover, it can be shown that the first option – for the primacy of the *logos* as opposed to mere matter – is not possible without the second and third, or, to be more accurate, the first, taken on its own, would remain mere idealism; it is only the addition of the second and third options – primacy of the particular, primacy of freedom – that marks the watershed between idealism and Christian belief, which now denotes something different from mere idealism. Much could be said about this. Let us content ourselves with the indispensable elucidations by first asking what it really means to say that this *logos*, whose thought is the world, is a person and therefore faith is the option in favour of the primacy of the particular over the universal. In the last analysis the answer can be put quite simply: It means nothing else than that the creative thinking which we found to be the precondition and ground of all being is truly conscious thinking and that it knows not only itself but also its whole thought. It means further that this thinking not only knows but loves; that it is creative because it is love; and that because it can love as well as think it has given its thought the freedom of its own existence, objectivized it, released it into self-being. So the whole thing means that this thinking knows its thought in its self-being, loves it and, loving, bears it up. Which brings us back to the saying to which our reflections keep leading: not to be encompassed by the greatest, but to let oneself be encompassed by the smallest – that is divine.

But if the *logos* of all being, the being that bears up and encompasses everything, is consciousness, freedom and love, then it follows automatically that the supreme factor in the world is not cosmic necessity but freedom. The implications of this are very extensive. For this leads to the appearance of freedom and the necessary structure, as it were, of the world, and this again means that one can only comprehend the world as incomprehensible, that it must be incomprehensibility. For if the supreme point in the world's design is a freedom which bears up, wills, knows and loves the whole world as freedom, then this means that together with freedom the incalculability implicit in it is an essential part of the world. Incalculability is an implication of freedom; the world can never – if this is the position – be completely reduced to mathematical logic. With the boldness and greatness of a world defined by the structure of freedom there comes also the sombre mystery of the demonic, which emerges from it to meet us. A world created and willed on the risk of freedom and love is no longer just mathematics. As the arena of love it is also the playground of freedom and also incurs the risk of evil. It accepts the mystery of darkness for the sake of the great light constituted by freedom and love.

Once again it becomes evident here how the categories of minimum and maximum, smallest and greatest, change in a perspective of this sort. In a world which in the last analysis is not mathematics but love, the minimum is a maximum; the smallest thing that can love is one of the biggest things; the particular is more than the universal; the person, the unique and unrepeatable, is at the same time the ultimate and highest thing. In such a view of the world the person is not just an individual, a reproduction arising by the diffusion of the idea into matter, but, precisely, a "person". Greek thought always regarded the many individual creatures, including the many individual human beings, only as individuals, arising out of the splitting-up of the idea in matter. The reproductions are thus always secondary; the real thing is the one and universal. The Christian sees in man not an individual but a person; and it seems to me that this passage from individual to person contains the whole span of the transition from antiquity to Christianity, from Plato to faith. This definite being is not at all something secondary, giving us a fragmentary glimpse of the universal, which is the real. As the minimum it is a maximum; as the unique and unrepeatable it is something supreme and real.

From this follows one last step. If it is the case that the person is more than the individual, that the many is something real and not something secondary, that there exists a primacy of the particular over the universal, then oneness is not the unique and final thing; plurality too has its own and definitive right. This assertion, which follows by an inner necessity from the Christian option, leads of its own accord to the overstepping of the concept of a God who is mere oneness. The internal logic of the Christian belief in God compels us to overstep mere monotheism and leads to the belief in the triune God, who must now, in conclusion, be discussed.

Chapter V

BELIEF IN THE TRIUNE GOD

OUR previous reflections have brought us to the point at which the Christian confession of faith in the one God passes over by a kind of inner necessity to the confession of faith in the triune God. On the other hand we cannot overlook the fact that we are now touching a realm in which Christian theology must be more aware of its limits than it has often been in the past; a realm in which any falsely-directed attempt to gain too precise a knowledge is bound to end in disastrous foolishness; a realm in which only the humble admission of ignorance can be true knowledge and only wondering attendance before the incomprehensible mystery can be the right confession of faith in God. Love is always "*mysterium*" – more than one can reckon or grasp by subsequent reckoning. Love itself – the uncreated, eternal God – *must* therefore be in the highest degree a mystery – "the" *mysterium* itself.

Yet – despite the necessary moderation of reason, which here is the only way in which thinking can remain true to itself and to its task – the question must be posed what is really meant by the confession of faith in the triune God. We cannot here attempt – as we really should in order to reach a satisfactory answer – to trace the individual stages by which it developed or even to display the individual formulas in which faith strove to protect it from misinterpretation. A few indications must suffice.

I. A START AT UNDERSTANDING

(a) The point of departure of the belief in the triune God

The doctrine of the Trinity did not arise out of speculation about God, out of an attempt by philosophical thinking to

explain to itself what the fount of all being was like; it developed
out of the effort to digest historical experiences. The biblical
faith was concerned at first – in the Old Covenant – with God,
who was encountered as the Father of Israel, the Father of the
peoples, the creator of the world and Israel's Lord. In the
formative period of the New Testament comes a completely
unexpected event in which God shows himself from a hitherto
unknown side: in Jesus Christ one meets a man who at the
same time knows and professes himself to be the Son of God.
One finds God in the shape of the ambassador who is completely
God and not some kind of intermediary being, yet with us says
to God "Father". The result is a curious paradox: on the one
hand this man calls God his Father and speaks to him as to
someone else facing him; if this is not to be a piece of empty
theatricality but truth, which alone befits God, then Christ
must be someone other than this Father to whom *he* speaks and
to whom *we* speak. But on the other hand he is himself the real
proximity of God coming to meet us, God's mediation to us,
and that precisely because he himself is God as man, in human
form and nature, God-with-us ("Emmanuel"). His mediation
would indeed basically cancel itself out and become a separation
instead of a mediation if he were someone other than God, if he
were an intermediate being. He would then be guiding us not
towards God but away from him. It thus turns out that as
mediator he is God himself and "man himself" – both with
equal reality and totality. But this means that God meets me
here not as Father but as Son and as my brother, whereby –
both incomprehensibly and quite comprehensibly – a duality
appears in God: God as "I" and "You" in one. This new
experience of God is followed finally by a third, the experience
of the Spirit, the presence of God in us, in our innermost being.
And again it turns out that this "Spirit" is not simply identical
either with the Father or the Son, nor yet a third thing erected
between God and us; it is the mode in which God gives himself to us, in which he enters into us, so that he is *in* man, yet
in the midst of this "indwelling" is infinitely *above* him.

We can thus observe that the Christian faith first comes to
deal with God in this triple shape in the course of its historical
development, as a matter of sheer fact. It is clear that it had to

begin straightway to consider how these different pieces of data were to be reconciled with each other. It had to ask itself how these three forms of historical encounter with God were related to the reality proper of God himself. Is the triplicity of the form in which God is experienced perhaps only his historical mask, in which he approaches man in different roles yet always as the One? Does this triplicity only tell us something about man and the various modes of his relationship to God, or does it shed light on what God is like in himself? If today we might swiftly feel inclined to regard only the former as conceivable and with that to consider all the problems solved, before taking refuge in such a solution we ought to make ourselves aware of the scope of the question. The point at issue here is whether man in his relations with God is only dealing with the reflections of his own consciousness or whether it is given to him to reach out beyond himself and to encounter God himself. In either case the consequences are far-reaching. If the first hypothesis is true, then prayer too is only an occupation of man with himself; there are no more grounds for worship proper than there are for prayers of petition – and this inference is in fact drawn to an increasing degree. This renders all the more pressing the question whether it does not rest in the end on comfortable thinking which takes the line of least resistance without asking too many questions. For if the other answer is the correct one worship and prayer are not only possible; they are enjoined, that is, they are a postulate of the being "man" who is open to God.

Anyone who sees the profundity of the question will at the same time understand the passionate nature of the struggle that was fought out round it in the ancient Church; he will understand that anything but hair-splitting and formula-worship was involved, as a superficial view might easily suggest. Indeed, he will realize that the strife of those days is flaring up afresh today in just the same form – the one constant struggle of man for God and for himself – and that we cannot endure as Christians if we think it permissible to make it easier for ourselves today than it was then. Let us anticipate the answer found in those days to the parting between the path of faith and a path bound to lead to the mere appearance of faith: God *is* as he *shows* himself; God does not show himself in a way in which he is not. On this assertion rests the Christian relation with God; in it is grounded the doctrine of the Trinity; indeed, it *is* this doctrine.

(b) The guiding motives

What led to this conclusion? Two basic attitudes were decisive. The first could be described as faith in man's immediate proximity to God, the belief that the man who has to do with Christ meets in his fellow man Jesus, who as a fellow man is attainable and accessible to him, God himself, not a hybrid being inserting itself in between. The anxiety in the early Church about the true divinity of Jesus springs from the same root as the anxiety about his true humanity. Only if he was really a man like us can he be *our* mediator, and only if he is really God, like God, does the mediation reach its goal. It is not at all difficult to see that the fundamental decision of monotheism, the previously described equation of the God of faith with the God of the philosophers, here comes into the question and becomes exceptionally acute: only the God who on the one hand is the real ground of the world and on the other totally the One near to us can be the goal of a piety devoted to the truth. Thus the second basic attitude has already been described by implication: the unyielding loyalty to a strictly monotheistic decision, to the confession "There is only *one* God". Care had to be taken at all costs not to erect again, *via* the mediator, a whole region of middle beings and with it a region of false gods where man worships what is not God.

The third basic attitude could be described as the striving to give the story of God's dealings with man its proper seriousness. This means that when God appears as Son, who says "You" to the Father, it is not a play produced for man, it is not a masked ball on the stage of human history, but the expression of reality. The idea of a divine show had been canvassed in the ancient Church by the Monarchians. The three persons, they maintained, were three "roles" in which God shows himself to us in the course of history. Here it must be mentioned that the word *"persona"* and its Greek equivalent, *"prosopon"*, belong to the language of the theatre. They denoted the mask which made the actor into the embodiment of someone else. It was as a result of considerations of this sort that the word was first introduced into the language of Christianity and so transformed by the Christian faith itself in the course of a severe struggle that out of the word arose the idea of the person, a notion alien to antiquity.

Others – the so-called Modalists – thought that the three forms of God were three *modi*, ways, in which our consciousness perceives God and explains him to itself. Although it is true that we only know God as he is reflected in human thought, the Christian faith held firmly to the view that in this reflection it is *him* that we know. Even if we are not capable of breaking *out* of the narrow bounds of our consciousness, God can nevertheless break *into* this consciousness and show himself in it. All the same, it need not be denied that the efforts of the Monarchians and Modalists resulted in noteworthy progress towards a correct conception of God; after all, the language of Christianity adopted the terminology which they developed and in the confession of faith in the three *persons* in God it is still at work today. That the word "*prosopon*" or "*persona*" could not at once express the whole scope of what there is to express here was not, after all, their fault. The enlargement of the bounds of human thinking necessary to absorb intellectually the Christian experience of God did not come of its own accord. It demanded a struggle, in which even error was fruitful, here it followed the basic law that everywhere governs the human mind in its advances.

(c) *The hopelessness of the solutions*

In the light of what we have already said, the whole struggle of the first few centuries, with all its ramifications, can be traced back to the inadequacy of two paths, which had more and more to be recognized as dead ends: Subordinationism and Monarchianism. Both solutions *seem* logical; yet with their seductive simplifications both destroy the whole. The teaching of the Church, as it comes to us in the doctrine of the triune God, means at bottom renouncing any solution and remaining content with a mystery which cannot be plumbed by man. In truth this confession of faith is the only real way to renounce the arrogance of knowledge, which makes smooth solutions with their false modesty so tempting.

So-called Subordinationism escapes from the dilemma by saying: God himself is only a single being; Christ is not God but only a being particularly close to God. This removes the difficulty, but the consequence – as we explained at length a little earlier – is that man is cut off from God himself and confined, so to speak, to the antechamber. God becomes a sort of constitutional monarch; faith deals not with him but only with his ministers.[23] Anyone who is not content with this, who really believes in the Lordship of God, in the "greatest" in the smallest, will have to hold fast to the belief that God *is* man, that the being of God and man intermingle, and will thus adopt with the belief in Christ the starting-point of the doctrine of the Trinity.

Monarchianism, whose solution we have already touched on earlier, solves the dilemma by proceeding in the opposite direction. It too holds firmly to the oneness of God but at the same time also takes seriously the God who meets us, the God who comes towards us first as creator and father, then, in Christ, as son and redeemer, and finally as Holy Ghost. But these three figures are regarded only as masks of God which tell us something about ourselves but nothing about God himself. Tempting as such an approach seems, in the end it leads back to a situation in which man is only circling round in himself and not penetrating to God's own reality. The subsequent history of Monarchianism in modern thinking has only confirmed this once again. Hegel and Schelling, in their efforts to interpret Christianity philosophically and to re-think philosophy from Christian premises, went back to this early Christian attempt at a philosophy of Christianity and hoped by starting from here to make the doctrine of the Trinity rationally analysable and useful, to elevate it in its allegedly pure philosophical sense into the true key to all understanding of Being. Obviously we cannot try here to give a full picture of these attempts, the most exciting so far made, to validate the Christian faith in purely intellectual terms. All we can do is indicate how they

---

[23] E. Peterson, *Theologische Traktate*, Munich, 1951, pp. 45–147; for monotheism as a political problem, see especially pp. 52f.

too, like Monarchianism (and Modalism), run up again, for all practical purposes, against a dead end.

The point of departure of this whole approach remains the idea that the doctrine of the Trinity is the expression of the historical side of God and therefore of the way in which God appears in history. Inasmuch as Hegel and – in a different way – Schelling push this idea to its logical conclusion, they reach the point where they no longer distinguish this process of the historical self-revelation of God from a God quietly resting in himself behind it all; instead, they now understand the process of history as the process of God himself. The historical form of God then becomes the gradual self-realization of the divine; thus history certainly becomes the process of the *logos*, but even the *logos* is only real as the process of history. In other words, this means that it is only gradually in the course of history that the *logos* – the meaning of all being – brings itself forth to itself. Thus the "historicization" of the doctrine of the Trinity, as contained in Monarchianism, now becomes the "historicization" of God. This again signifies that meaning is no longer simply the creator of history, instead, history becomes the creator of meaning and the latter becomes its creation. Karl Marx is the only one who continued to think resolutely along these lines, by asserting that if meaning does not precede man then it lies in the future, which man must himself bring about by his own struggles.

It thus becomes clear that the logic of Monarchianism is just as unhelpful to faith as Subordinationism is. For such a view does away with the confrontation of freedoms, so essential to faith; it does away with the dialogue of love and its incalculability; and it does away with the "personal" structure of meaning, with its interplay of greatest and smallest, of world-encompassing meaning and creature in quest of meaning. All this – the personal element, the dialogue, the freedom and the love – is merged into the inevitability of the one process of reason. But something else too comes to light here: the attempt to understand the doctrine of the Trinity quite clearly, the thoroughly logical approach which ends in the "historicization" of the *logos* itself, and with the comprehension of God also wants to abolish mystery and comprehend the history of

God, to construct it itself according to its own logic – this grandiose attempt to lay hands on the logic of the *logos* itself leads us back to a mythology of history, to the myth of a God who brings himself to birth historically. The attempt at total logic ends in the reverse of logic, in the self-dissolution of logic into myth.

The history of Monarchianism also has another side to it which must at least be briefly mentioned here. Even in its early Christian form and then again in its revival by Hegel and Marx it has a decidedly political tinge; it is "political theology". In the ancient Church it served the attempt to give the imperial monarchy a theological foundation; in Hegel it becomes the apotheosis of the Prussian state, and in Marx a programme of action to secure a sound future for humanity. Conversely, it could be shown how in the old Church the victory of belief in the Trinity over Monarchianism signified a victory over the political abuse of theology: the ecclesiastical belief in the Trinity shattered the politically usable moulds, destroyed the potentialities of theology as a political myth, and disowned the misuse of the Gospel to justify a political situation.[24]

(d) *The doctrine of the Trinity as negative theology*

If one surveys the whole question it is possible to observe that the ecclesiastical doctrine of the Trinity can be justified first and foremost on the negative side, as a demonstration of the hopelessness of all other approaches. Indeed, perhaps this is all we can really accomplish here. The doctrine of the Trinity would in that case be essentially negative – the only remaining way to reject all attempts to understand clearly; a sort of cipher for the insolubility of the mystery of God. It would become questionable if it were to move over to a simple, positive desire for knowledge. If the painful history of the human and Christian striving for God proves *anything*, it surely proves this: that any attempt to reduce God to the scope of our own

[24] *Op. cit.* p. 102ff. Peterson's concluding remark (p. 147, note 168) is also important: "The concept of 'political theology' was introduced, so far as I know, by Carl Schmitt, *Politische Theologie*, Munich, 1922. . . . We have tried here, by means of a concrete example, to demonstrate the theological impossibility of a 'political theology'. "

comprehension leads to the absurd. We can only speak rightly about him if we renounce the attempt to comprehend and leave him as the uncomprehended. Any doctrine of the Trinity cannot therefore aim at being a perfect comprehension of God. It is a frontier notice, a discouraging gesture pointing over to unchartable territory. It is not a definition that confines a thing to the pigeon-holes of human knowledge, nor is it a concept which would put the thing within the grasp of the human mind.

This character of allusion, in which the concept becomes a mere hint, and comprehension a mere reaching out to apprehend the incomprehensible, could be accurately mapped by the ecclesiastical formulas themselves and their early history. Every one of the big basic concepts in the doctrine of the Trinity was condemned at one time or another; they were all adopted only after the frustration of a condemnation; they are accepted only inasmuch as they are at the same time branded as unusable and admitted simply as poor stammering utterances – and no more.[25] The concept *"persona"* (or *prosopon*) was once condemned, as we have seen; the crucial word that in the fourth century became the standard of orthodoxy, *homousios* (=of one substance with the Father), had been condemned in the third century; the concept of "proceeding" has a condemnation behind it – and so one could go on. One must say, I think, that these condemnations of the later formulas of faith form an intimate part of them: it is only through the negation, and the infinite indirectness implicit in it, that they are usable. The doctrine of the Trinity is only possible as a piece of baffled theology, so to speak.

A further observation should be added. When one looks at the history of the dogma of the Trinity as it is reflected in a present-day manual of theology, it looks like a graveyard of heresies, whose emblems theology still carries round with it

[25] The history of the *homousios* will suffice to illustrate the point; see the summary by A. Grillmeier, in LThK, V, pp. 467f; and also the survey of the history of trinitarian dogma in A. Adam, *loc. cit.*, pp. 115–254 (p. 85, note 13). On the subject of man's stammering before God, cf. the beautiful story "Das Stammeln" from the Chassidic stories in M. Buber, *Works*, Vol. III, Munich, 1963, p. 334.

like the trophies from battles fought and won. But such a view does not represent a proper understanding of the matter, for all the attempted solutions which in the course of a long struggle were finally thrown out as dead-ends and hence heresies are not just mere gravestones to the vanity of human endeavour, monuments which confirm how often thinking has come to grief and at which we can now look back in retrospective – and in the last analysis fruitless – curiosity. On the contrary, every heresy is at the same time the cipher for an abiding truth, a cipher which we must now preserve with other simultaneously valid statements, separated from which it produces a false impression. In other words, all these statements are not so much gravestones as the bricks of a cathedral, which are of course only useful when they do not remain alone but are inserted in something bigger, just as even the positively accepted formulas are only valid if they are at the same time aware of their own inadequacy.

The Jansenist Saint-Cyran once made the thought-provoking remark that faith consists of a series of contradictions held together by grace.[26] He thereby expressed in the realm of theology a discovery which today in physics, as the law of complementarity, belongs to the realm of scientific thought.[27] The physicist is becoming increasingly aware today that we cannot embrace given realities – the structure of light, for example, or matter as a whole – in *one* form of experiment and so in *one* form of statement; that on the contrary from different sides we glimpse different aspects, which cannot be traced back to each other. We have to take the two together – say the structure of corpuscle and wave – without being able to find any all-embracing aspect – as a provisional assessment of the whole,

[26] Quoted by H. Dombois, "Der Kampf um das Kirchenrecht", in H. Asmussen and W. Stählin, *Die Katholizität der Kirche*, Stuttgart, 1957, pp. 285–307. The quotation is on p. 297.

[27] H. Dombois, *loc. cit.*, points out that Niels Bohr, who introduced the law of complementarity into physics, referred for his part to theology – to the complementarity of God's justice and mercy; cf. N. Bohr, *Atomtheorie und Naturbeschreibung*, Berlin, 1931; *Atomphysik und menschliche Erkenntnis*, Brunswick, 1958. Further references and literature are provided by C. F. von Weizsäcker in his article "Komplementarität", in *Die Religion in Geschichte und Gegenwart* (RGG), Vol. III, pp. 1744f.

which is not accessible to us as a unified whole because of the limitations implicit in our point of view. What is true here in the physical realm as a result of the deficiencies in our vision is true in an incomparably greater degree of the spiritual realities and of God. Here too we can always look from *one* side and so grasp only one particular aspect, which seems to contradict the other, yet only when combined with it is a pointer to the whole which we are incapable of stating or grasping. Only by circling round, by looking and describing from different, apparently contrary angles can we succeed in alluding to the truth, which is never visible to us in its totality.

The intellectual approach of modern physics may offer us more help here than the Aristotelian philosophy was able to give. Physicists know today that one can only talk about the structure of matter in approximations starting from various different angles. They know that the position of the beholder at any one time affects the result of his questioning of nature. Why should we not be able to understand afresh, on this basis, that in the question of God we must not look, in the Aristotelian fashion, for an ultimate concept encompassing the whole, but must be prepared to find a multitude of aspects which depend on the position of the observer and which we can no longer survey as a whole but only accept alongside each other, without being able to make any statement about the ultimate truth? We meet here the hidden interplay of faith and modern thought. That present-day physicists are stepping outside the structure of Aristotelian logic and thinking in this way is surely an effect already of the new dimension which Christian theology has opened up, of its need to think in "complementarities".

In this connection I should like to mention briefly two other aids to thought provided by physics. E. Schrödinger has defined the structure of matter as "parcels of waves" and thereby fallen upon the idea of a being that has no substance but is purely actual, whose apparent "substantiality" really results only from the pattern of movement of superimposed waves. In the realm of matter such a suggestion may well be physically, and in any case philosophically, highly contestable. But it remains an exciting simile for the *actualitas divina*, for the absolute "being-act" of God, and for the idea that the densest being –

God – can subsist only in a multitude of relations, which are not substances but simply "waves", and therein form a perfect unity and also the fullness of being. We shall have to consider this idea more fully later on; it is already formulated to all intents and purposes in St Augustine, when he develops the idea of the pure act-existence (the "parcel of waves").

But first let me mention the second aid to understanding provided by science. We know today that in a physical experiment the observer himself enters into the experiment and only by doing so can arrive at a physical experience. This means that there is no such thing as pure objectivity even in physics, that even here the result of the experiment, nature's answer, depends on the question put to it. In the answer there is always a bit of the question and a bit of the questioner himself; it reflects not only nature-in-itself, in its pure objectivity, but also gives back something of man, of our individuality, a bit of the human subject. This too, *mutatis mutandis*, is true of the question of God. There is no such thing as a mere observer. There is no such thing as pure objectivity. One can even say that the higher an object stands in human terms, the more it penetrates the centre of individuality, and the more it engages the beholder's individuality, then the smaller the possibility of the mere distancing involved in pure objectivity. Thus, wherever an answer is presented as unemotionally objective, as a statement that finally goes beyond the prejudices of the pious and provides purely factual, scientific information, then it has to be said that the speaker has here fallen a victim to self-deception. This kind of objectivity is quite simply denied to man. He cannot ask and and exist as a mere observer. He who tries to be a mere observer experiences nothing. Even the reality "God" can only impinge on the vision of him who enters into the experiment with God – the experiment that we call faith. Only by entering does one experience; only by co-operating in the experiment does one ask at all, and only he who asks receives an answer.

Pascal set this out in his famous argument of the wager with an almost uncanny clarity and an acuteness verging on the unbearable. The verbal strife with the unbelieving interlocutor has finally reached the point at which the latter admits that he must make a choice about God. But he would like to avoid the leap, to possess a mathematical certainty: "Is there no way of illuminating the darkness and of seeing the face of the cards?" "Yes, Scripture and all the other testimony of religion." "Yes, but my hands are tied and my lips are closed . . . I am so made that I cannot believe. What am I to do?" "So you admit that your inability to believe does not come from reason; on the contrary, reason leads you to belief; the reason for your refusal lies elsewhere. There is therefore no point in trying to convince you any further by piling up the proofs of the existence of God; you must above all fight against your passions. You would like to reach faith, but do not know the way? You want to cure yourself of unbelief and you ask for a remedy? Take a lesson from those who were earlier racked by doubts like yourself. . . . Follow the way by which they began; by acting as if they believed, by taking holy water, by having Masses said, etc. This will bring you quite naturally to believe and will stupefy you."[28]

In this curious passage this much at any rate is right: the mere neutral curiosity of the mind which wants to remain uninvolved can never enable one to see – even in dealing with a human being, and much less in dealing with God. The experiment with God cannot take place without man.

Certainly it is true here, even more than it is in physics, that anyone who enters into the experiment of belief receives an answer that reflects not only God but also his own questioning and through the refraction of his own personality lets us know something about God. Even dogmatic formulas such as "one being in three persons" include this refraction of the human element, they reflect in this case the man of late antiquity, whose questions and experiments are governed by the categories of late antique philosophy, which provide him with his

[28] B. Pascal, *Pensées*, Fragment 233 (ed. Brunschvicg, pp. 137f.). Cf. Brunschvicg, p. 333, note 53, who contrary to V. Cousin, shows that to Pascal "*s'abêtir*" ("make simple") means: "*retourner à l'enfance, pour atteindre les vérités supérieures qui sont inaccessibles à la courte sagesse des demi-savants*". On this basis Brunschvicg can say in Pascal's sense: "*Rien n'est plus conforme à la raison que le désaveu de la raison*" ("Nothing is in more conformity with reason than the disavowal of reason"). Pascal does not speak here, as Cousin thought he did, as a sceptic, but out of the conviction and certainty of the believer; cf. also H. Vorgrimler, *loc. cit.*, pp. 383f. (see p. 99, note 17, of this book).

angle of vision. Indeed, we must go a stage further: that we put any questions or make any experiments at all is due to the fact that God for his part has agreed to the experiment, has entered into it himself as man. Through the human refraction of this one man we can thus come to know more than the mere man; in him, he who is man and God has demonstrated his humanity and in the man has let himself be known.

2. POSITIVE SIGNIFICANCE

The inner limitation of the doctrine of the Trinity in the sense of a negative theology, a facet of it on which we have tried to throw some light above, cannot mean all the same that its formulas remain impenetrable, empty strings of words. They can and must be understood as meaningful statements, representing, it is true, indications about the ineffable, not its incorporation in our mental world. To conclude our reflections on the doctrine of the Trinity we shall now try to elucidate the character of these indications by means of three theses.

1st Thesis: The paradox "una
essentia tres personae" − one Being in
three persons − is subordinate to the
question of the original meaning of
unity and plurality

What is meant by this is best illustrated by a glance at the background of pre-Christian Greek thought against which faith in the triune God emerges. To ancient thought only unity (i.e. oneness) is divine; plurality seems in contrast to be secondary, the disintegration of unity. It proceeds from disintegration and tends towards it. The Christian confession of faith in God as the Three-in-One, as him who is simultaneously the *"monas"* and the *"trias"*, absolute unity and fullness, signifies the conviction that divinity lies beyond our categories of unity and plurality. Although to us, the non-divine, it is one and single, the one and only divine as opposed to all that is not divine, nevertheless in itself it is truly fullness and plurality, so that creaturely unity and plurality are both in the same degree copy and share of the divine. Not only unity is divine; plurality is not just primordial and has its inner ground in God. Plurality is not just disintegration which sets in outside the divinity; it does not arise simply through the intervention of the *"dyas"*, of disintegration; it is not the result of the dualism of two opposing powers; it corresponds to the creative fullness of God, who himself stands above plurality and unity, encompassing both.[29] So at bottom the belief in the Trinity, which recognizes the plural in the unity of God, is the only way to the final elimination of dualism as a means of explaining plurality alongside unity; only through this belief is the positive validation of plurality given a definitive base. God stands above singular and plural. He bursts both categories.

This has a further important consequence. To him who believes in God as tri-une, the highest unity is not the unity of inflexible monotony. The model of unity or oneness towards which one should strive is consequently not the indivisibility of the atom, the smallest unity, too small to be divided up; the authentic acme of unity is the unity created by love. The multi-unity which grows in love is a more radical, truer unity than the unity of the "atom".

> *2nd Thesis: The paradox "una*
> *essentia tres personae" is a function of*
> *the person and is to be understood as an*
> *intrinsic implication of the concept of person*

Inasmuch as Christian faith acknowledges God, the creative meaning, as person it acknowledges him as knowledge, word and love. But the confession of faith in God as a person necessarily includes the acknowledgement of God as relatedness, as communicability, as fruitfulness. The unrelated, unrelatable, absolutely one could not be person. There is no such thing as person in the categorical singular. This is already apparent in the words in which the concept of person grew up: the Greek word *"prosopon"* means literally "(a) look towards"; with the prefix *"pros"* (towards) it includes the notion of relatedness as an integral part of itself. It is the same with the Latin *"persona"*

---

[29] Cf. on this point W. Kern, "Einheit-in-Manningfaltigkeit", in *Gott in Welt* (Essays presented to K. Rahner), Vol. I, Freiburg, 1964, pp. 207–239; see also what we said on p. 84, note 13, about Maximus Confessor.

="sounding through"; again the *"per"*="through . . . to" expresses relatedness, this time in the form of communication through speech. In other words, if the absolute is person it is not an absolute singular. To this extent the overstepping of the singular is implicit in the concept of person. Of course, we shall have to say at the same time that the acknowledgement that God is a person in the guise of a triple personality explodes the naïve, anthropomorphic concept of person. It declares in a sort of cipher that the personality of God infinitely exceeds the human kind of personality; so that the concept of person, illuminating as it is, once again reveals itself as an inadequate image.

> *3rd Thesis: The paradox "una essentia*
> *tres personae" is subordinate to the problem of*
> *absolute and relative and emphasizes the*
> *absoluteness of the relative, of*
> *relativity*

(a) Dogma as speech form

Let us try to feel our way to this idea by means of the following reflections. If faith has expressed the three-in-oneness of God since the fourth century in the formula "one being – three persons", this distribution of the concepts is first of all largely just a form of words.[30] The only thing certain at first was that the element of oneness, that of three-ness and the complete simultaneity of both in the all-embracing dominance of oneness had all to be expressed. That the two things were allotted to the concepts of substance and person, as they were, is in a certain sense accidental; in the last resort it is only a case of ensuring that both are put into words and not left to individual whim, which at bottom could always dissipate and destroy the thing itself as well as the words. In face of this discovery one is not entitled to go too far in the direction of taking these words as the only possible ones and deducing that the matter can be stated only in this way and in no other. That would mean a failure to recognize the negative character of the language of theology, the purely tentative fashion in which it speaks.

[30] Cf. the article by K. Rahner mentioned above, p. 62, note 26.

(b) The concept of person

On the other hand it remains true that this speech-form is more than just a final decision to cling to some string of letters or other. The struggle over the language of the profession of faith involved settling the struggle over the thing itself, so that in this language, inadequate as it may be, contact with the reality does take place. We can say from the history of ideas that it was here that the reality "person" was first fully sighted; the concept and idea of "person" dawned on the human mind in no other way than in the struggle over the Christian image of God and the interpretation of the figure of Jesus of Nazareth. If we try to test the intrinsic suitability of our formula while bearing these points in mind we find that it was imposed by two basic premises. First it was clear that, seen absolutely, God is only One, that there is not a plurality of divine principles. Once this has been established it is also clear that the oneness lies on the plane of substance; consequently the three-ness which must also be mentioned is not to be sought here. It must therefore exist on a different level, on that of relation, of the "relative".

This result was also recommended above all by the evidence of the Bible. Here one met the fact that God seems to converse with himself. There is a "We" in God – the Fathers found it on the very first page of the Bible in the words "Let us make man" (Gen. 1.26); there are an "I" and a "You" in him – the Fathers found this in the Psalms ("The Lord said to my lord": Ps. 110.1) as well as in Jesus' conversations with the Father. The discovery of the dialogue within God led to the assumption of the presence in God of an "I" and a "You", an element of relationship, of co-existent diversity and affinity, for which the concept *"persona"* absolutely dictated itself. It thereby acquired, over and above its theatrical and literary significance, a new depth of meaning without losing the vagueness which made it suitable for such a use.[31]

[31] Cf. C. Andresen, "Zur Entstehung und Geschichte des trinitarischen Personbegriffs", in *Zeitschrift für die neutestamentliche Wissenschaft*, 52 (1961), pp. 1–38; J. Ratzinger, "Zum Personverständnis in der Dogmatik", in J. Speck, *Das Personverständnis in der Pädagogik und ihren Nachbarwissenschaften*, Münster, 1966, pp. 157–171.

With the perception that, seen as substance, God is One, but that there exists in him the phenomenon of dialogue, of differentiation and of relationship through speech, the category of *relatio* gained a completely new significance for Christian thought. To Aristotle it was among the "accidents", the chance circumstances of being, which are separate from substance, the sole sustaining form of the real. The experience of the God who conducts a dialogue, of the God who is not only *logos* but also *dia-logos*, not only idea and meaning but speech and word in the reciprocal exchanges of conversation – this experience exploded the ancient division of reality into substance, the real thing, and accidents, the merely circumstantial. It now became clear that the dialogue, the *relatio*, stands beside the substance as an equally primordial form of being.

With that, the wording of the dogma was to all intents and purposes settled. It expresses the perception that God as substance, as "being", is absolutely one. If we nevertheless have to speak of him in the category of triplicity this does not imply any multiplication of substances but means that in the one and indivisible God there exists the phenomenon of dialogue, the reciprocal exchange of word and love. This again signifies that the "three persons" who exist in God are the reality of word and love in their attachment to each other. They are not substances, personalities in the modern sense, but the relatedness whose pure actuality ("parcel of waves"!) does not impair the unity of the highest being but fills it out. St Augustine once enshrined this idea in the following formula: "He is not called Father with reference to himself but only in relation to the Son; seen by himself he is simply God."[32] Here the decisive point comes beautifully to light. "Father" is purely a concept of relationship. Only in being-for the other is he Father; in his own being-in-himself he is simply God. Person is the pure relation of being related, nothing else. Relationship is not something extra added to the person, as it is with us; it only exists at all as relatedness.

Expressed in the imagery of Christian tradition, this means that the First Person does not beget the Son in the sense of the

[32] Augustine, *Enarrationes in Psalmos 68*, p. 1, 5, in CChr 39, 905 (Patrologia Latina [PL] 36, 845).

act of begetting coming on top of the finished Person; it *is* the act of begetting, of giving oneself, of streaming forth. It is identical with the act of giving. Only as this act is it person, and therefore it is not the giver but the act of giving, "wave" not "corpuscle". . . . In this idea of relativity in word and love, independent of the concept of substance and not to be classified among the "accidents", Christian thought discovered the kernel of the concept of person, which describes something other and infinitely more than the mere idea of the "individual". Let us listen once again to St Augustine: "In God there are no accidents, only substance and relation".[33] Therein lies concealed a revolution in man's view of the world: the undivided sway of thinking in terms of substance is ended; relation is discovered as an equally valid primordial mode of reality. It becomes possible to surmount what we call today "objectifying thought"; a new plane of being comes into view. It is probably true to say that the task imposed on philosophy as a result of these facts is far from being completed – so much does modern thought depend on the possibilities thus disclosed, but for which it would be inconceivable.

(c) *The backward link with biblical thought and the question of Christian existence*

But let us return to our question. The ideas just described can easily give the impression that one has here arrived at the outermost point of speculative theology, which in elaborating on what is found in Scripture has moved far away from Scripture and lost itself in purely philosophical speculation. It will be all the more surprising to hear that closer inspection discloses that here the most extreme speculation leads directly back to biblical thought. For at bottom the ideas just outlined are to a large extent already present in Johannine thought, if expressed in different concepts and with a somewhat different

---

[33] Cf. *De Trinitate*, V, 5, 6 (PL 42, 913f.): ". . . In Deo autem nihil quidem secundum accidens dicitur, quia nihil in eo mutabile est; nec tamen omne quod dicitur, secundum substantiam dicitur . . . quod tamen relativum non est accidens, quia non est mutabile." See also on the whole question M. Schmaus, *Katholische Dogmatik* I, 3rd ed., Munich, 1948, pp. 425–432 (§58).

aim. A brief indication will have to suffice. In St John's gospel Christ says of himself: "The Son can do nothing of his own accord" (5.19 and 30). This seems to rob the Son of all power; he has nothing of his own; precisely because he is the Son he can only *operate* by virtue of him to whom he owes his whole existence. What first becomes evident here is that the concept "Son" is a concept of relation. By calling the Lord "Son", John gives him a name that always points away from him and beyond him; he thus employs a term that denotes essentially a relationship. He thereby puts his whole Christology into the context of the idea of relation. Formulas like the one just mentioned only emphasize this; they only, as it were, draw out what is implicit in the word "son", the relativity which it contains. On the face of it, a contradiction arises when the same Christ says of himself in St John: "I and the Father are one" (10.30). But anyone who looks more closely will see at once that in reality the two statements are complementary. In that Jesus is called "Son" and is thereby made relative to the Father, and in that Christology is ratified as a statement of relation, the automatic result is the total reference of Christ back to the Father. Precisely because he does not stand in *himself* he stands in *him*, constantly one with him.

What this signifies, not just for Christology but for the illumination of the whole meaning of being a Christian at all, comes to light when John extends these ideas to Christians, who proceed from Christ. It then becomes apparent that he explains by Christology what the Christian's situation really is. We find here precisely the same interplay of the two series of statements as before. Parallel to the formula "The Son can do nothing of his own accord", which illumines Christology from the son-concept as a doctrine of relativity, is the statement about those who belong to Christ, the disciples: "Apart from me you can do nothing" (John 15.5). Thus Christian existence is put with Christ into the category of relationship. And parallel to the logic which makes Christ say, "I and the Father are one", we find here the petition "that they may be one, even as we are one" (17.11 and 22). The significant difference from Christology comes to light in the fact that the unity of Christians is mentioned not in the indicative but in the form of a prayer.

Let us now try briefly to consider the significance of the line of thought that has become visible. The Son as Son, and in so far as he is Son, does not proceed in any way from himself and so is completely one with the Father; since he is nothing beside him, claims no special position of his own, confronts the Father with nothing belonging only to him, retains no room for his own individuality, therefore he is completely equal to the Father. The logic is compelling: if there is nothing in which he is just he, no kind of fenced-off private ground, then he coincides with the Father, is "one" with him. It is precisely this totality of interplay that the word "Son" aims at expressing. To John "Son" means being-from-another; thus with this word he defines the being of this man as being from another and for others, as a being that is completely open on both sides, knows no reserved area of the mere "I". When it thus becomes clear that the being of Jesus as Christ is a completely open being, a being "from" and "towards", that nowhere clings to itself and nowhere stands on its own, then it is also clear at the same time that this being is pure relation (not substantiality) and, as pure relation, pure unity. This fundamental statement about Christ becomes, as we have seen, at the same time the explanation of Christian existence. To John, being a Christian means being like the Son, becoming a son; that is, not standing on one's own and in oneself, but living completely open in the "from" and "towards". In so far as the Christian is a "Christian", this is true of him. And certainly such utterances will make him aware to how small an extent he is a Christian.

It seems to me that this illuminates the ecumenical character of the passage from a quite unexpected angle. Everyone knows, it is true, that Jesus' "high priestly prayer" (John 17), of which we are speaking, is the basic charter of all efforts for the unity of the Church. But do we not often take far too superficial a view of it? Our reflections have shown that Christian unity is first of all unity with Christ, which becomes possible where insistence on one's own individuality ceases and is replaced by pure, unreserved being "from" and "for". From such a being with Christ, that enters completely into his openness, that would want to hold on to nothing of its own individuality (cf. also

Phil. 2.6f.), follows the complete "at-one-ness" – "that they may be one, even as we are one". All not-at-one-ness, all division, rests on a concealed lack of real Christliness, on a retention of individuality which hinders the coalescence into unity.

I think it is not unimportant to note how the doctrine of the Trinity here passes over into a statement about existence, how the assertion that relation is at the same time pure unity becomes transparently clear to us. It is the nature of the Trinitarian personality to be pure relation and so the most absolute unity. That there is no contradiction in this is probably now perceptible. And one can understand from now on more clearly than before that it is not the "atom", the indivisible smallest piece of matter,[34] that possesses the highest unity; that on the contrary pure oneness can only occur in the spirit and embraces the relativity of love. Thus the profession of faith in the oneness of God is just as radical as in any other monotheistic religion; indeed only in Christianity does it reach its full stature. But it is the nature of Christian existence to receive and to live life as relatedness, and thus to enter into that unity which is the ground of all reality and sustains it. This will perhaps make it clear how the doctrine of the Trinity, when properly understood, can become the nodal point of theology and of Christian thought in general.

Let us turn here once again to St John's gospel, which offers the decisive assistance. One can well say that the line indicated forms the dominant one in his theology. As well as in the "Son" idea it appears especially in two further christological concepts which must at least be briefly outlined here for the sake of completeness. These are the idea of the "mission" and the description of Jesus as the "word" (*logos*) of God. "Mission" theology is again theology of being as relation and of relation as mode of unity. There is a well-known late Jewish saying: "The ambassador of a man is like the man himself."[35] Jesus appears in St John as the Father's ambassador, in whom is really fulfilled what all other ambassadors can only aim at asymptotically: he really loses his own identity in the role of

[34] Cf. the short survey of the history of the concept "atom" by C. F. von Weizsäcker, in RGG I, pp. 682–686.
[35] Quoted in K. H. Schelkle, *Jüngerschaft und Apostelamt*, Freiburg, 1957.

ambassador; he is nothing but the ambassador who represents the other without interposing his own individuality. And so, as the true ambassador, he is one with him who sends him. Once again, through the concept of the mission, being is interpreted as being "from" and as being "for"; once again being is conceived as absolute openness without reservation. And again we find the extension to Christian existence in the words, "As the Father has sent me, even so I send you" (13.20; 17.18, 20, 21). In the classification of this existence as mission it is again expounded as being "from" and "for", as relatedness and hence as unity. Finally, a remark on the concept of *logos* would also be appropriate. When John characterizes the Lord as *logos* he is employing a term widely current in both Greek and Jewish thought and taking over with it a series of ideas implicit in it which are to that extent transferred to Christ. But perhaps one can say that the new element that John has added to the *logos*-concept lies not least in the fact that to him "*logos*" does not mean simply the idea of the eternal rationality of being, as it did essentially in Greek thought. By its application to Jesus of Nazareth the concept "*logos*" acquires a new dimension. It no longer denotes simply the permeation of all being by meaning; it characterizes this man: He who is here is "Word". The concept "*logos*", which to the Greeks meant "meaning" (*ratio*), changes here really into "word" (*verbum*). He who is here is Word; he is consequently "spoken" and hence the pure relation between the speaker and the spoken to. Thus "*logos*"-Christology, as "word"-theology, is once again the opening up of being to the idea of relationship. For again it is true that "word" comes essentially "from some one else" and "to some one else"; word is an existence that is entirely way and openness.

Let us round off the whole discussion with a passage from St Augustine which elucidates splendidly what we mean. It occurs in his commentary on St John and hinges on the sentence in the gospel which runs, "*Mea doctrina non est mea*" – "My teaching is not my teaching, but that of the Father who sent me" (7.16). Augustine has used the paradox in this sentence to illuminate the paradoxical nature of the Christian image of God and of Christian existence. He asks himself first

whether it is not a sheer contradiction, an offence against the
elementary rules of logic, to say something like "Mine is not
mine". But, he goes on to say, digging deeper, what really is
the teaching of Jesus which is simultaneously his and not his?
Jesus is "word", and thus it becomes clear that his teaching is
he himself. If one reads the sentence again from this angle it
then says: I am by no means just I; I am not mine at all; my I
is that of another. With this we have moved on out of Christology and arrived at ourselves: "*Quid tam tuum quam tu, quid tam non
tuum quam tu*" – "What is so much yours as yourself and what
is so little yours as yourself?"[36] The most individual element
in us – the only thing that belongs to us in the last analysis –
our own "I", is at the same time the least individual element
of all, for it is precisely our "I" that we have neither from ourselves nor for ourselves. The "I" is simultaneously what I have
completely and what least of all belongs to me. Thus here
again the concept of mere substance (=what stands in itself!)
is shattered and it is made apparent how being that truly
understands itself grasps at the same time that *in* its self-being
it does not belong to itself; that it only comes to itself by moving
away from itself and finding its way back as relatedness to its
true primordial state.

Ideas such as these do not make the doctrine of the Trinity
unmysteriously comprehensible, but they do help, I think,
to open up a new understanding of reality, of what man is and
of what God is. Just when we seem to have reached the extreme
limit of theory the extreme of practicality comes into view:
talking about God discloses what man is; the most paradoxical
approach is at the same time the most illuminating and helpful
one.

---

[36] Augustine, *In Ioannis Evangelium tractatus* 29, 3 (on John 7.16), in CChr
36, 285.

PART TWO

JESUS CHRIST

Chapter I

"I BELIEVE IN JESUS CHRIST, HIS ONLY-BEGOTTEN SON, OUR LORD"

1. THE PROBLEM OF FAITH IN JESUS TODAY

IT is only in the second section of the Creed that we come up against the real difficulty – already considered briefly in the introduction – about Christianity: the confession of faith that the man Jesus, an individual executed in Palestine round about the year 30, the *"Christus"* (anointed, chosen) of God, indeed God's own Son, is the central and decisive point of all human history. It seems both presumptuous and foolish to assert that one single figure who is bound to disappear further and further into the mists of the past is the authoritative centre of all history. If faith in the *"logos"*, the meaningfulness of being, corresponds perfectly with a tendency in the human reason, this second article of the Creed proclaims the absolutely staggering alliance of *logos* and *sarx*, of meaning and a single historical figure. The meaning that sustains all being has become flesh; that is, it has entered history and become one individual in it; it is no longer simply what encompasses and sustains history but a point in it. According to this the meaning of all being is first of all no longer to be found in the sweep of mind which rises above the individual, the limited, into the universal; it is no longer simply given in the world of ideas, which transcends the individual and is reflected in it only in a fragmentary fashion; it is to be found in the midst of time, in the countenance of one man. One is reminded of the moving conclusion of Dante's *Divine Comedy*, where, looking on the mystery of God, in the midst of that "all-powerful love which, quiet and united, leads round in a circle the sun and all the stars", the poet discovers in blissful wonder his own likeness, a human countenance.[1] The transformation of the path from being to meaning which results from this will have to be considered later. For the time being, let us note that alongside the union of the God of faith and the God of the philosophers, which we recognized in the first article as the basic assumption and structural form of the Christian faith, a second, no less decisive alliance appears, namely that of the *logos* and *sarx*, of word and flesh, of faith and history. The historical man Jesus is the Son of God, and the Son of God is the man Jesus. God comes to pass for man through men, nay, even more concretely, through *the* man in whom the quintessence of humanity appears and who for that very reason is at the same time God himself.

Perhaps it is already clear at this point that even in the paradox of word and flesh we are faced with something meaningful and in accordance with the *logos*. Yet at first this article of faith represents a stumbling-block for human thinking. In this have we not fallen victims to an absolutely staggering kind of positivism? Can we cling at all to the straw of one single historical event? Can we dare to base our whole existence, indeed the whole of history, on the straw of one happening in the great sea of history? Such a notion, which even in itself is an adventurous one and seemed equally improbable to both ancient and Asiatic thought, is rendered still more difficult in the intellectual climate of modern times, or at any rate rendered difficult in a different way, by the fashion in which history is now dealt with by scholars: that is to say, by the critical method. This means that the encounter with history is affected by the same sort of problem that has arisen in the search for being and for the ground of being as a result of the methods employed by physics and of the scientific approach to the investigation of nature. We have seen in our reflections on this subject that physics has renounced the discovery of being itself and confines itself to the "positive",

[1] *Paradiso* XXXIII, 127 to the end. See the decisive passage in V, 130ff.: Dentro da sè del suo colore istesso / Mi parve pinta della nostra effige / Per che il mio viso in lei tutto era messo.

to what can be proved. The impressive gain in precision thus made has to be paid for by a renunciation of truth which in the end can go so far that behind the prison bars of positivism, being, truth itself, disappears, ontology becomes visibly more impossible and even philosophy has to yield in large measure to phenomenology, to the investigation of mere appearances.

A very similar position threatens to arise in the encounter with history. The methods of physics are followed as far as they possibly can be, though a limit is set to the process by the fact that history cannot carry verification, which forms the core of the modern scientific approach, to the point of repetition, on which the unique certainty of scientific statements rests. The historian is denied this satisfaction; past history cannot be re-enacted and verification must be content with the demonstrable soundness of the evidence on which the historian bases his view. The consequence of this methodical approach is that – as in natural science – only the "phenomenal" or outer surface of what has happened comes into view. But this "phenomenal" aspect, that is, the surface that can be checked by documentary evidence, is more questionable than the positivism of physics from two points of view. It is more questionable first because it has to rely on the availability of the documents, that is, on chance statements, while physics at any rate always has the necessary material realities before it. It is also more questionable because the expression of the human element in the written evidence is less accurate than the self-expression of nature; its reflection of human depths is inadequate and often positively conceals them; and its interpretation involves man and his personal mode of thinking far more extensively than the interpretation of physical phenomena does. Accordingly, although one must agree that the imitation of scientific methods in the realm of history undoubtedly heightens the accuracy of its assertions, on the other hand it cannot be overlooked that here too this approach involves a grievous loss of truth which is even more extensive than it is in physics. Just as in physics being retires behind appearance, so here to a large extent the only past events that are still accepted as valid are those that are presented as "historical", that is, tested and passed by historical methods. It is quite often forgotten that the full truth of history eludes documentary verification just as much as the truth of being escapes the experimental approach. So it must be said that historical science in the narrowest sense of the term not only reveals but also conceals history. The automatic result is that it can see the man Jesus all right, but can only with difficulty discover the Christ in him, which as a truth of history cannot simply be checked as right or wrong by reference to the documentary evidence.

II. JESUS THE CHRIST: THE BASIC FORM OF THE CHRISTOLOGICAL CONFESSION OF FAITH

I. THE DILEMMA OF MODERN THEOLOGY: JESUS OR CHRIST?

It is hardly surprising, after all we have said, that the more the barrier of historical science tends to divide faith and history, the more theology seeks to escape in one way or the other from the dilemma of the simultaneous existence of both. Thus today we meet here and there the attempt to establish Christology securely on the historical plane, to make it visible in spite of everything, by this method of the "accurate" and demonstrable[2]; or the very much simpler enterprise of straightforwardly reducing it to the demonstrable.[3] The first course cannot succeed because, as we have seen, the "historical" in the strict sense of the word denotes a mode of thought which implies a limitation to the phenomenon (the demonstrable) and thus can no more produce faith than physics can produce the confession of belief in God. But the second course can bring no satisfaction because the whole of what happened then cannot be grasped in this fashion, and what is offered as a statement of fact is in reality the expression of a personal view, not the

[2] This is the approach of the group centred round W. Pannenberg; cf. W. Pannenberg, *Grundzüge der Christologie*, 2nd ed., Gütersloh, 1966, especially definition No. 23: "It is therefore the task of Christology to base on the history of Jesus the true perception of his significance. . . ."

[3] This was the approach of earlier liberal theology; cf. its classical expression in A. v. Harnack, *Das Wesen des Christentums* (new edition ed. by R. Bultmann), Stuttgart, 1950. English trans.: *What is Christianity?* (*Lectures 1899–1900*), trans. by T. B. Saunders, 1958.

pure result of historical research.[4] So these efforts are being paralleled more and more by a third, the attempt to escape the dilemma of the historical altogether and to leave it behind as superfluous. This already happens on a grand scale in Hegel; and much as Bultmann's work differs from that of Hegel he shares this same tendency. It is certainly not quite the same thing whether one confines oneself to the idea or the kerygma, but the difference is not quite so sweeping as the exponents of kerygma-theology themselves seem to assume.[5]

The dilemma of the two courses – on the one hand that of transposing or reducing Christology to history and on the other that of escaping history completely and abandoning it as irrelevant to faith – could be quite accurately summarized in the two alternatives by which modern theology is vexed: Jesus or Christ? Modern theology begins by turning away from Christ and taking refuge in Jesus as a figure who is historically comprehensible, only to make an about-turn at the climax of this movement – in Bultmann – and flee in the opposite direction back to Christ, a flight, however, which at the present moment is already starting to change back into the new flight from Christ to Jesus.

Let us try to follow this zig-zag movement of modern theology a little more closely, because by doing so we shall come nearer

---

[4] This was pointed out with all possible emphasis by A. Schweitzer in his *Geschichte der Leben-Jesu-Forschung* (Tübingen, 1906; Eng. trans. *The Quest of the Historical Jesus*, 1922), which thus also drew a provisional line under this enterprise. Let me just quote the following *locus classicus* in this work: "There is nothing more negative than the result of the research into the life of Jesus. The Jesus of Nazareth who appeared upon the scene as the Messiah, proclaimed the morality of the kingdom of God, founded the kingdom of Heaven upon earth and died to consecrate his work never existed. He is a figure sketched by rationalism, brought to life by liberalism and clothed by modern theology with historical scholarship. This image has not been destroyed from outside; it has collapsed internally, shaken and riven by the actual historical problems. . . ." (quoted from W. G. Kümmel, *Das Neue Testament. Geschichte der Erforschung seiner Probleme*, Freiburg and Munich, 1958, p. 305).

[5] This becomes quite clear in Bultmann's last great utterance on the question of Jesus: *Das Verhältnis der urchristlichen Christusbotschaft zum historischen Jesus*, Heidelberg, 1960; and still more in the work of his disciple H. Braun, to whom, however, he often draws near in the book mentioned.

to the heart of the matter. The first tendency – flight from Jesus to Christ – produced Harnack's *Wesen des Christentums* at the beginning of the century, a book that offers a form of Christianity drenched in the pride and optimism of reason, the Christianity to which liberalism had reduced the original Creed by a process of "purification". One of the crucial sentences in this work runs thus: "Not the Son but only the Father belongs in the Gospel as Jesus preached it".[6] How simple, how liberating this seems! Where faith in the Son had divided people – Christians and non-Christians, Christians of various different tendencies – knowledge of the Father can unite. While the Son belongs only to a few, the Father belongs to all and all to him. Where faith has parted people, love can bind them together. Jesus *versus* Christ, and this means "away from dogma, over to love". According to Harnack, what caused the decisive rupture was the fact that the preaching Jesus, who told all men of their common father and so made them brothers, had been turned into the preached Jesus, who then demanded faith and became dogma: Jesus had proclaimed the undoctrinal message of love, and therein lay the great revolution with which he had split the armour of pharisaical orthodoxy, setting in place of intolerant right-thinking the simplicity of trust in the Father, of the brotherhood of man and of the call to one love. For this had been substituted the doctrine of the God-man, of the "Son", and so patience and brotherly love, which is salvation, had been replaced by a doctrine of salvation, which can only signify the contrary and has unleashed conflict upon conflict, cleavage after cleavage. So the watchword is obvious: back past the preached Christ, the object of the divisive belief, to the preaching Jesus, back to the summons to the unifying power of love under the one Father with all our brothers. One certainly cannot deny that these are impressive and stirring assertions, which cannot be lightly dismissed. And yet – while Harnack was still proclaiming his optimistic message about Jesus, those

[6] New impression, 1950, p. 86. In the 56th-60th thousand (1908), Harnack endorsed this statement emphatically in a note (183) ("I have nothing to alter in it") and at the same time emphasized that it is obviously only true of the Gospel "as Jesus preached it", not "as Paul and the Evangelists preached it".

who were to bury his work were already knocking at the door. At the very same time proof was produced that the plain Jesus of whom he spoke was a romantic dream, a *Fata Morgana* of the historian, a mirage induced by thirst and longing which dissolved as he approached it.

So Bultmann resolutely chose the other path. The only thing that is important about Jesus, he says, is the fact of his having existed; for the rest, faith does not rest on such uncertain hypotheses, which can yield no historical certainty, but only on the verbal happening of the preaching of the Gospel, through which closed human existence is opened up to its true nature. But is an empty event any easier to swallow than one filled with content? Is anything gained when the question who, what and how this Jesus was is dismissed as meaningless and man is tied instead to a mere verbal event? The latter certainly takes place, for it is *preached;* but this way its authenticity and content of reality remain extremely dubious.

Such questions will enable us to understand why it is that more and more people are fleeing back from the pure kerygma and from the pale ghost of the historical Jesus to the most human of all human beings, whose humanity seems to them in a secularized world like the last shimmer of the divine left after the "death of God". This is what is happening today in the "Death of God" theology, which tells us that, although we no longer have God, Jesus remains to us as the symbol of trust that gives us courage to go on.[7] In the midst of a world emptied of God his humanity is to be a sort of proxy for the God who is no longer to be discovered. But how uncritical here are those who before were so critical that they were only willing to accept a theology without God, just so as not to appear old-fashioned in the eyes of their progressive contemporaries! Perhaps one should really put the question a bit earlier and consider whether a gravely uncritical attitude is not already reflected in the attempt to pursue theology – the science of God – without God. We do not need to argue about that here;

[7] See the survey by G. Hasenhüttl, "Die Wandlung des Gottesbildes" in *Theologie im Wandel* (Tübingen Festschrift, ed. by J. Ratzinger and J. Neumann), Munich, 1967, pp. 228–253; W. H. van de Pol, *Das Ende des konventionellen Christentums*, Vienna, 1967, pp. 438–443.

so far as our question is concerned, it is at any rate certain that
we cannot undo the work of the last forty years and that the
way back to a mere Jesus is irrevocably barred. The attempt to
outflank historical Christianity and out of the historian's retorts
to construct a pure Jesus by whom one should then be able to
live is intrinsically absurd. Mere history creates no present;
it only confirms what happened in the past. In the last analysis,
therefore, the romantic approach to Jesus is just as devoid of
value for the present or future as the flight to the pure verbal
event was bound to be.

Yet the shuttle movement of the modern mind between Jesus
and Christ, the main stages of which in the present century I
have just tried to sketch, was not entirely wasted. I believe
that it can even become a very useful pointer to something,
namely to the fact that the one (Jesus) cannot exist without
the other (Christ), that on the contrary one is bound to be
continually pushed from one to the other because in reality
Jesus only subsists as the Christ and the Christ only subsists
in the shape of Jesus. We must advance a step further and
before we do any reconstructing, which after all can only
produce reconstructions, that is, supplementary artificial creations, we must simply try to understand what is stated by the
Christian faith, which is not a reconstruction or a theory but
a present, a living reality. After all, perhaps we should put
more trust in the presence of the faith, which has endured for
centuries and by its very nature had no other aim but that of
understanding – understanding who and what this Jesus really
was – than in the activity of reconstruction, which goes its
own way, aloof from reality; at the very least one must try for
once to appreciate clearly what this faith really says.

2. THE CREED'S IMAGE OF CHRIST

The Creed, which we are following in this book as a repres-
entative summary of the faith, formulates its faith in Jesus in the
quite simple phrase "and (I believe) in Christ Jesus". The only
striking thing about it for us is that, as in St Paul's preferred
form of words, the word Christ, which was originally not a

name but a title ("Messiah"), is put first.* It can be shown that
the Christian community at Rome, which formulated our
Creed, was still completely aware of the significance of the
word's content. The transformation into a mere proper name,
which it is for us today, was certainly completed at a very early
period, but here "Christ" is still used as the definition of what
this Jesus is. The fusion with the name Jesus is well advanced,
it is true; we stand here at the last stage, so to speak, in the
change of meaning of the word Christ.

Ferdinand Kattenbusch, the great student of the Apostles'
Creed, illustrates the process with a neat example from his own
time (1897): he points to the comparison with the phrase
"Kaiser Wilhelm". The words "Kaiser" and "Wilhelm" go so
closely together that the title "Kaiser" had itself already
become almost a part of the name; yet everyone was still aware
that the word was not just a name but denoted a function.[8]
The phrase "Christ Jesus" is an exactly similar case and shows
just the same development: Christ is a title and yet also already
part of the unique name for the man from Nazareth. This
fusion of the name with the title, the title with the name, is far
from being just another example of history's forgetfulness. On
the contrary, it spotlights the very heart of that process of
understanding which faith went through with regard to the
figure of Nazareth. For what faith really states is precisely that
with Jesus it is not possible to distinguish office and person;
with him, this differentiation simply becomes inapplicable.
The person *is* the office, the office *is* the person. The two are no
longer divisible. Here there is no private area reserved for an
"I" which remains in the background behind the deeds and
actions and thus at some time or other can be "off duty";
here there is no "I" separate from the work; the "I" *is* the work
and the work *is* the "I".

Jesus did not leave behind him (again as the faith expressed
in the Creed understood it) a body of teaching that could be
separated from his "I", as one can collect and evaluate the
ideas of great thinkers without going into the personalities of
the thinkers themselves. The Creed offers no teachings of Jesus;

* Though not in the usual English version (trans.).
[8] Kattenbusch, II, p. 491; cf. pp. 541–562.

evidently no one even conceived the – to us – obvious idea of
attempting anything like this, because the operative understanding pointed in a completely different direction. Similarly,
as faith understood the position, Jesus did not perform a work
that could be distinguished from his "I" and depicted separately. On the contrary, to understand him as the Christ means
to be convinced that he has put himself into his word. Here
there is no "I" (as there is with all of us) which utters words;
he has identified himself so closely with his word that "I" and
word are indistinguishable: he *is* word. In the same way, to
faith, his work is nothing else than the unreserved way in which
he merges himself into this very work; he performs *himself* and
gives *himself*; his work is the giving of himself.

Karl Barth once expressed this perception on the part of faith
in the following way:

> Jesus is utterly holder of an office. He is therefore not first man
> and then in addition holder of this office. . . . There is no such
> thing as the neutral humanity of Jesus. . . . The remarkable state-
> ment of Paul in 2 Cor. 5.16, "Even though we once regarded
> Christ from a human point of view, we regard him thus no longer",
> could also be uttered in the name of all four evangelists. The latter
> were quite uninterested in anything that this man might have
> been or done outside his function as Christ and therefore aside from
> its fulfilment. . . . Even when they recount of him that he hungered
> and thirsted, that he ate and drank, that he grew tired and rested
> and slept, that he loved, mourned, showed anger and even wept,
> they are touching on accompanying circumstances which nowhere
> betrayed anything like a personality independent of its work,
> with definite tendencies, inclinations and emotions peculiar to
> itself. . . . His being as man is his work.[9]

In other words, faith's decisive statement about Jesus lies in
the indivisible unity of the two words "Jesus Christ", a unity
which conceals the experience of the identity of existence and
mission. In this sense one can certainly speak of a "functional
Christology": the whole being of Jesus is a function of the

---

[9] K. Barth, *Kirchliche Dogmatik*, Vol. III, 2, Zürich, 1948, pp. 66–69;
quoted from H. U. von Balthasar, "Zwei Glaubensweisen" in *Spiritus
Creator*, Einsiedeln, 1967, pp. 76–91; quot. on pp. 89f. Balthasar's whole
contribution should be compared.

"for us", but the function too is – for this very reason – all being.[10]

As a fitting conclusion one could indeed assert that, thus understood, the teaching and the deeds of the historical Jesus are not as such important, but that the mere fact of his having existed is sufficient – so long as one realizes that this "fact" implies the whole reality of the person who as such is his own teaching, who as such coincides with his deeds and thereby possesses his unparalleled individuality and uniqueness. The person of Jesus *is* his teaching, and his teaching is he himself. Christian faith, that is, faith in Jesus as the Christ, is therefore truly "personal faith". What this means can really be understood only from this angle. Such faith is not the acceptance of a system but the acceptance of this person who is his word; of the word as person and of the person as word.

3. THE POINT OF DEPARTURE OF FAITH IN JESUS: THE CROSS

What has been said so far will be clarified if we go back a step further, past the Apostles' Creed to the origin of the Christian faith as a whole. Today we can establish with some certainty that the birthplace of the faith in Jesus as the Christ, that is, the birthplace of "Christ"-ian faith as a whole, is the cross. Jesus himself had not proclaimed himself directly as the Christ ("Messiah"). This certainly somewhat – to us – surprising assertion now emerges with some clarity from the frequently confusing quarrels of the historians; it cannot be eluded even if, indeed especially if, one faces with an appropriately critical attitude the hasty process of subtraction current in present-day research into Jesus. So Jesus did not call himself unequivocally the Messiah (Christ); the man who gave him this name was Pilate, who for his part associated himself with the accusation of the Jews by yielding to this accusation and proclaiming Jesus on the cross, in an execution notice drawn up in all the international languages of the day, as the executed king (= Messiah, Christus) of the Jews. This execution notice, the

[10] H. U. von Balthasar, *loc. cit.*, esp. p. 90; *idem*, *Verbum caro*, Einsiedeln, 1960, pp. 11–72, esp. 32f., 54ff.

death sentence of history, became with paradoxical unity the
"confession of faith", the real starting-point and rooting-point
of the Christian faith, which holds Jesus to be the Christ: as the
crucified criminal this Jesus is the Christ, the king. His crucifixion is his coronation; his coronation or kingship is his
surrender of himself to men, the identification of word, mission
and existence in the yielding up of this very existence. His
existence is thus his word. He *is* word because he is love. From
the cross faith understands in increasing measure that this Jesus
did not just do and say *something;* that in him message and person
are identical, that he always already is what he says. John
needed only to draw the final straightforward inference: if
that is so – and this is the christological basis of his gospel –
then this Jesus Christ is "word"; but a person who not only *has*
words but *is* his word and his work is the *logos* ("the Word",
meaning, mind) itself; that person has always existed and will
always exist; he is the ground on which the world stands – if we
ever meet such a person, then he is the meaning which sustains
us all and by which we are all sustained.

The unfolding of the understanding that we call faith thus
happens in such a way that Christians first hit upon the identification of person, word and work through the cross. Through
it they recognized the really and finally decisive factor, before
which all else becomes of secondary importance. For this reason
their confession of faith could be restricted to the simple
association of the words Jesus and Christ – this combination
said it all. Jesus is seen from the cross, which speaks louder
than any words: he *is* the Christ – no more need be said. The
crucified "I" of the Lord is such an abundant reality that all
else can retire into the background. A second step was then
taken and from the understanding of Jesus thus acquired people
looked back at his words. When the community began to
think back like this it was forced to note, to its amazement, that
the same concentration on his "I" was to be found in the words
of Jesus; that his message itself, studied retrospectively, is such
that it always leads to and flows into this "I", into the identity
of word and person. Finally John was able to take one last
step and link the two movements. His gospel is, as it were, the
thorough reading of the words of Jesus from the angle of the

person and of the person from the words. That he treats "Christology", the assertion of faith in the Christ, as the message of the story of Jesus and, *vice-versa*, the story of Jesus as Christology indicates the complete unity of Christ and Jesus, a unity which is and remains formative for the whole further history of faith.[11]

4. JESUS THE CHRIST

It will probably be clear from what has been said in what sense and to what point one can follow Bultmann's movement. There does exist such a thing as a concentration on the fact of Jesus' existence, a fusion of the fact of Jesus with faith in the Christ – his most characteristic word is indeed he himself. But this does mean skating rather swiftly over the question posed by Harnack. What about the opposite of Christology, the message about the Father-God, about the love of all men that oversteps and surmounts the boundaries of faith? Has it been swallowed up in a christological dogmatism? In this attempt to re-define the faith of early Christendom and of the Church of all ages has the important element brought to the fore by liberal theology not been pushed into the background again and overlaid by a faith that causes love to be forgotten? That this can happen, and has indeed happened more than once in history, we are well aware. But that it corresponds to the intention of this conception of faith must be most emphatically denied.

For anyone who recognizes the Christ in Jesus, and only in him, and who recognizes Jesus as the Christ, anyone who grasps the total oneness of person and work as the decisive factor, has abandoned the exclusiveness of faith and its antithesis to love; he has combined both in one and made their mutual separation unthinkable. The hyphen between Jesus and Christ, the inseparability of person and work, the identity of one man with the act of sacrifice – these also signify the hyphen between love

[11] Cf. the illuminating remarks of E. Käsemann, in *Exegetische Versuche und Besinnungen*, Vol. II, Göttingen, 1964, p. 47. Käsemann points out that the mere fact that John sets down his kerygma in the form of a gospel says a great deal.

and faith. For the peculiarity of Jesus' "I", of his person, which now certainly moves right into the centre of the stage, lies in the fact that this "I" is not at all something exclusive and independent but Being completely derived from the "Thou" of the Father and lived for the "You" of men. It is identity of *logos* (truth) and love, and thus makes love into the *logos*, the truth of human existence. The essence of the faith demanded by a Christology so understood is consequently entry into the universal openness of unconditional love. For to believe in a Christ so understood means simply to make love the content of faith, so that from this angle one can perfectly well say, love is faith.

This corresponds with the picture sketched by Jesus in his great parable of the last judgment (Matt. 25.31–46): the confession of faith in Christ demanded by the Lord when he sits in judgment is explained as the discovery of Christ in the least of men, in those who need my help. From here onwards to confess one's faith in Christ means to recognize the man who needs me as the Christ in the form in which he comes to meet me here and now; it means understanding the challenge of love as the challenge of faith. The apparent re-interpretation here – in Matthew 25 – of the christological confession of faith into the unconditionality of human service and mutual help is not to be regarded, after what we have said, as an escape from otherwise prevailing dogma; it is in truth the consequence that arises from the hyphen between Jesus and Christ, and therefore from the heart of Christology itself. For this hyphen – let me repeat – is at the same time the hyphen between faith and love. Therefore it is also true that faith which is not love is not a really *Christian* faith; it only seems to be such – a fact which must redound both against any doctrinalistic misunderstanding of the Catholic concept of faith and against the secularization of love which proceeds in Luther from the notion of justification by faith.[12]

---

[12] Cf. P. Hacker, *Das Ich im Glauben bei Martin Luther*, Graz, 1966, especially the section "Säkularisierung der Liebe", pp. 166–174. Hacker shows there with an abundance of textual references that Luther as reformer (i.e., from about 1520 onwards) allots love to the "outward life", to "the use of the second table", to life not with God but "with men", and thus to the

III. JESUS CHRIST – TRUE GOD AND TRUE MAN

1. THE FORMULATION OF THE QUESTION

Let us return once again to the christological question in the narrower sense, so that what we have said does not rest as mere assertion or even seem like an attempt to take refuge in an opportune interpretation. We had established that the Christian "yes" to Jesus affirms that he is the Christ, that is, he in whom person and work are identical; from this point we then came up against the unity of faith and love. Inasmuch as Christian faith leads us away from all mere ideas, from any independent body of teaching, to the "I" of Jesus, it leads towards an "I" which is complete openness, all "Word", all "Son". We had also already considered the fact that the concepts "word" and "son" are intended to convey the dynamic character of this existence, its pure "*actualitas*". Word never stands on its own; it comes from someone, is there to be heard, and is therefore meant for others. It can only subsist in this totality of "from" and "for". We had discovered the same meaning in the concept "son", which signifies a similar tension between "from and "for". We could accordingly summarize the whole in the formula, "Christian faith is not related to ideas but to a person, an 'I', and to one that is defined as 'word' and 'son', that is, as 'total openness' ". But this now leads to a double consequence, in which the drama of faith in Christ (in the sense of a faith in Jesus as *Christ*, that is, as Messiah) and its necessary historical development into the scandal of faith in the Son (as faith in the true divinity of Jesus) come to light. For if this is the case, if this "I" is believed in as pure openness, as total being

realm of the profane, to what is called today "pure worldliness", and therefore to the "righteousness of the law". He thus secularizes it and excludes it from the realm of grace and salvation. Hacker is thereby able to demonstrate convincingly that Gogarten's programme of secularization can base itself quite justifiably on Luther. It is clear that at this point Trent had to draw a firm dividing line and that where the secularization of love is retained the dividing line continues to run as it did before. On Gogarten, see A. V. Bauer's survey and evaluation of his work in *Freiheit zur Welt (Säkularisation)*, Paderborn, 1967.

derived from the Father; if with its whole existence it is "son" – *actualitas* of pure service; if – in other words – this existence not only has but *is* love – must it not then be identical with God, who *alone is* love? Is Jesus, the Son of God, not then himself God? Is it not true that "the Word was with God, and the Word was God" (John 1.1)? But the opposite question also arises, so that we must say: If this man is all he does, if he stands behind all he says, if he is all for others and yet in such self-abandonment still completely with himself; if he is he who in losing himself has found himself (cf. Mark 8.35), is he not the most human of men, the fulfilment of the whole concept of humanity? Is it then permissible to resolve Christology (= study of Christ) into theology (= study of God)? Must we not much rather claim Jesus enthusiastically as a man, and treat Christology as humanism and anthropology? Or should the real man, precisely because he *is* wholly and properly such, be God, and God be the real man? Ought it to be possible that the most radical humanism and faith in the God who reveals himself here meet and even merge?

I think it is clear that these questions, whose tremendous import shook the Church of the first five centuries, emerge quite simply from the christological confession of faith itself; that period's dramatic arguments about these questions led in the ecumenical councils of those days to the answering of *all three questions* in the affirmative. This triple "yes" forms the content and final shape of the classical christological dogma, which was only trying in this way to be completely loyal to the straightforward original confession of faith in Jesus as the "Christ". In other words, developed christological dogma acknowledges that the radical Christship of Jesus postulates the Sonship, and that the Sonship includes the Godship; only if it is thus understood does it remain "*logos*-like", that is, a rational statement; without this logical consistency one sinks into myth. But it also acknowledges no less resolutely that in the radicality of his service Jesus is the most human of men, the true man, and it thus subscribes to the identity of theology and anthropology, an identity in which ever since then the truly exciting part of Christ-ian faith has resided.

But yet again a question arises. Even if one must admit the

soundness of the argument just expounded and thus simply recognize the intrinsic logic of the dogma, there yet remains the all-important step of looking at the facts. Have we not perhaps raised ourselves aloft on a splendid system of ideas but left reality behind us, so that the indisputable coherence of the system is of no use to us because the foundation is missing? In other words, we must ask whether the findings of the Bible and its critical illumination of the facts empower us to conceive the Sonship of Jesus in the way we have just done and in the way christological dogma does. Today the answer usually given to this question is an even more decided and self-evident "no"; to many people the "yes" seems to have sunk to a pre-critical position hardly worth attention. I should like to try to show, in contrast to this, that one not only can but must answer with "yes" if one is not to slip either into rationalistic trivialities or mythological son-ideas which were long ago overtaken and overcome by biblical faith in the Son and the way it was expounded in the early Church.[13]

2. A MODERN STOCK IDEA OF THE "HISTORICAL JESUS"

We must proceed slowly. Who was Jesus of Nazareth really? What view did he take of himself? According to the stock idea, which today, as the vulgarized form of modern theology, is beginning to gain wide currency,[14] things happened like this. This historical Jesus is to be visualized as a sort of prophetic teacher who appeared on the scene in the eschatologically overheated atmosphere of the late Judaism of his time and preached, in accordance with this eschatologically pregnant situation, the proximity of the Kingdom of God. This had been at first an assertion to be understood in an entirely temporal

[13] Naturally this does not mean taking up again by way of an appendix the attempt, already rejected as impossible, at a historical construction of faith; what we *are* concerned with is demonstrating the historical legitimacy of faith.

[14] When we speak here of a "vulgarized form of modern theology", this in itself implies that in specialized fields of research things are seen in varying lights and often in detail quite differently. But the impasses remain the same and for this reason there is no validity in the popular excuse that "it is not quite so simple as that".

sense: the Kingdom of God, the end of the world, was now coming very soon. But the "now" had received so much emphasis in Jesus' words that for anyone who looked deeper the element of "future" could no longer be regarded as the essential one, which seemed rather to reside – even if Jesus himself was thinking of a future, of a Kingdom of God – in the call to make a decision: man's whole duty was to the "now" that thrust itself upon him at any particular time.

Let us not pause to wonder how such an empty message, which is alleged to reflect a better understanding of Jesus than he had himself, could have ever meant anything to anyone. Let us rather hear what is supposed to have happened next. For reasons which can no longer be properly established, Jesus was condemned to death and died a failure. Afterwards, in a way that can no longer be clearly perceived, the belief in a resurrection arose, the notion that he lived on or at any rate still signified something. Gradually this belief increased and the idea developed – an idea that can be shown to have arisen in other places in a similar way – that Jesus would return in the future as the Son of Man, Messiah. The next step was finally to project this hope back on to the historical Jesus, put it on his own lips and re-interpret him accordingly. The picture was now rearranged to make it look as if Jesus had proclaimed himself as the coming son of Man or Messiah. Very quickly – according to our stock idea – the tidings passed over from the Semitic world into the Hellenistic world. This had the following consequences. In the Jewish world Jesus had been explained along Jewish lines (Son of Man, Messiah). In the Hellenistic area these categories were incomprehensible and consequently Hellenistic patterns of thought were pressed into service. The Semitic notions, Son of Man and Messiah, were replaced by the Hellenistic idea of the "divine person" or "God-man" (θεῖος ἀνήρ) and the figure of Jesus was thus rendered comprehensible.

But the "God-man" in the Hellenistic sense was characterized chiefly by two qualities: he was a miracle-worker and he was of divine origin. The latter idea means that in some way or other God is his Father; it is precisely his half divine, half human origin that makes him a God-man, a divine man. The consequence of the utilization of the category of divine man was that the attributes just described above had also to be transferred to Jesus. So people now began to portray him as a miracle-worker; the "myth" of the virgin birth was created for the same reason. The latter for its part led afresh to the description of Jesus as the Son of God, since God now appeared in mythical style as his Father. In this fashion the Hellenistic interpretation of Jesus as a "divine man", together with the inevitable accompanying phenomena, finally transformed the phenomenon of proximity to God, which had been character-istic of Jesus, into the "ontological" descent from God. The faith of the old Church then advanced along these mythical lines up to the final ratification of the whole in the dogma of Chalcedon, with its concept of the ontological worship of Jesus. With the idea of the ontological origin of Jesus from God the myth was turned by this Council into dogma and sur-rounded with so much abstruse learning that in the end it was raised to the status of shibboleth of orthodoxy; the starting-point was thus finally stood on its head.

To anyone accustomed to think historically the whole theory is absurd, even if today hordes of people believe it; for my part I must confess that, quite apart from the Christian faith and simply from my acquaintance with history, I find it preferable and easier to believe that God became man than that such a conglomeration of hypotheses represents the truth. In the space at our disposal here we cannot, I fear, go into the details of the historical problems involved; this would demand a very com-prehensive and tedious investigation. Instead, we must (and are entitled to) confine ourselves to the crucial point round which the whole question revolves: the Sonship of Jesus. If one goes to work carefully from a linguistic point of view and does not mix together things that it would be convenient to find cohering, the following points can be established.

3. THE CLAIM OF CHRISTOLOGICAL DOGMA

(a) The question of the "divine man"

The concept of the divine man or God-man ($\theta\epsilon\tilde{\iota}o\varsigma$ $\alpha\nu\acute{\eta}\varrho$) occurs *nowhere* in the New Testament. Conversely, *nowhere* in antiquity is the "divine man" described as the "Son of God". These are two important facts. Historically the two concepts are in no way connected; they have nothing to do with each other either in language or content. The Bible is not familiar with the divine man, nor is antiquity familiar, in the realm of divine men, with the idea of "Son of God". Indeed, recent researches show in addition that even the concept of the "divine man" can hardly be attested in the pre-Christian period but only turns up later.[15] But even apart from this observation the fact remains that the title Son of God and the things implicit in it cannot be explained from the content of the title and idea of the divine man; from a historical point of view the two patterns of thought are completely alien to each other and had no contact with each other.

(b) Biblical terminology and its relation to dogma

In the language of the New Testament a rigorous distinction must be made between the description "Son of God" and the description "the Son". To anyone who does not proceed with linguistic precision the two seem to mean just the same thing. The two descriptions do indeed in a certain sense have something to do with each other; but originally they belong to quite different contexts, have different origins, and express different things.

(i) "Son of God." The expression "Son of God" stems from the "king" theology of the Old Testament, which itself rests on the demythologization of oriental "king" theology and expresses its transformation into the "Chosen People" theology of Israel. The classical example of this procedure (that is, of the borrowing of ancient oriental "king" theology and its biblical demythologization into the idea of election) is provided by Psalm 2.7, and thus by the text which at the same time became one of the points of departure of christological thinking. In this verse the following oracle is delivered to the king of Israel: "I will tell of the decree of the Lord: He said to me, 'You are my son, today I have begotten you. Ask of me, and I will make the nations your heritage, and the ends of the earth

[15] W. v. Martitz, "υἱός im Griechischen", in Theologisches Wörterbuch zum NT (ed. Kittel-Friedrich), Vol. VIII, pp. 335–340, esp. 339f.

your possession.'" This dictum, which belongs in the context of the enthronement of the kings of Israel, stems, as we have said, from ancient oriental coronation rites, in which the king was declared the son begotten of God, though the full scope of the notion of begetting seems to have been retained only in Egypt. There the king was regarded as a being mythically begotten by God, while in Babylon the same ritual was largely demythologized and the idea that the king was the son of God was already conceived as the conferment of a legal sanction.[16]

When the formula was taken over by the Davidic court the mythological sense was certainly set completely aside. The idea of a physical begetting of the king by the godhead is replaced by the notion that the king becomes son here and now; the act of procreation consists in the act of election by God. The king is son not because he has been begotten by God but because he has been chosen by God. The reference is not to a physical event but to the power of the divine will that creates new being. In the idea of sonship so conceived the whole theology of the Chosen People is now also concentrated. In older passages of the Bible (Exod. 4.22, for example) Israel as a whole had been called Yahweh's first-born, beloved son. When in the age of the kings this description is transferred to the ruler, this means that in him, the successor of David, Israel's vocation is summed up; that he stands for Israel and unites in himself the secret of the promise, the call, the love that lies over Israel.

Then there is a further point. The application of the oriental royal ritual to the king of Israel, as we find it applied in the psalm, must have seemed like a cruel mockery in face of the actual situation of Israel. When people called out to Pharaoh or to the king of Babylon at his enthronement, "The nations are your heritage and the ends of the earth your possession; you shall break them with a rod of iron, and dash them in pieces like a potter's vessel", there was some sense in it. Such words corresponded to these kings' claims to world power. But when what was meaningful for the great powers of Babylon and Egypt is applied to the king on Mount Zion it turns into pure irony, for the kings of the earth do not tremble before

[16] Cf. H. J. Kraus, *Psalmen* I, Neukirchen, 1960, pp. 18ff. (on Ps. 2.7).

him; on the contrary he trembles before them. Mastery of the world, expressed as it was by a petty prince, must have sounded ridiculous. To put it another way, the mantle of the psalm, borrowed from oriental royal ritual, was far too big for the shoulders of the real king on Mount Zion. So it was historically inevitable that this psalm, which seen from the angle of the present must have appeared almost unbearable, should grow more and more into a profession of hope in him of whom it would one day really be true. This means that the "royal" theology, which had first been transformed from a theology of procreation into one of election, now went through a further change and turned from a theology of election into a theology of hope in the king to come. The coronation oracle became more and more a reiteration of the promise that one day that king would come of whom it could rightly be said: "You are my son, today I have begotten you. Ask of me, and I will make the nations your heritage."

At this point the re-employment of the passage by the original Christian community begins. The words of the psalm were probably first applied to Jesus in the framework of the belief in his resurrection. The event of Jesus' awakening from the dead, in which this community believed, was conceived by the first Christians as the moment at which the happenings of Psalm 2 had become a factual reality. The paradox is certainly no less striking here, for to believe that he who died on Golgotha is at the same time he to whom *these* words are addressed seems an extraordinary contradiction. What does this application of the psalm mean? It means that people know that Israel's royal hope is fulfilled in him who died on the cross and, to the eye of faith, rose again from the dead. It implies the conviction that to him who died on the cross, to him who renounced all earthly power (and this must be heard against the background of the talk about kings trembling and being broken with a rod of iron!), to him who laid aside the sword and instead of sending others to their death, as earthly kings do, himself went to his death for others, to him who saw the meaning of human existence not in power and self-assertion but in existing utterly for others – who indeed was, as the cross shows, existence for others – to him and to him alone God has said, "You are my son, today I have begotten you". In the crucified Christ those who believe see what the meaning of that oracle, what the meaning of being chosen is: not privilege and power for oneself but service to others. In him it becomes clear what the meaning of the story of being chosen, what the true meaning of kingship is. It has always aimed at standing for others, at being "representation". The "representation", the standing as proxy for others, now acquires a changed meaning. It is of him, the complete failure, who no longer has an inch of ground under his feet as he hangs from the cross, for whose garments lots are drawn and who himself seems to be abandoned by God, that the oracle speaks: "You are my son; today – on *this* spot – I have begotten you. Ask of me, and I will make the nations your heritage and the ends of the earth your possession."

The Son of God idea which in this way and in this form – the explanation of cross and resurrection by Psalm 2 – entered into the confession of faith in Jesus of Nazareth has truly nothing to do with the Hellenistic idea of the divine man and is not to be explained in any way from it. On the contrary, it is the second stage in the demythologization of the oriental concept of kingship, an idea already partly demythologized in the Old Testament. It defines Jesus as the true heir to the universe, as heir to the promise in which Davidic theology culminates. At the same time it becomes evident that the idea of the king, which to this extent is transferred to Jesus in the title of "son", becomes intertwined with the idea of the servant. As king he is a servant and as the servant of God he is king. This interplay, so fundamental to belief in Christ, is adumbrated in the Old Testament and anticipated linguistically in the Greek translation of it. The word *"pais"*, which the latter uses to denote the servant of God, can also mean "child"; in the light of the event of Christ this ambiguity must have become a pointer to the way in which the two roles coincide in Jesus.[17]

The interchangeability of son and servant, of glory and service, which thus resulted, signifying a completely new interpretation of the concepts both of king and son, probably

[17] Cf. the important article by J. Jeremias, *"παῖς θεοῦ"*, in *Theologisches Wörterbuch zum NT*, Vol. V, pp. 653–713, exp. p. 702f.

received its most impressive formulation in the Epistle to the Philippians (2.5–11), that is, in a text still springing solely from the soil of Palestinian Christianity. The passage in question points to the basic example of the attitude of Jesus Christ, who did not jealously cling to the equality with God which is proper to him but accepted the humble position of servant, right to the point of complete self-emptying; the word "*evacuatio*" used here by the Latin text points to this translation, to the assertion that he "emptied" himself and, surrendering existence-for-himself, entered into the pure movement of the "for". But precisely therein, the passage goes on to say, he has become the lord of all, of the whole cosmos, before whom the latter performs the *proskynesis*, the rite and act of submission, which is the due only of the real king. The willing subject thus appears as the true ruler; he who humbled himself to the final point of emptying himself of his own being is for that very reason the ruler of the world. What we had already discovered in our reflections on the triune God appears again here at the end of a different train of reasoning: he who does not cling to himself but is pure relatedness coincides in this with the absolute and thus becomes lord. The lord before whom the universe bows is the slaughtered lamb, the symbol of existence that is pure act, pure "for". The cosmic liturgy, the adoring homage of the universe, centres round this lamb (Apoc. 5).

But let us return once again to the question of the title "Son of God" and its position in the ancient world. For we must after all observe that there was in fact *one* linguistic and objective parallel to it in the Graeco-Roman world. The only thing is that this parallel did not consist in the idea of the "divine man", which simply has nothing to do with it. The only real ancient parallel to the description of Jesus as the Son of God (which expresses a new understanding of power, kingship, election, indeed of humanity) occurs in the description of the Emperor Augustus as "son of God" (Θεοῦ υἱός = Divi [Caesaris] filius).[18] Here we do indeed encounter the exact phrase with which the New Testament describes the significance of Jesus of Nazareth. In the cult of the Roman emperor, and not before, we see the return in late antiquity, in conjunction with

[18] Cf. W. v. Martitz, *loc. cit.*, pp. 330ff., 336.

the oriental concept of monarchy, of the title "son of God", which otherwise did not exist and could not exist simply because of the many possible meanings of the word "god".[19] It only reappears with the return of the oriental concept of monarchy from which the designation stems. In other words, the title "son of god" belongs to the political theology of Rome and thus refers to the same basic context that also gave rise, as we have seen, to the New Testament "Son of God". Both usages proceed in fact, if independently and by different paths, from the same native soil and point back to one and the same source. So both in the ancient East and again in imperial Rome the title "son of God" is – let us be quite clear about this – a piece of political theology. In the New Testament the phrase has been transferred to another dimension of thought as a result of its reinterpretation in Israel by a theology of election and hope. So from the same root completely different things grew up; and the conflict – soon to become unavoidable – between the acknowledgement of *Jesus* as the Son of God and the acknowledgement of the *emperor* as the son of God represented for all practical purposes a clash between demythologized myth and myth that has remained myth. The Roman god-emperor, with his all-embracing claims, could certainly not allow the continued existence alongside his own pretensions of the transformed "king" and "emperor" theology which lives on faith in Jesus as the Son of God. To that extent *"martyria"* (testimony) was bound to turn into *"martyrium"*, the challenge to the self-deification of political power.[20]

(ii) "The Son." Jesus' own description of himself as "the Son" is something quite distinct from the concept "son of God" which we have just discussed. This phrase, "the Son", has a different etymology and belongs to a different kind of language, namely that of the coded parable, which Jesus employed in the wake of the prophets and teachers of wisdom of Israel. And

[19] For this reason similar formulas also contain some determinant. Cf. the material in W. Bauer, *Wörterbuch zum NT*, 5th ed., Berlin, 1958, pp. 1649ff., and in W. v. Martitz, *loc. cit.*

[20] Cf. on this the important materials in A. A. T. Ehrhardt, *Politische Metaphysik von Solon bis Augustin*, 2 vols, Tübingen, 1959; E. Peterson, "Zeuge der Wahrheit", in *Theologische Traktate*, Munich, 1951, pp. 165–224; N. Brox, *Zeuge und Märtyrer*, Munich, 1961.

here again the phrase is not to be located in the public preaching but in Jesus' conversations with the inner circle of disciples. Its real source is probably to be found in Jesus' prayers; it forms the natural corollary to his new mode of addressing God, "*Abba*".[21] Joachim Jeremias has shown by means of careful analyses that the few words which have been handed down to us by the Greek New Testament in Jesus' mother-tongue, Aramaic, form a particularly good key to his original mode of speech. They struck those who heard them as so surprisingly new, and mirrored so well the special quality of the Lord, his uniqueness, that they were remembered word for word; in them we can still hear him, as it were, speaking in his own voice.

Among the few small treasures in which the original Christian community preserved Jesus' Aramaic words untranslated, because they seemed a particularly striking reflection of his personality, is the form of address "*Abba*" – "Father". It differs from the modes of address possible in the Old Testament inasmuch as "*Abba*" is a term of intimate familiarity (comparable with the word "Papa", if rather more elevated);[22] the intimacy implicit in the word excluded for the Jew the possibility of relating it to God; such a close approach was not seemly in man. That Jesus prayed in this way, that he used this word in his converse with God, thereby expressing a new form of intimacy with God belonging only to him personally – this was what gripped the first Christians and caused them to preserve the word in its original sound.

But this form of address finds its intrinsically appropriate corollary, as we have already indicated, in Jesus' description

[21] This has been convincingly demonstrated by F. Hahn, *Christologische Hoheitstitel*, 3rd ed., Göttingen, 1966, pp. 319–333; see also the important observations of J. Jeremias, in *Abba. Studien zur neutestamentlichen Theologie und Zeitgeschichte*, Göttingen, 1966, pp. 15–67.

[22] J. Jeremias, *op. cit.*, pp. 58–67. Jeremias here amends his own earlier view – according to which *Abba* was a pure childish stammer – in the *Theologisches Wörterbuch zum NT*, Vol. V, pp. 984f.; but the fundamental perception remains valid: "To the Jewish way of thinking it would have been disrespectful and therefore unthinkable to address God with this familiar word. It was something new and unheard of that Jesus should have dared to take this step. . . . The 'Abba' of Jesus' prayers reveals the very heart of his relationship to God."

of himself as Son. The two words together express the particular way in which Jesus prayed, his awareness of God, into which, in however restrained a fashion, he let his closest circle of friends have an insight. If, as we have seen, the title "Son of God" is taken from Jewish Messianology and is thus a phrase with a rich historical and theological content, here we are confronted with something quite different, something infinitely simpler and at the same time infinitely more personal and more profound. Here we see into Jesus' experience of prayer, into the nearness to God which, while distinguishing his relations with God from those of all other men, yet does not aim at any kind of exclusiveness but is designed to include the others in its own relationship to God. It wishes to incorporate them, as it were, in its own kind of attitude to God, so that with Jesus and in him they can say "*Abba*" to God just as he does: no set distance shall separate them any longer; they are to be embraced in that intimacy which in Jesus is reality.

St John's gospel puts this self-description of Jesus, which in the first three gospels occurs only in a few places (at moments when the disciples are being instructed) at the heart of its picture of Jesus; this corresponds with the basic tendency of this text, which is much more "inward" in character than the other three gospels. Jesus' own description of himself as "the Son" now becomes the guiding thread of the depiction of the Lord; and at the same time, as the gospel progresses, the full meaning of the phrase is unfolded. Since the most important aspects of this have already been covered in our consideration of the doctrine of the Trinity, it will be sufficient here if we just remind ourselves briefly of the conclusions at which we arrived there.

To John, the description of Jesus as Son is not the expression of any power of his own claimed by Jesus but the expression of the total relativity of his existence. When Jesus is put completely into this category this means that his existence is explained as completely relative, nothing other than "being from" and "being for", coinciding in this very totality of its relativity with the absolute. In this the title "Son" is identical with the descriptions "the Word" and "the envoy". And when John describes the Lord in the words of God's dictum in Isaiah, "I am (it)", again the same thing is meant, the total unity with the "I am" which results from an attitude of complete surrender. The heart of this Son-Christology of John's, the basis of which in the synoptic gospels and through them in the historical Jesus ("*Abba!*") was made plain earlier, lies accordingly in what has become clear to us as being the starting-point of all Christology: in the identity of work and being, of deed and person, of the total merging of the person in his work and in the total coincidence of the doing with the person himself, who keeps back nothing for himself but gives himself completely in his work.

To that extent it can indeed be maintained that in John there is an "ontologization", a reaching back to the being behind the "phenomenal" character of the mere happening. It is no longer simply a question of speaking about the doings, sayings and teaching of Jesus; on the contrary, it is now established that at bottom his teaching is he himself. He as a totality is Son, Word and mission; his activity reaches right down to the ground of being and is one with it. And it is precisely in this unity of being and doing that his special character lies. This radicalization of the statement, this inclusion of the ontological element, does not imply, to anyone who can see the context and the background, any sacrifice of the earlier conclusions; above all, it does not imply any kind of triumphalist Christology of glorification in place of the Christology of service, which could do nothing with the crucified and serving man and would like to invent instead another ontological myth about God. On the contrary, anyone who has properly understood the train of ideas must see that the earlier aspect is now grasped in its full profundity. The "servant" aspect is no longer explained as a deed, behind which abides the person of Jesus; it is made to embrace the whole existence of Jesus, so that his *being* itself is service. And precisely because this being, as a totality, is nothing but service, it is sonship. To that extent it is not until this point that the Christian revaluation of values reaches its final goal; only here does it become fully clear that he who surrenders himself completely to service for others, to complete selflessness and self-emptying, clearly *becomes* these things – that this very person is the true man, the man of the future, the commixture of man and God.

This leads to the next step: the meaning of the dogmas of Nicaea and Chalcedon becomes evident. These dogmas were intended to express nothing else than this identity of service and being, in which the whole content of the prayer-relationship *"Abba*–Son" comes to light. These dogmatic formulations with their so-called ontological Christology are not prolongations of mythical notions of begetting. Anyone who makes that assumption only proves that he has no idea of the Council of Chalcedon, of the real meaning of ontology or even of the mythological concepts opposed to them. These assertions were not developed out of mythological notions of procreation but out of the Johannine testimony, which for its part simply represents the prolongation of Jesus' converse with the Father and of Jesus' existence for men to the point of sacrificing himself on the cross.

If one pursues these connections further it is not difficult to see that the "ontology" of the fourth gospel and of the old creeds embraces a much more radical "actualism" that anything appearing today under the label "actualism". I shall content myself with one example, a statement of Bultmann's on the question of Jesus' worship: "Just as the ἐκκλησία, the eschatological community, is only ever really ἐκκλησία as an event, so too Christ's Lordship, his Godhood, is always only ever event."[23] In this form of actualism the real *being* of the man Jesus remains static behind the event of "being-God" and "being-Lord", like the being of any man, fundamentally untouched by the event and only the chance kindling-point at which it comes to pass that for some one as he hears the Word an actual encounter with God himself becomes reality. And just as the being of Jesus remains static behind the act, so the being of man too can be affected by the divine only "now and then", by something in the nature of an "event". Here too the encounter with God only comes to pass in the momentary flash of an event; the "being" is excluded from the meeting. Theology of this sort seems to me to display a kind of despair

---

[23] *Glauben und Verstehen*, Vol. II, Tübingen, 1952, p. 258. Cf. G. Hasenhüttl, *Der Glaubensvollzug. Eine Begegnung mit R. Bultmann aus katholischem Glaubensverständnis*, Essen, 1963, p. 127.

in face of what *is*; it leaves no hope that being itself could ever become act.

The Christology of John and of the Church's Creed, on the other hand, goes much further in its radicalism, inasmuch as it acknowledges being itself as act and says, "Jesus is his work". Then there is no man behind it all to whom nothing has really happened. His being is pure *actualitas* of "from" and "for". But precisely because this "being" is no longer separable from its *actualitas* it coincides with God and is at the same time the exemplary man, the man of the future, through whom it becomes evident how very much man is still the coming creature, a being still, so to speak, waiting to˙ be realized; and what a short distance man has even now progressed towards being himself. When this is understood it also becomes clear why phenomenology and existential analyses, helpful as they are, cannot suffice for Christology. They do not reach deep enough, because they leave the realm of real "being" untouched.

IV. THE DIFFERENT PATHS TAKEN BY CHRISTOLOGY

1. THEOLOGY OF THE INCARNATION AND THEOLOGY OF THE CROSS

The insights so far acquired also provide access to those basic assertions of Christology that still remain to be considered. In the history of the Christian faith two divergent lines of approach to the contemplation of Jesus have appeared again and again: the theology of the incarnation, which sprang from Greek thought and became dominant in the Catholic tradition of East and West, and the theology of the cross, which based itself on St Paul and the earliest forms of Christian belief and made a decisive break-through in the thinking of the Reformers. The former talks of "being" and centres round the fact that here a man *is* God and that accordingly at the same time God is man; this astounding fact is seen as the all-decisive one. All the individual events that followed pale before this one event of the one-ness of man and God, of God's becoming man. In face of this they can only be secondary; the interlocking of God and man appears as the truly decisive, redemptive factor, as the real future of man, on which all lines must finally converge.

Theology of the cross, on the other hand, will have nothing to do with ontology of this kind; it speaks instead of the event; it follows the testimony of the early days, when people did not yet enquire about *being* but about the *activity* of God in the cross and resurrection, an activity which conquered death and pointed to Jesus as the Lord and as the hope of humanity. The differing tendencies of these two theologies result from their respective approaches. Theology of the incarnation tends towards a static, optimistic view. The sin of man appears quite easily as a transitional stage of fairly minor importance. The decisive factor is then not that man is in a state of sin and must be saved; the aim goes far beyond any such atonement for the past and lies in making progress towards the convergence of man and God. The theology of the cross, on the other hand, leads rather to a dynamic, topical, anti-world conception of Christianity, a conception which understands Christianity only as a discontinuously but constantly appearing breach in the self-confidence and self-assurance of man and of his institutions, including the Church.

Anyone at all familiar with these two great historical forms of Christian self-comprehension will certainly not be tempted to try his hand at a simplifying synthesis. The two fundamental structural forms of "incarnation" and "cross" theology reveal polarities which cannot be surmounted and combined in a neat-looking synthesis without the loss of the crucial points in each; they must remain present as polarities which mutually correct each other and only by complementing each other point towards the whole. Nevertheless, our reflections may perhaps have given us a glimpse of that unity which makes these polarities possible and prevents them from falling apart as contradictions. For we have found that the *being* of Christ ("incarnation" theology!) is *actualitas*, stepping beyond and out of oneself, the exodus of departure from self; it is not a being that rests in itself, but the act of being sent, of being son, of serving. Conversely, this "doing" is not just "doing" but "being"; it reaches down into the depths of being and coincides with it. This being is exodus, transformation. So at this point a properly understood theology of being and of the incarnation must pass over into the theology of the cross and become one with it; conversely, a theology of the cross that gives its full measure must pass over into the theology of the Son and of being.

2. CHRISTOLOGY AND THE DOCTRINE OF REDEMPTION

From the position thus gained it is at last also possible to perceive the operation of another antithesis erected by history; it is in fact closely related to the one we have just considered. In the course of the historical development of the Christian faith two aspects of it which people became accustomed to call "Christology" and "soteriology" visibly parted company. The former term came to denote the doctrine of the being of Jesus, which was treated more and more as a self-contained ontological exception and thus transformed into an object of speculation over something special, incomprehensible and confined to Jesus alone. Soteriology then came to denote the doctrine of the redemption: after dealing with the ontological crossword puzzle – the question how man and God could in Jesus be one – people went on to enquire quite separately what Jesus had really done and how the effect of his deed impinges on us. That the two questions parted company, that the person and his work were made the subjects of separate enquiries and treatises, led to both problems becoming incomprehensible and insoluble. A brief inspection of the manuals of dogmatic theology is sufficient to confirm how complicated the theories dealing with both problems were, because it had been forgotten that they can only be understood when considered together. Let me just recall the form which the doctrine of redemption mostly takes in the Christian consciousness. It is based on the so-called "satisfaction theory", which was developed by St Anselm of Canterbury on the threshold of the Middle Ages and moulded the Western consciousness more and more exclusively. Even in its classical form it is not devoid of one-sidedness, but when contemplated in the vulgarized form which has extensively moulded the general consciousness it looks cruelly mechanical and less and less feasible.

Anselm of Canterbury (c. 1033–1109) had been concerned

to deduce the work of Christ by a train of necessary reasons (*rationibus necessariis*) and thus to show irrefutably that this work *had* to happen in the precise way in which it in fact did. His argument may be roughly summarized like this: by man's sin, which was aimed against God, the order of justice was infinitely damaged and God infinitely offended. Behind this is the idea that the measure of the offence is determined by the status of the offended party; if I offend a beggar the consequences are not the same as they would be if I offended a head of state. The importance of the offence varies according to the addressee. Since God is infinite the offence to him implicit in humanity's sin is also infinitely important. The right thus damaged must be restored, because God is a God of order and justice; indeed, he is justice itself. But the measure of the offence demands an infinite reparation, which man is not capable of making. He can offend infinitely – his capacity extends that far – but he cannot produce an infinite reparation; what he, as a finite being, gives will always be only finite. His powers of destruction extend further than his capacity to reconstruct. Thus between all the reparations that man may attempt and the greatness of his guilt there remains an infinite gulf which he can never bridge. Any gesture of expiation can only demonstrate his powerlessness to close the infinite gulf which he himself opened up.

Is order to be destroyed for ever, then, and man to remain eternally imprisoned in the abyss of his guilt? At this point Anselm hits on the figure of Christ. His answer runs thus: God himself removes the injustice; not (as he could) by a simple amnesty, which cannot after all overcome from inside what has happened, but by the infinite Being's himself becoming man and then as a man – who thus belongs to the race of the offenders yet possesses the power, denied to man, of infinite reparation – making the required expiation. Thus the redemption takes place entirely through grace and at the same time entirely as restoration of the right. Anselm thought he had thereby given a compelling answer to the difficult question of "*Cur Deus homo*", the wherefore of the incarnation and the cross. His view has put a decisive stamp on the second millennium of Western Christendom, which takes it for granted that

Christ had to die on the cross in order to make good the infinite offence which had been committed and in this way to restore the damaged order of things.

Now it cannot be denied that this theory takes account of crucial biblical and human perceptions; anyone who studies it with a little patience will have no difficulty in seeing this. To that extent it will always command respect as an attempt to synthesize the individual elements in the biblical evidence in one great all-embracing system. It is not hard to see that in spite of all the philosophical and juridical terminology employed, the guiding thread remains that truth which the Bible expresses in the little word "For", in which it makes clear that we as men live not only directly from God but from one another, and in the last analysis from the One who lived for all. And who could fail to see that thus in the schematization of the "satisfaction" theory the breath of the biblical idea of election remains clear, the idea that makes election not a privilege of the elected but the call to live for others? It is the call to that "For" in which man confidently lets himself fall, ceases to cling to himself and ventures on the leap away from himself into the infinite, the leap through which alone he can come to himself. But even if all this is admitted it cannot be denied on the other hand that the perfectly logical divine-cum-human legal system erected by Anselm distorts the perspectives and with its rigid logic can make the image of God appear in a sinister light. We shall have to go into this in detail when we come to talk about the meaning of the cross. For the time being it will suffice to say that things immediately look different when, in place of the division of Jesus into work and person, it becomes clear that with Jesus Christ it is not a question of a piece of work separate from himself, of a feat which God must demand because he himself is under an obligation to the concept of order; that with him it is not a question – to use Gabriel Marcel's terminology – of *having* humanity, but of *being* human. And how different things look further on when one picks up the Pauline key, which teaches us to understand Christ as the "last man" (ἔσχατος ᾿Αδάμ: 1 Cor. 15.45) – the final man, who takes man into his future, which consists of his being not just man but one wi h God.

3. CHRIST, "THE LAST MAN"

We have now reached the point at which we can try to summarize what we mean when we confess, "I believe in Jesus Christ, only begotten Son of God, our Lord". After all that has gone before we shall dare to say first: Christian faith believes in Jesus as the exemplary man (this is probably the best way to translate accurately the above-mentioned Pauline concept of the "last Adam"). But precisely because he is the exemplary, the authoritative man, he oversteps the bounds of humanity; only thus and only thereby is he the truly exemplary man. For man is the more himself the more he is with "the other". He only comes *to* himself by moving away *from* himself. Only through "the other" and through "being" with "the other" does he come to himself.

In the last analysis there is one final depth to this truth. If "the other" is just anyone he can also cause man to lose himself. Man is finally intended for *the* other, the truly other, for God; he is all the more himself the more he is with the *quite* other, with God. Accordingly he is completely himself when he has ceased to stand in himself, to shut himself off in himself and to assert himself, when in fact he is pure openness to God. To put it again in different terms: man comes to himself by moving out beyond himself. Jesus Christ is he who has moved right out beyond himself and *thus* the man who has truly come to himself.

The Rubicon of becoming man, of "hominization", was first crossed by the step from animal to *logos*, from mere life to mind. Man came into existence out of the "clay" at the moment when a creature was no longer merely "there" but, over and above just being there and filling his needs, was aware of the whole. But this step, through which "*logos*", understanding, mind, first came into this world, is only completed when the *logos* itself, the whole creative meaning, and man merge into each other. Man's full "hominization" presupposes God's becoming man; only by this event is the Rubicon dividing the "animal" from the "logical" finally crossed for ever and the highest possible development accorded to the process which began when a creature of dust and earth looked out beyond itself and its environment and was able to address God as

"You". It is openness to the whole, to the infinite, that makes man complete. Man is man by reaching out infinitely beyond himself and he is consequently more of a man the less enclosed he is in himself, the less "limited" he is. For – let me repeat – that man is most man, indeed *the* true man, who is most unlimited, who not only has contact with the infinite – the infinite being! – but is one with him: Jesus Christ. In him "hominization" has truly reached its goal.[24]

But now there is a second point to be considered. We tried earlier, *via* the idea of the "exemplary man", to understand that first fundamental overstepping of one's own individuality which faith knows to be the decisive feature in the figure of Jesus; the feature which in him binds humanity and divinity into a unity. But in that concept there was already a hint of the abolition of yet another frontier. If Jesus is the exemplary man, in whom the true figure of man, God's intention for him, comes fully to light, then he cannot be destined to be merely an absolute exception, a curiosity, in which God demonstrates to us just what is possible. His existence concerns all mankind. The New Testament makes this perceptible by calling him an "Adam"; in the Bible this word expresses the unity of the whole creature "man", so that one can speak of the biblical idea of a "corporate personality".[25] So if Jesus is called "Adam" this implies that he is intended to gather the whole creature "Adam" in himself. But this means that the reality which Paul calls, in a way that is largely incomprehensible to us today, the "body of Christ" is an intrinsic postulate of this existence, which cannot remain an exception but must "draw to itself" the whole of mankind (cf. John 12.32).

[24] Cf. on this subject B. Welte, "Homousios hemin. Gedanken zum Verständnis und zur theologischen Problematik der Kategorien von Chalkedon", in A. Grillmeier–H. Bacht, *Das Konzil von Chalkedon*, Vol. III, Würzburg, 1954, pp. 51–80; K. Rahner, "Zur Theologie der Menschwerdung", in *Schriften zur Theologie*, Vol. IV, Einsiedeln, 1960, pp. 137–155; *Idem*, "Die Christologie innerhalb einer evolutiven Weltanschauung", in *Schriften*, Vol. V, Einsiedeln, 1962, pp. 183–221.

[25] Cf. J. Pedersen, *Israel, its Life and Culture*, 2 vols., London, 1926 and 1940; H. W. Robinson, "The Hebrew Conception of Corporate Personality", in *Beihefte zur Zeitschrift für die alttestamentliche Wissenschaft* 66 (Berlin, 1936), pp. 49–62; J. de Fraine, *Adam und seine Nachkommen*, Cologne, 1962.

It must be regarded as an important service of Teilhard de Chardin's that he re-thought these ideas from the angle of the modern view of the world and, in spite of a not entirely unobjectionable tendency towards the biological approach, nevertheless on the whole grasped them correctly and in any case made them accessible once again. Let us listen to his own words: the human monad "can only be absolutely itself by ceasing to be alone".[26] In the background is the idea that in the cosmos, alongside the two orders or classes of the infinitely small and the infinitely big, there is a third order, which determines the real drift of evolution, namely the order of the infinitely complex. It is the real goal of the ascending powers of growth or becoming; it reaches a first peak in the genesis of living things and then continues to advance to those highly complex creations which give the cosmos a new centre: "Imperceptible and accidental as the position which they hold may be in the history of the heavenly bodies, in the last analysis the planets are nothing less than the vital points of the universe. It is through them that the axis now runs, on them is henceforth concentrated the main effort of an evolution aiming principally at the production of large molecules."[27]

The examination of the world by the dynamic criterion of complexity thus signifies "a complete inversion of values. A reversal of the perspective."[28]

But let us return to man. He is so far the maximum in complexity. But even he as mere man-monad cannot represent an end; his growth itself demands a further advance in complexity: "At the same time as he represents an individual centred on himself (that is, a 'person'), does not Man also represent an *element* in relation to some new and higher synthesis?"[29] That is to say, man is indeed on the one hand already an end that can no longer be reversed, no longer be melted down again; yet in the juxtaposition of individual men he is not yet at the

[26] Quoted by C. Tresmontant, *Introduction à la pensée de Teilhard de Chardin*, Paris, 1956, p. 68 (the quotation in fact comes from Teilhard's *La Vie Cosmique*, 1916 – Translator).

[27] *Ibid.*, p. 38 (Teilhard, *Vie et Planètes*, Etudes, May 1946, p. 157 – trans.).

[28] *Ibid.*, p. 37 (Teilhard, *Vie et Planètes*, p. 155 – Trans.).

[29] *Ibid.*, p. 68 (Teilhard, *La Place de l'Homme dans l'Univers*, 1942 – Trans.).

goal but shows himself to be an element, as it were, that longs
for a whole which will embrace it without destroying it. Let us
look at a further text, in order to see in what direction such
ideas lead: "Contrary to the appearances still accepted by
Physics, the Great Stability is not below – in the infra-elemental
– but above – in the ultra-synthetic."[30]

So it must be discovered that "If things hold and hold together, it is only by virtue of 'complexification', from the top".[31]
I think we are confronted here with a crucial statement; at this
point the dynamic view of the world destroys the positivistic
conception, so near to all of us, that stability is located only in
the "mass", in hard material. That the world is in the last
resort put together and held together "from above" here becomes evident in a way that is particularly striking because we
are so little accustomed to it.

This leads to a further passage in Teilhard de Chardin which
it is worth quoting in order to give at least some indication
here, by means of a few fragmentary excerpts, of his general
outlook. "The Universal Energy must be a Thinking Energy
if it is not to be less highly evolved than the ends animated by
its action. And consequently . . . the attributes of cosmic value
with which it is surrounded in our modern eyes do not affect in
the slightest the necessity obliging us to recognize in it a trans-
cendent form of Personality."[32] From here it is possible to
understand the final aim of the whole movement as Teilhard
sees it: the cosmic drift moves "in the direction of an incredible
'mono-molecular' state, so to speak, in which . . . each *ego* is
destined to attain its climax in a sort of mysterious super-
ego".[33] As an "I", man is indeed an end, but the whole tendency
of his being and of his own existence shows him also to be a creation belonging to a "super–I" that does not blot him out but
encompasses him; only such an association can bring out the
form of the future man, in which humanity will achieve complete
fulfilment of itself.

One can safely say that here the tendency of Pauline Christ-

[30] *Ibid.*, p. 72 (Teilhard, *Le Phénomène humain*, p. 301 – Trans.).
[31] *Ibid.*, p. 72 (Teilhard, *Le Phénomène humain*, p. 37 – Trans.).
[32] *Ibid.*, p. 78 (Teilhard, *L'Esprit de la Terre* – Trans.).
[33] *Ibid.*, p. 69 (Teilhard, *Le Cœur de la Matière*, 1950 – Trans.).

ology is in essentials correctly grasped from the modern angle and rendered comprehensible again, even if the vocabulary employed is certainly rather too biological. Faith sees in Jesus the man in whom – on the biological plane – the next evolutionary leap, as it were, has been accomplished; the man in whom the breakthrough out of the limited scope of humanity, out of its monadic enclosure, has occurred; the man in whom personalization and socialization no longer exclude each other but support each other; the man in whom perfect unity – "The body of Christ", says St Paul, and even more pointedly "You are all one in Christ Jesus" (Gal. 3.28) – and perfect individuality are one; the man in whom humanity comes into contact with its future and in the highest extent itself becomes its future, because through him it makes contact with God himself, shares in him and thus realizes its most instrinsic possibility. From here onwards faith in Christ will see the beginning of a movement in which dismembered humanity is gathered together more and more into the being of one single Adam, one single body – the man to come. It will see in him the movement to that future of man in which he is completely "socialized", incorporated in one single being, but in such a way that the separate individual is not extinguished but brought completely to himself.

It would not be difficult to show that Johannine theology points in the same direction. One has only to recall the words briefly touched on earlier: "And I, when I am lifted up from the earth, will draw all men to myself" (John 12.32). This sentence is intended to explain the meaning of Jesus' death on the cross; it thus expresses, since the cross forms the centre of Johannine theology, the direction in which the whole Gospel is intended to point. The event of the crucifixion appears there as a process of opening, in which the scattered man-monads are drawn into the embrace of Jesus Christ, into the wide span of his outstretched arms, in order to arrive, in this union, at their goal, the goal of humanity. But if this is so, then Christ as the man to come is not man for himself but essentially man for others; it is precisely his complete openness that makes him the man of the future. The man for himself, who wants to stand only in himself, is then the man of the past whom we must leave behind us in order to stride forward. In other words, this means that the future of man lies in "being-for". This fundamentally confirms once again what we recognized as the meaning of the talk of sonship and, before that, as the meaning of the doctrine of three persons in one God, namely a reference to the dynamic, "actual" existence, which is essentially openness in the movement between "from" and "for". And once again it becomes clear that Christ is the completely open man, in whom the dividing-walls of existence are torn down, who is all "transition" (Passover, "Pasch").

This brings us straight back again to the mystery of the cross and Easter, a mystery that is indeed viewed by the Bible as a mystery of transition. John, who in particular reflects these ideas, concludes his portrait of the earthly Jesus with the image of an existence whose walls are torn down, which knows no more firm boundaries but is essentially openness. "One of the soldiers thrust a lance into his side and immediately blood and water came out" (John 19.34). For John, the picture of the pierced side forms the climax not only of the crucifixion scene but of the whole story of Jesus. Now, after the lance-thrust that ends his earthly life, his existence is completely open; now he is entirely "for", now he is truly no longer a single individual but "Adam", from whose side Eve, a new mankind, is formed. That profound description in the Old Testament according to which the woman is taken from the side of the man (Gen. 2.21ff.) – an inimitable expression of their perpetual dependence on each other and their unity in the one humanity – that story seems to be echoed here in the recurrence of the word "side" ($\pi\lambda\varepsilon\upsilon\varrho\acute{a}$, usually translated – wrongly – by "rib"). The open side of the new Adam repeats the creative mystery of the "open side" of man: it is the beginning of a new definitive community of men with one another, a community symbolized here by blood and water, in which John points to the basic Christian sacraments of baptism and Eucharist and through them to the Church as the sign of the new community of men.[34] The fully opened

[34] Cf. O. Cullmann, *Urchristentum und Gottesdienst*, Zürich, 1950, pp. 110ff.; J. Betz, *Die Eucharistie in der Zeit der griechischen Väter*, Vol. II, 1: "Die Realpräsenz des Leibes und Blutes Jesu im Abendmahl nach dem NT", Freiburg, 1961, pp. 189–200.

Christ, who completes the transformation of being into reception and transmission, is thus visible as what at the deepest level he always was: as "Son". So Jesus on the cross has truly entered on *his* hour, as once again John says. This enigmatic mode of speech may now perhaps become to some extent comprehensible.

But the whole thing also shows what demands the talk of the man to come involves, and how little it really has to do with the cheerful romanticism of progress. For to be the man for others, the man who is open and thereby opens up a new beginning, means being the man in the sacrifice, sacrificed man. The future of man hangs on the cross – the redemption of man is the cross. And he can only come to himself by letting the walls of his existence be broken down, by looking on him who has been pierced (John 19.37), and by following him who as the pierced and opened one has opened the path into the future. This means in the end that Christianity, which as belief in the creation acknowledges the primacy of the *logos*, the creative meaning as beginning and origin, also acknowledges it in a specific way as the end, the future, the coming one. Indeed, in this gaze at him who is coming lies the real historical dynamism of the Christian approach, which in the Old and New Testaments perfects faith into hope in the promise.

Christian faith is not just a backward gaze at what has happened in the past, an anchorage in a source that lies behind us in time; a conception of this sort would finally end in mere romanticism and reaction. Nor is it just gazing out at the eternal; that would be Platonism and metaphysics. It is also above all things a looking forward, a reaching-out of hope. Not only that, certainly; hope would become utopianism, with only man's own product as the goal. It is true hope precisely because it is located at the intersection of all three dimensions: the past, that is, the breakthrough that has already taken place; the present of the eternal, which makes divided time like unity; and him who is to come, in whom God and world will touch each other and thus God in world, world in God will truly be the omega of history.

From the standpoint of Christian faith one may say that for *history* God stands at the end, while for *being* he stands at the beginning. This indicates Christianity's all-embracing horizon, which distinguishes it both from mere metaphysics and from the future-orientated ideology of Marxism. Since Abraham and until the return of the Lord, faith advances to meet him who is coming. But in Christ the countenance of him who is to come is already revealed: it will be the man who can embrace all men because he has lost himself and them to God. For this reason the emblem of him who is to come must be the cross, and his face in this era of the world must be a countenance of blood and wounds: the "last man", that is, the real, the future man reveals himself in this age in *the* last men; whoever wishes to stand on *his* side must therefore stand on *their* side (cf. Matt. 25.31–46).

EXCURSUS: CHRISTIAN STRUCTURES

Before we proceed to work through the separate christological assertions in the Creed which follow the basic acknowledgement of Jesus as the Christ it will be as well to pause for a moment. The individual questions are only too apt to make us forget to look at the whole, and it is clear how essential such a general survey is today, especially when we are trying to talk to anyone who does not believe. Sometimes one can get the impression from contemporary theology that it is so pleased with its progress – certainly very welcome – in the ecumenical field, and so glad that it is succeeding in moving old boundary stones (if only in most cases to erect them again at a different spot), that it does not pay sufficient attention to the direct questions of the men of today, questions which often have little to do with the traditional points of conflict between the various denominations. For example, who can ever tell an enquirer comprehensibly and reasonably briefly what "being a Christian" really means? Who can explain comprehensibly to someone else why he believes and what the plain direction, the nub, of the decision implicit in faith is?

When people do begin, as they have done recently, to put such broad questions to themselves, they quite often simultaneously slip into watering down Christianity into sweet-sounding generalities, which certainly flatter the ears of their contemporaries (cf. 2 Tim. 4.3) but deny them the strong meat of the faith to which they are entitled. Theology is not measuring up to its task when it concentrates happily on itself and its own erudition; it is failing even more radically when it invents "doctrines to its own taste" (2 Tim. 4.3) and thus offers stones instead of bread, its own talk instead of the word of God. The task which thus presents itself – between this Scylla and this Charybdis – is immeasurably big. Nevertheless – or rather for this very reason – let us try to rethink things along these lines and to summarize the basic content of Christianity in a few easily graspable statements. Even if the results remain somewhat unsatisfactory the enterprise may perhaps have the advantage of stimulating others to put further questions and thus of helping things forward.[35]

1. *The individual and the whole*

For us men of today the basic stumbling-block of Christianity lies first of all simply in the outwardness which the religious element seems to have assumed in it. It irritates us that God should have to be passed on to us through outward forms: through Church, sacrament, dogma or even just through the Gospel (kerygma), to which people like to withdraw to reduce the irritation and which is nevertheless itself something outward. All this provokes the question, Does God dwell in institutions, events or words? As the eternal Being, does he not make contact with each of us from within? To this we must first of all simply say "yes", and then go on to say that if there were only God and a collection of individuals Christianity would be unnecessary. The salvation of the individual *as* individual can and could always be looked after directly and immediately by God, and this does happen again and again. He needs no intermediary channels by which to enter the soul of the individual, to which he is more intrinsic than he is to himself; nothing can reach more intimately and deeply into man than he, who touches this creature man in the very innermost heart of his

---

[35] What follows makes considerable use of ideas which I first developed in my little book *Vom Sinn des Christseins*, 2nd ed., Munich, 1966. I have tried to systematize what I said there and to incorporate it in the larger context of the reflections contained in this present book.

being. For the salvation of the mere individual there would be no need of either a Church or a history of salvation, an incarnation or a passion. But precisely at this point we must also add the further statement: Christian faith is not based on the atomized individual but comes from the knowledge that there is no such thing as the mere individual, that on the contrary man is himself only when he is fitted into the whole: into mankind, history, the cosmos, as is right and proper for a being who is "spirit in body".

The principle of "body" and "corporality" by which man is governed means two things: on the one hand the body separates men from one another, makes them impenetrable to each other. As a space-filling and sharply defined shape the body makes it impossible for one to be completely in the other; it erects a dividing line which signifies distances and limit; it keeps us at a distance from one another and is to that extent a dissociating principle. But at the same time existence in a corporal form necessarily also embraces history and community, for if pure spirit can be thought of as existing strictly for itself, corporality implies descent from one another: human beings live and depend in a very real and at the same time very complex sense on one another. For if this dependence is first of all a physical one (and even in this sphere it extends from parentage down to the manifold exchanges of mutual daily care), it means for him who is spirit only in a body and as body that the spirit too – in short, the one, whole man – is deeply marked by his membership of the whole of mankind – the one "Adam".

It thus becomes clear that man is a being that can only "be" by virtue of others. Or to put it in the words of the great Tübingen theologian, Möhler: "Man, as a being set entirely in a context of relationship, cannot come to himself through himself, although he cannot do it without himself either."[36] This was expressed even more pointedly by Möhler's contemporary, the Munich philosopher Franz von Baader, when he declared that it was just as absurd "to deduce the knowledge

[36] This is how J. R. Geiselmann summarizes the ideas developed by Möhler in the *Theologische Quartalschrift*, 1830, pp. 582f.; J. R. Geiselmann, *Die Heilige Schrift und die Tradition*, Freiburg, 1962, p. 56.

of God and the knowledge of all other intelligences and non-intelligences from self-knowledge (self-awareness) as to deduce all love from self-love".[37] Here we are confronted with a sharp rejection of the mode of thinking adopted by Descartes, whose grounding of philosophy in self-awareness (*"Cogito, ergo sum"*: "I think, therefore I am") has decisively influenced the fate of the modern spirit right down to the present-day forms of transcendental philosophy. Just as self-love is not the primordial form of love but at the most a derivative of it, just as one has only arrived at the specific nature of love when one has grasped it as a relation, that is, something coming from another, so too human knowledge is only reality when it is *being* known, being brought to knowledge, and thus again "from another". The real man does not come into it at all if I only plumb the loneliness of the "I", of self-knowledge, for then I clamp off in advance the point of departure of his ability to come to himself and thus his most specific characteristic. That is why Baader, consciously and quite rightly, changed the Cartesian *"Cogito, ergo sum"* into *"Cogitor, ergo sum"*: not "I think, therefore I am" but "I am thought, therefore I am". Only from man's being-known can his knowledge and he himself be understood.

Let us go a step further: being a man means being a fellow man in every aspect, not just in the respective present but in such a way that every man also contains the past and future of mankind, which really does emerge, the closer one looks, as one single "Adam". We cannot go into this in detail here; a few indications must suffice. One needs only to point to the fact that our mental life depends entirely on the medium of language and to add then that language was not invented today. It comes from a long way off; the whole of history has contributed to it and through it enters into us as the unavoidable premise of our present, indeed as a constant part of it. And, *vice versa*, man is a being who lives for the future, who continually takes care to plan ahead beyond the passing moment and could no longer exist if he suddenly found himself without

[37] According to J. R. Geiselmann, *op. cit.*, p. 56; F. von Baader, *Vorlesungen über spekulative Dogmatik* (1830), 7th lecture, in *Werke*, Vol. VIII, p. 231; cf. Möhler, *loc. cit.*

a future.[38] We are therefore bound to say that such a thing as
the mere individual, the man-monad of the Renaissance, the
pure *Cogito-ergo-sum*-being does not exist. Humanity comes to
man only in the web of history that impinges on the individual
through speech and social communication; and the individual
for his part lives his life on the collective pattern in which he is
already previously included and which forms the scene of his
self-realization. It is simply not the case that every man plans
himself anew from the zero of his own freedom, as it seemed to
the German idealist philosophers. He is not a being who keeps
starting again from scratch; he can only work out his own new
approach within the framework of the already existing whole
of human life which stamps and moulds him.

This brings us back to the question with which we started,
and we can now say: The Church and being a Christian have
to do with man so understood. They would have no function to
fulfil if the only thing that existed was the man-monad, the
being implied by *"Cogito, ergo sum"*. They are related to the
man who is a fellow being and only subsists in the collective
entanglements that follow from the principle of corporality.
Church and Christianity itself exist on account of history, because of the collective involvements which stamp man; they
are to be understood on this plane. Their purpose is to save
history as history and to break through or transform the collective grid that forms the site of human existence. According to
the Epistle to the Ephesians, Christ's work of salvation consisted precisely in bringing to their knees the forces and powers
seen by Origen in his commentary on this passage as the collective powers which encircle man: the power of the milieu, of
national tradition; the conventional "they" or "one" that
oppresses and destroys man.[39] Terms like original sin, resur-

[38] Cf. the observation by E. Mounier in *L'Esprit*, January 1947: a wireless
announcer had succeeded only too well in creating the idea that the end of
the world was at hand. Peak of absurdity: people took their own lives so as
not to die. This quite obviously senseless reaction proves that we live far
more on the future than on the present. A man who is violently robbed of
the future is a man already robbed of life itself. – In "Sein des Daseins als
Sorge", M. Heidegger, *Sein und Zeit*, Tübingen, 11th ed., 1967, pp. 191–196.

[39] Cf. J. Ratzinger, "Menschheit und Staatenbau in der Sicht der frühen
Kirche", in *Studium generale*, 14 (1961), pp. 664–682, especially 666–674;

rection of the flesh, last judgment, and so on, are only to be understood at all from this angle, for the seat of original sin is to be sought precisely in this collective net that precedes the individual existence as a sort of spiritual *datum,* not in any biological legacy passed on between otherwise utterly separated individuals. Talk of original sin means just this, that no man can start from scratch any more, in a *status integritatis* (=completely unimpaired by history). No one starts off in an unimpaired condition in which he would only need to develop himself freely and lay out his own grounds; everyone lives in a web that is a part of his existence itself. Last judgment is the answer to these collective entanglements. Resurrection expresses the idea that the immortality of man can only exist and be thought of in the fellowship of men, in man as the creature of fellowship, as we shall see in more detail later on. Finally, even the concept of redemption, as we have already said, only has a meaning on this plane; it does not refer to the detached, monadic destiny of the individual. If therefore the plane of reality of Christianity is to be sought here, in a realm which can be summarily described, in the absence of a better term, as that of historicity, then we can now clarify further and say: Being a Christian is in its first aim not an individual but a social charisma. One is not a Christian because only Christians are saved; one is a Christian because for history the Christian diaconate has a meaning and is a necessity.

At this point there occurs an absolutely decisive further step, which at first seems to represent a complete about-turn, but in fact is the necessary corollary of our reflections up to now. If one is a Christian in order to share in a diaconate for the whole, then this means at the same time that precisely because of this relation to the whole Christianity lives from the *individual* and for the individual, because only by the action of the individual can the transformation of history, the destruction of the dictatorship of the milieu come to pass. It seems to me that this is the reason for what to the other world religions and to the man

---

H. Schlier, *Mächte und Gewalten im Neuen Testament,* Freiburg, 1958, especially pp. 23f., 27, 29. On the "one": Heidegger, *Sein und Zeit,* 11th ed., Tübingen, 1967, pp. 126–130.

of today is always completely incomprehensible, namely that in Christianity *everything* hangs in the last resort on one *individual*, on the man Jesus of Nazareth, who was crucified by the milieu – public opinion – and who on his cross broke this very power of the conventional "one", the power of anonymity, which holds man captive. This power is now confronted by the name of this individual, Jesus Christ, who calls on man to follow him, that is, to take up the cross like him, and by being crucified to overcome the world and contribute to the renewal of history. Precisely because Christianity wants history as a whole its challenge is directed fundamentally at the individual; precisely for this reason it hangs on *the* single individual in whom the bursting of the bondage to the forces and powers took place. In other words, because Christianity relates to the whole and can only be understood from the idea of community and with reference to it, because it does not mean the salvation of the isolated individual but acceptance of service to the whole, which he neither can nor may escape, for this very reason it is committed to the principle of "the individual" in its most radical form. *Here* lies the intrinsic necessity of the unheard-of scandal that a single individual, Jesus Christ, is acknowledged as the salvation of the world. The individual is the salvation of the whole, and the whole receives its salvation only from the individual who *truly* is it and who precisely for this reason ceases to exist for himself alone.

I believe that this is also the key to understanding why there is no similar recourse to the individual in other religions. In the last analysis Hinduism seeks not the whole but the individual who saves himself, who escapes from the world, the wheel of Maja. Precisely because at bottom it does not want the whole but only to rescue the individual from wickedness it can never recognize any *other* individual as finally significant and decisive for *my* salvation. Its devaluation of the whole thus becomes a devaluation of the individual as well, in that "For" disappears as a category.[40]

To summarize the conclusions of our reflections so far, we

---

[40] Cf. the instructive investigation by J. Neuner, "Religion und Riten. Die Opferlehre der Bhagavadgita", in *Zeitschrift für Katholische Theologie*, 73 (1951), pp. 170–213.

have established that Christianity proceeds from the principle
of "corporeality" (historicity), that it is to be thought of on
the plane of "the whole" and only has a meaning on this plane,
and that nevertheless for this very reason it sets up and must
set up "the individual" as a principle, which is its scandal, yet
whose instrinsic necessity and rationality are here evident.

2. The principle of "For"

Because Christian faith demands the individual, but wants him
for the whole and not for himself, the real basic law of Christian
existence is expressed in the preposition "For": this is the final
conclusion that necessarily emerges from what we have said so
far. That is why in the chief Christian sacrament, which forms
the centre of Christian worship, the existence of Jesus Christ
is explained[41] as existence "for the many", "for you", as an
open existence which makes possible and creates the communication of all between one another through communication
in him. That is why Christ's existence, as exemplary existence,
is fulfilled and perfected, as we have seen, in his being opened
on the cross. That is why he can say, announcing and expounding his death: "I go away, and I will come to you" (John 14.28):
by my going away the wall of my existence which now bounds
me in will be broken down, and thus this happening is my real
coming, in which I make a reality of what I really am, he who
draws all into the unity of his new being, he who is not boundary but unity.

This is how the Fathers interpreted the arms of the Lord
outstretched on the cross. They saw in them first of all the
primordial form of the Christian position of prayer, the attitude
of the *orantes* so movingly portrayed in the pictures in the
catacombs. The arms of the crucified Christ thus show him to
be the worshipper, but at the same time they also add a new
dimension to worship, a dimension which forms the specifically
Christian element in the glorification of God: these open arms
are also the expression of worship precisely because they express
complete devotion to men, because they are a gesture of
embrace, of full and undivided brotherliness. On the cross the

[41] In the canon of the Mass, for example, in accordance with the sacramental words, Mk. 14.24.

theology of the Fathers found symbolically depicted in the
Christian gesture of prayer the coincidence of worship and
brotherliness, the indivisibility of service for man and the
glorification of God.

Being a Christian means essentially changing over from being
for oneself to being for one another. This also explains what is
really meant by the often rather odd-seeming concept of
election ("predestination"). It does not mean a preference that
leaves the individual undisturbed in himself and divides him
from the others, but entrance on the common task of which we
spoke earlier. Accordingly the basic Christian decision signifies the assent to being a Christian, the abandonment of self-
centredness and accession to Jesus Christ's existence with its
concentration on the whole. The same thing is meant by the
phrase "the way of the cross", which does not indicate a private
devotion at all but is in harmony with the basic idea that man,
leaving behind the privateness and peace of his "I", departs
from himself in order by this frustration of his "I" to follow the
crucified Christ and exist for others. All the great images of the
history of salvation, which represent at the same time the great
basic forms of the Christian religion, are expressions of this
principle of "For". Think for example of the image of the
exodus ("departure"), which from Abraham onwards and far
beyond the classic Exodus of the history of salvation, the
departure from Egypt, remains the basic idea governing the
existence of the people of God and of him who belongs to it:
he is called to the continual exodus of stepping outside himself.
There is an echo of the same thing in the image of the Pasch,
in which the Christian faith has crystallized the connection
between the mystery of Jesus' cross and resurrection and the
exodus-idea of the Old Covenant.

John expressed the whole thing in an image borrowed from
nature. With this the horizon widens out beyond anthropology
and the history of salvation to embrace the cosmic: what is
here called the basic structure of Christian life already represents
at bottom the stamp of the creation itself. "Truly, truly, I say
to you, unless a grain of wheat falls into the earth and dies, it
remains alone; but if it dies, it bears much fruit" (John 12.24).
Even on the cosmic plane the law holds good that life comes

only through death, through loss of self. What is thus hinted at in the creation is fulfilled in man and finally in *the* man *par excellence*, Jesus Christ: by embracing the fate of the grain of wheat, by going through the process of being sacrificed, by letting himself be broken down and by losing himself he opens up access to true life. The findings of the history of religion, which precisely at this point approach very close to the testimony of the Bible, would also justify one in saying that the world lives on sacrifice. Those great myths which assert that the cosmos was built up out of an original sacrifice and that the cosmos only goes on existing through self-sacrifice, that it is dependent on sacrifice,[42] are here confirmed as true and valid. Through this mythological imagery the Christian exodus-principle become visible: "He who loves his life loses it, and he who hates his life in this world will keep it for eternal life" (John 12.25; cf. Mark 8.35 par.). In conclusion it must be stated that all man's own efforts to step outside himself can never suffice. He who only wants to give and is not ready to receive, he who only wants to exist for others and is unwilling to recognize that he for his part too lives on the unexpected, unprovokable gift of others' "For", fails to recognize the basic mode of human existence and is thus bound to destroy the true meaning of living "for one another". To be fruitful, all self-sacrifices demand acceptance by others and in the last analysis by *the* other who is the truly "other" of all mankind and at the same time completely one with it: the God-man Jesus Christ.

3. *The law of disguise*

The fact that "For" is to be regarded as the decisive principle of human existence, and in coinciding with the principle of love becomes the real point at which the divine manifests itself

[42] Cf. the Purusa myth of the Vedic religion; see on this P. Régamey, in F. König, *Christus und die Religionen der Erde. Handbuch der Religionsgeschichte*, 3 vols., Freiburg, 1951, Vol. III, p. 172f.; *Idem*, in F. König, *Religionswissenschaftliches Wörterbuch*, Freiburg, 1956, pp. 470f.; J. Gonda, *Die Religionen Indiens*, Vol. I, Stuttgart, 1960, pp. 186f. and passim. The chief text for this is the *Rigveda*, 10, 90.

in the world, brings a further consequence with it. It has the result that the "quite otherness" of God, which man can work out for himself, becomes the total otherness, the complete unknowability of God. It means that the concealment of God, on which man counts, assumes the scandalous form of his touchability and visibility as the crucified one. To put it in another way, the result is that God, the first principle, the alpha of the world, appears as the omega, the last letter in the alphabet of creation, as the lowliest creature in it. Luther speaks in this connection of God's concealment "*sub contrario*", that is, in what seems to be the opposite of God. He thereby emphasizes the peculiarity of the Christian form of negative theology, the form determined by the cross, as opposed to the negative theology of philosophical thinking. Even philosophy, man's own reflections on God, leads to the realization that God is the quite other, the absolutely hidden and unparalleled. "As blind as the eyes of night-birds", Aristotle had already said, "are our eyes before what is in itself the very brightest thing of all."[43] In fact, on the basis of faith in Jesus Christ, we shall reply: "God is the quite other, invisible, unrecognizable. But when he really did appear upon the scene, so other, so invisible in regard to his divinity, so unrecognizable, it was not the kind of otherness and strangeness that we had foreseen and expected, and he thus remained in fact unrecognized. But should not that in itself prove him to be the *really* quite other, he who casts overboard our notions of otherness and thereby shows himself to be the one and only genuinely quite other?"

All through the Bible one can find again and again the notion of God's double mode of appearing in the world.[44] God affirms his presence first of all of course in the cosmic power. Its greatness, the *logos* of the world that exceeds all our thinking and yet embraces it, points to him whose thought this world is; to whom, before whom the peoples are like "drops from a bucket", "like dust on the scales" (Is. 40.15). There really is such a thing

[43] Quoted by H. Meyer, *Geschichte der abendländischen Weltanschauung*, Vol. I, Würzburg, 1947, p. 231 (=ed. Bekker 993 b 9ff.).

[44] Cf. Ph. Dessauer, "Geschöpfe von fremden Welten", in *Wort und Wahrheit*, 9 (1954), pp. 569–589, J. Ratzinger, *Vom Sinn des Christseins*, 2nd ed., Munich, 1966, pp. 32ff.

as the reference of the universe to its creator. However much we may rebel against proofs of the existence of God and whatever objections philosophical reflection may justifiably make to individual steps in the arguments, the fact remains that the radiance of the original creative idea and of its power to build does shimmer through the world and its spiritual structure.

But this is only one way in which God appears in the world. The other sign which he has adopted and which, by concealing him more, shows more truly his intrinsic nature, is the sign of the lowly, which, measured cosmically, quantitatively, is completely insignificant, actually a pure nothing. One could cite in this connection the series Earth–Israel–Nazareth–Cross–Church, in which God seems to keep disappearing more and more, and precisely in this way becomes more and more manifest as himself. First there is the Earth, a mere nothing in the cosmos, which was to be the point of divine activity in the cosmos. Then comes Israel, a cipher among the powers, which was to be the point of his appearance in the world. Then comes Nazareth, again a cipher within Israel, which was to be the point of his definitive arrival. Then at the end there is the cross, on which a man was to hang, a man whose life had been a failure; yet this was to be the point at which one can actually touch God. Finally there is the Church, the questionable creation of human history, which claims to be the abiding site of his revelation. We know today only to well how little, even in it, concealment of the divine presence is abolished. Precisely when the Church believed, in all the glory of the Renaissance princedom, that it could strip away this concealment and be directly the "gate of heaven", the "house of God", it has become once again, and almost more than before, God's disguise, with God scarcely to be found behind it. Thus what is small by a cosmic or even worldly scale represents the real sign of God wherein the quite other shows itself, which even in relation to our expectations is once again the completely unrecognizable. The cosmic Nothing is the true All, because "For" is the really divine thing. . . .

4. *The law of excess or superfluity*

In the ethical statements of the New Testament there is a

tension which looks as if it cannot be resolved: the tension between grace and ethos, between total forgiveness and just as total a demand on man, between the complete endowment of man, who gets everything thrown at him because he can achieve nothing, and the equally complete obligation to give himself, an obligation that culminates in the unheard-of demand, "You, therefore, must be perfect, as your heavenly Father is perfect" (Matt. 5.48). When, confronted with this exciting polarity, one looks for a connecting link one comes across again and again, especially in Pauline theology, but also in the first three gospels, the word "excess" ($\pi\epsilon\varrho\iota\sigma\sigma\epsilon\upsilon\mu\alpha$), in which the talk of grace and that of demands meet and merge.

In order to take a good look at this principle let us seize on that central passage in the Sermon on the Mount which acts as a sort of superscription and distinguishing mark for the six great antitheses ("You have heard that it was said to the men of old . . . But I say to you . . .") in which Jesus rewrites the Table of the Law. The text runs thus: "For I tell you, unless your righteousness exceeds that of the scribes and Pharisees, you will never enter the kingdom of heaven" (Matt. 5.20). This statement means first of all that all human righteousness is dismissed as inadequate. Who could honestly boast of having really and without reserve absorbed the full meaning of the individual demands and of having fulfilled them, completely fulfilled them in all their profundity, let alone fulfilled them to excess? True, there exists in the Church a "state of perfection", in which one undertakes to go beyond what is commanded, to go to excess. But those who belong to it would be the last to deny that for this very reason they are always finding themselves at the beginning again and full of deficiencies. The "state of perfection" is in reality the most dramatic depiction of the abiding imperfection of man.

Anyone not satisfied with this reference has only to read the next few verses of the Sermon on the Mount (Matt. 5.21–48) to find himself exposed to a terrifying examination of conscience. In these paragraphs it becomes clear what it means when one takes really seriously the principles, at first sight apparently so simple, of the second decalogue, three of which are expounded here: "Thou shalt not kill. Thou shalt not commit adultery.

Thou shalt not bear false witness." At first glance it seems quite easy to feel righteous about these things. After all, one has not killed anyone, one has not broken one's marriage vows, one has not sworn any false oaths. But as Jesus illuminates the depths of these demands it becomes evident that man shares in these sins through anger, hatred, failure to forgive, envy and covetousness. It becomes clear how very much man in his apparent righteousness is besmirched with what goes to make the unrighteousness of the world. If one takes the words of the Sermon on the Mount seriously one realizes what happens to a man who moves over from party politics to reality. The beautiful black and white into which one is accustomed to divide men changes into the grey of a universal twilight. It becomes clear that with men there is no such thing as black and white, and that in spite of all the possible gradations, which do in fact span a wide range, nevertheless all men stand somewhere in the twilight. To change the imagery, one could say that if the moral differences between men can be found to be total in the "macroscopic" realm, a microscopic, "micromoral" inspection discloses a different picture, in which the distinctions begin to look questionable. At any rate, there can be no further talk of an excess of righteousness.

Thus if it depended on man no one could enter heaven, that is, the realm of real, full righteousness. Heaven would have to remain an empty Utopia. And in fact it *does* have to remain an empty Utopia so long as it depends only on the good will of men. How often people say, "with a little bit of good will, everything in the world would be fine". This is true; a little bit of good will would really suffice; but it is the tragedy of mankind that it does not possess the strength for this very thing. Is Camus right, then, when he chooses as a symbol of humanity Sisyphus, who keeps trying to push the stone up the mountain and must continually see it slip down again? So far as human capacities are concerned, the Bible is as sober as Camus, but it does not stop at his scepticism. To the Bible, the limits of human righteousness, of human power as a whole, become an indication of the way in which man is thrown back upon the unquestioning gift of love, a gift which unexpectedly opens itself to him and thereby opens up man himself, and without which man would remain shut up in all his "righteousness" and thus unrighteous. Only the man who accepts this gift can come to himself. Thus the proved speciousness of man's "righteousness" becomes at the same time a pointer to the righteousness of God, the excess of which is called Jesus Christ. He is the righteousness of God, which goes far beyond what need be, which does not calculate, which really overflows; the "notwithstanding" of his greater love, in which he infinitely surpasses the failing efforts of man.

Nevertheless, it would be a complete misunderstanding of the whole to deduce from this a devaluation of man and to feel inclined to say: "Then without this it is all one and any attempt to attain righteousness or esteem in God's eyes is pointless." To this we must reply, "Not at all". In spite of everything and indeed just because of what we have just considered, the requirement to have an excess holds good, even if one can never attain full righteousness. But what is this supposed to mean? Is it not a contradiction? Well, it means, in short, that he who is always calculating how much he must do to be just adequate and to be able to regard himself, after a few casuistical flicks, as a man with a nice, white shirt-front, is still no Christian. And similarly, he who tries to reckon where duty ends and where he can gain a little extra merit by an *opus supererogatorium* (work of supererogation) is a Pharisee, not a Christian. Being a Christian does not mean duly making a certain obligatory contribution and perhaps, as a specially perfect person, even going a little further than is required for the fulfilment of the obligation. On the contrary, a Christian is someone who knows that apart from all this he lives first and foremost as the beneficiary of a bounty; and that consequently all righteousness can only consist in being himself a donor, like the beggar who is grateful for what he receives and generously passes part of it on to others. The calculatingly righteous man, who thinks he can keep his own shirt-front white and build himself up inside it, is the unrighteous man. Human righteousness can only be attained by abandoning one's own claims and being generous to man and to God. It is the righteousness of "Forgive, as we have forgiven" – this request turns out to be the proper formula of human righteousness as understood in the Christian sense: it consists in continuing to forgive, since man himself lives essentially on the forgiveness he has received himself.[45]

But when it is studied in the New Testament the theme of excess leads up another path where its meaning first becomes completely clear. We find the word occurring again in connection with the miracle of the loaves, where an "excess" of seven baskets is mentioned (Mark. 8.8 par.). It forms an essential factor in the story of the multiplication of the loaves and is to be connected with the idea of the superfluous, of the more-than-necessary. One thinks at once of a related miracle preserved in the Johannine tradition: the changing of water into wine at the marriage-feast at Cana (John 2.1–11). It is true that the *word* "excess" does not occur here, but the fact certainly does: according to the evidence of the gospel the new-made wine amounted to between 130 and 190 gallons, a somewhat unusual quantity for a private banquet! In the evangelists' view both stories have to do with the central element in Christian worship, the Eucharist. They show it as the divine excess or abundance, which infinitely surpasses all needs and legitimate demands.

In this way both stories are concerned, through their reference to the Eucharist, with Christ himself: Christ is the infinite self-expenditure of God. And both point back, as we found with the principle of "For", to the law governing the structure of creation, in which life squanders a million seeds in order to save one living one; in which a whole universe is squandered in order to prepare at one point a place for spirit, for man. Excess is God's trade mark in his creation; as the Fathers put it, "God does not reckon his gifts by the measure". At the same time excess is also the real foundation and form of the history of salvation, which in the last analysis is nothing other than the truly breathtaking fact that God, in an incredible outpouring of himself, expends not only a universe but his own self in order to lead man, a speck of dust, to salvation. So excess or superfluity – let us repeat – is the real definition or mark of the history of salvation. The purely calculating mind

---

[45] This is probably the best angle from which to tackle the theme of law and Gospel; cf. G. Söhngen, *Gesetz und Evangelium*, Freiburg, 1957, pp. 11–22.

will always find it absurd that for man God himself should be expended. Only the lover can understand the folly of a love to which prodigality is a law and excess alone is sufficient. Yet if it is true that the creation lives from excess or superfluity, that man is a being for whom excess is necessity, how can we wonder that revelation is the superfluous and for that very reason the necessary, the divine, the love in which the meaning of the universe is fulfilled?

5. *Finality and hope*

Christian faith says that in Christ the salvation of man is accomplished, that in him the true future of mankind has irrevocably begun and thus, although remaining future, is yet also perfect, a part of our present. This assertion embraces a principle of finality which is of the highest importance for the form of Christian existence or for the attitude implied by Christianity to decisions about existence. Let us try to work this out in more detail. We have just established that Christ is the beginning of the future, the already inaugurated finality of the being "man". This idea was expressed in the language of scholastic theology by the statement that with Christ revelation is concluded. Naturally this cannot mean that a certain number of truths have now been imparted and God has decided to make no further communications. On the contrary, it means that God's dialogue with man, God's entry into mankind in Jesus, the man who is God, has achieved its goal. The point of this dialogue was not, and is not, to say *something*, many kinds of things, but to utter himself in the Word. Thus his purpose is not fulfilled when the greatest possible sum of knowledge has been communicated, but when through the Word love becomes visible, when in the Word "You" and "You" make contact. Its meaning does not lie in a third thing, in some kind of factual knowledge, but in the partners themselves. It is called "union". In the man Jesus, God has once and for all uttered himself: he *is* his Word and, as his Word, himself. Revelation does not end here because God deliberately puts an end to it, but because it has reached its goal; as Karl Rahner puts it, "Nothing fresh is said, not in spite of there being still much to say, but because everything is said, indeed everything is given, in the Son of love in whom God and the world have become one".[46]

If one looks more carefully at this conclusion a further point emerges. The fact that in Christ the goal of revelation and the goal of humanity is attained, because in him divine existence and human existence touch and unite, means at the same time that the goal attained is not a rigid boundary but an open space. For the union which has taken place at the one point "Jesus of Nazareth" must attain the whole of mankind, the whole one "Adam", and transform it into the "body of Christ". So long as this totality is not achieved, so long as it remains confined to one point, what has happened in Christ remains simultaneously both end and beginning. Mankind can advance no further or higher than it has, for God is the furthest and highest; any apparent progress beyond him is a plunge into the void. Humanity cannot go beyond him – to that extent Christ is the end; but it must enter into him – to that extent he is the real beginning.

We do not need to ponder here on the interlacing of past and future which results from this for the Christian consciousness; or to reflect that while looking back at the historical Jesus the Christian faith is accordingly looking forward at the same time to the new Adam – to the future which comes to the world and to man from God. We have already considered all this earlier. Here we are concerned with something different. The fact that God's final decision for man has already been made means – according to the conviction of the Christian faith – that there is such a thing as finality in history, even if this finality is of such a kind that it does not exclude a future but inaugurates it. This has the further consequence that there is and must be such a thing as the final, the irrevocable in the life of man too, especially where he encounters the divine finality of which we were just speaking. The confidence that the final already exists, and that precisely therein the future of man is kept open, is characteristic of the whole Christian attitude to reality: the Christian can find no validity in the circling movement of

[46] K. Rahner, *Schriften zur Theologie*, I, Einsiedeln, 1954, p. 60, cf. J. Ratzinger, "Kommentar zur Offenbarungskonstitution", in LThK, supplementary Vol. II, p. 510.

actualism, which adapts itself to the respective "now" and never discovers finality. On the contrary, he is certain that history marches forward; but progress demands finality of direction – that is what distinguishes it from the circular movement that leads nowhere. The struggle for the irrevocability of Christianity was fought and won in the Middle Ages as a struggle against the idea of the "third realm", according to which Christianity so far represented the second realm, that of the Son, which was better than that of the Old Testament, the "realm of the Father", but had to be succeeded by the third realm, the age of the spirit.[47] Faith in the incarnation of God in Jesus Christ can admit no "third realm"; it believes in the finality of what has already occurred and knows that for this very reason it is open to the future.

We have already touched on the fact that this also brings with it decisive consequences for the life of the individual. It means that faith makes a definitive claim on man and cannot be succeeded one day, after the reign of the Father in childhood and that of the Son in youth, by an enlightened age of the spirit that would obey only its own reason and insinuate that it was the Holy Ghost. To be sure, faith has its terms and stages, but it is precisely in this way that it constitutes the abiding ground of man's existence, a ground which is always one and the same. This is also how it comes about that faith can have final statements – dogma and Creed – in which its instrinsic finality is articulated. Again, this does not mean that these formulas cannot open further in the course of history and thus be understood in fresh ways, just as the individual must continually learn to understand the faith afresh as a result of his own experience in life. But it does mean that in the course of this understanding and maturing the unity of what is understood neither can nor may be destroyed.

Last, it could be demonstrated that the finality of the alliance of two human beings, which Christian faith knows to be established by the "yes" of love on which marriage is based,

[47] Cf. A. Dempf, *Sacrum Imperium*, Darmstadt, 1954 (unchanged reprint of the first, 1929, edition), pp. 269–398; E. Benz, *Ecclesia spiritualis*, Stuttgart, 1934; J. Ratzinger, *Die Geschichtstheologie des hl. Bonaventura*, Munich, 1959.

also has its roots here. Indissoluble marriage is in fact only comprehensible and feasible on the basis of faith in God's henceforward irrevocable decision, embodied in Christ, in favour of "marriage" with mankind (cf. Eph. 5.22–33). It stands or falls with this faith; in the long run it is just as impossible outside this faith as it is necessary within it. And once again it should be stated that it is precisely this apparent fixation on the decision of one moment in life that enables man to march forward, to consolidate himself stage by stage, while the continual annulment of such decisions keeps sending him back to the beginning again and condemns him to a circular motion that encloses itself in the fiction of eternal youth and thus refuses to accept the totality of human existence.

6. *The primacy of acceptance and Christian positivity*

Man is redeemed by the cross; the crucified Christ, as the completely opened being, is the true redemption of man – this central principle of Christian faith we have already striven in another context to make accessible to modern modes of thought. If we look at it now, not from the point of view of content but from that of structure, we see that, in the last analysis of man, it expresses the primacy of acceptance over action, over one's own achievement. Here lies possibly the deepest division between the Christian principle of hope and its Marxist modification. It is true that the Marxist principle too is based on the idea of passivity, in so far as according to Marxism the suffering proletariat is the redeemer of the world. But this suffering of the proletariat, which is supposed in the end to bring about the change to the classless society, has to be accomplished concretely in the active form of the class struggle. Only in this way can it become "redemptive" and lead to the downfall of the ruling class and the equality of all mankind. If the cross of Christ is a suffering-for, the passion of the proletariat, as the Marxist would call it, takes the form of a struggle-against, and if the cross is essentially the work of one individual for the whole, this Marxist "passion" is essentially the activity of a mass organized as a party on behalf of itself. Thus, although they start very close together, the two paths lead off in opposite directions.

Accordingly, from the point of view of the Christian faith, man comes in the profoundest sense to himself not through what he does but through what he accepts. He must wait for the gift of love, and love can only be received as a gift. It cannot be "made" on one's own, without anyone else; one must wait for it, let it be given to one. And one cannot become *wholly* man in any other way than by being loved, by letting oneself be loved. That love represents simultaneously both man's highest possibility and his deepest need, and that this most necessary thing is at the same time the freest and the most unenforceable, means precisely that for his "salvation" man is meant to rely on receiving. If he declines to let himself be presented with the gift, then he destroys himself. Activity that makes itself into an absolute, that aims at achieving humanity by its own efforts alone, is in contradiction with man's being. Louis Evely has expressed this perception splendidly:

> The whole history of mankind was led astray, suffered a break, because of Adam's false idea of God. He wanted to be like God. I hope that you never thought that Adam's sin lay in this. . . . Had God not invited him to nourish this desire? Adam only deluded himself about the model. He thought God was an independent, autonomous being sufficient to himself; and in order to become like him he rebelled and showed disobedience.
>
> But when God revealed himself, when God wished to show who he was, he appeared as love, tenderness, as outpouring of himself, infinite pleasure in another. Inclination, dependence. God showed himself obedient, obedient unto death.
>
> In the belief that he was becoming like God, Adam turned right away from him. He withdrew into loneliness, and God was fellowship.[48]

This whole thing indubitably signifies a relativization of works, of doing; St Paul's struggle against "justification by works" is to be understood from this angle. But one must add that this classification of human activity as only of penultimate importance gives it at the same time an inner liberation: man's activity can now be carried on in the tranquillity, detachment and freedom appropriate to the penultimate. The primacy of

[48] L. Evely, *Manifest der Liebe. Das Vaterunser*, 3rd ed., Freiburg, 1961, p. 26; cf. Y. Congar, *Wege des lebendigen Gottes*, Freiburg, 1964, p. 93.

acceptance is not intended to condemn man to passivity; it does not mean that man can now sit idle, as Marxism claims. On the contrary, it alone makes it possible to do the things of this world in a spirit of responsibility, yet at the same time in an uncramped, cheerful, free way, and to put them at the service of redemptive love.

Yet another point emerges from this train of reasoning. The primacy of acceptance includes Christian positivity and shows its intrinsic necessity. We established that man does not create his specific quality out of his own resources; it has to come to him as something not made by himself; not as his own product, but instead as a free exchange that gives itself to him. But if this is so, then it also means that our relation to God cannot rest in the last analysis on our own planning, on a speculative knowledge, but demands the positivity of what confronts us, what comes to us as something positive, something to be received. It seems to me that from here the squaring of the theological circle, so to speak, can be accomplished; that the intrinsic necessity of the apparently historical contingency of Christianity can be shown, the "must" of its – to us – objectionable positivity as an event that comes from outside. The antithesis, so heavily emphasized by Lessing, between *vérité de fait* (contingent factual truth) and *vérité de raison* (necessary intellectual truth) here becomes surmountable. The contingent, the external is what is necessary to man; only in the arrival of something from outside does he open up inwardly. God's disguise as man in history "must" be – with the necessity of freedom.

7. Summary: The "spirit of Christianity"

To summarize the whole, we are entitled to say that the six principles which we have tried to sketch may be described as the blueprint, so to speak, of the Christian existence and at the same time the formula for the essence of Christianity, the "spirit of Christianity". These principles may also help to make clear what we call, in a phrase that can easily be misunderstood, the Christian claim to absoluteness. What is really meant by this comes to light above all in the principles "individual", "for", "finality" and "positivity". These basic assertions make

clear the particular nature of the claim which the Christian
faith raises in face of the history of religion and must raise if it
is to remain true to itself.

But one other question is still left: if one keeps one's eyes on
the six principles, as we have done, will one have the same
experience as the physicists who looked for the primary stuff
of being and thought at first they had found it in the so-called
elements? But the further one looked, the more the number of
these elements increased; today over a hundred are known. So
they could not be the ultimate thing which it was thought had
been discovered in the atoms. They too turned out to be composed of particles, of which again so many are already known
that one cannot stop at them, but must launch out afresh in
the hope of still meeting the primary matter. In the six principles we have identified the particles, so to speak, of Christianity, but must there not exist behind these one single, simple
centre? Such a centre does exist, and I think we can say, after
all our investigations and without any danger of using a mere
sentimental phrase, that the six principles finally coalesce into
the one principle of love. Let us be plain, even at the risk of
being misunderstood: the true Christian is not the denomi-
national party-member but he who through being a Christian
has become truly human; not he who slavishly observes a
system of norms, thinking as he does so only of himself, but he
who has become freed to simple human goodness. Of course,
the principle of love, if it is to be genuine, includes faith. Only
thus does it remain what it is. For without faith, which we have
come to understand as a term expressing man's ultimate need
to receive and the inadequacy of all personal achievement,
love becomes an arbitrary deed. It cancels itself out and
becomes self-righteousness: faith and love condition and
demand each other reciprocally. Similarly, in the principle of
love there is also present the principle of hope, which looks
beyond the moment and its isolation, and seeks the whole.
Thus our reflections finally lead of their own accord to the
words in which Paul named the main supporting pillars of
Christianity: "So faith, hope, love abide, these three; but the
greatest of them is love" (1 Cor. 13.13).

Chapter II

THE DEVELOPMENT OF FAITH IN CHRIST IN THE CHRISTOLOGICAL ARTICLES OF THE CREED

1. "CONCEIVED BY THE HOLY GHOST, BORN OF THE VIRGIN MARY"

THE origin of Jesus is shrouded in mystery. It is true that in St John's gospel the people of Jerusalem object to his Messianic claim on the grounds that "we know where this man comes from; and when the Christ appears, no one will know where he comes from" (John 7.27). But Jesus' immediately following words disclose how inadequate this alleged knowledge of his origin is: "I have not come of my own accord; he who sent me is true, and him you do not know" (7.28). Certainly Jesus comes from Nazareth. But what does one know of his true origin just by being able to name the geographical spot from which he comes? St John's gospel emphasizes again and again that the real origin of Jesus is "the Father", that he comes from him more totally than any previous envoy of God's, and in a different way.

This descent of Jesus from the mystery of God, "which no one knows", is depicted in the so-called "childhood stories" in the gospels of St Matthew and St Luke, not with the object of emphasizing it but precisely to confirm its mystery. Both evangelists, but especially Luke, tell the beginning of the story of Jesus almost entirely in the words of the Old Testament, in order thus to demonstrate from within what happens here as the fulfilment of Israel's hope and to put it in the context of the whole story of God's covenant with men. The words with

which in Luke the angel addresses the Virgin are closely akin
to the greeting with which the prophet Sophonias hails the
saved Jerusalem of the last days (Soph. 3.14ff.), and they also
echo the words of blessing with which the great women of
Israel had been praised (Judg. 5.24; Judith 13.18f.). Thus
Mary is characterized as the holy remnant of Israel, as the
true Sion on which hopes had centred in the wildernesses of
history. With her begins, according to St Luke's text, the new
Israel; indeed, it does not just begin with her; she *is* it, the holy
"daughter of Sion" in whom God sets the new beginning.[49]

No less full is the central promise: "The Holy Spirit will
come upon you, and the power of the Most High will over-
shadow you; therefore the child to be born will be called holy,
the Son of God" (Luke 1.35). Our gaze is led beyond the
covenant with Israel to the creation: in the Old Testament the
spirit of God is the power of creation; he it was who hovered
over the waters in the beginning and shaped chaos into cosmos
(Gen. 1.2); when he is sent, living beings are created (Ps. 104
[103]. 30). So what is to happen here to Mary is new creation:
the God who called forth being out of nothing makes a new
beginning amid humanity: his Word becomes flesh. The other
image in this text – the "overshadowing by the power of the
Most High" – points to the temple of Israel and to the holy
tent in the wilderness where God's presence was indicated in
the cloud, which hides his glory as well as revealing it
(Exod. 40.34; 1 Kings 8.11). Just as Mary was depicted earlier
as the new Israel, the true "daughter of Sion", so now she
appears as the temple on to which descends the cloud in which
God walks into the midst of history. Whoever puts himself at
God's disposal disappears with him in the cloud, into oblivion
and insignificance, and precisely in this way acquires a share
in his glory.

The birth of Jesus from a virgin of whom things like these are
reported in the gospels has long been a thorn in the flesh of

---

[49] Cf. R. Laurentin, *Struktur und Theologie der lukanischen Kindheitsgeschichte*,
Stuttgart, 1967; L. Deiss, *Maria, Tochter Sion*, Mainz, 1961; A. Stöger, *Das
Evangelium nach Lukas*, Vol. I, Düsseldorf, 1964, pp. 38–42; G. Voss, *Die
Christologie der lukanischen Schriften in Grundzügen. Studia Neotestamentica*, Vol.
II, Paris and Bruges, 1965.

rationalizers of every kind. Clarifications of sources are supposed to minimize the New Testament testimony, references to the unhistorical thinking of the ancients are supposed to remove the event to the realm of the symbolical, and insertion into the context of the history of religions is supposed to show that it is a variant of a myth. The myth of the miraculous birth of the child saviour is indeed found all over the world. It expresses a longing on the part of humanity, the longing for the austere and pure embodied in the intact virgin; the longing for the truly maternal, protective, mature and kind, and finally the hope that always rises again when a man is born – the hope and joy signified by a child. It may be regarded as probable that Israel too had myths of this sort; Isaiah 7.14 ("Behold, a virgin shall conceive . . .") could certainly be explained as the echo of an expectation of this sort, even though it is not absolutely clear from the text of this passage that a virgin in the strict sense of the term is meant.[50] If the passage should properly be understood by reference to such sources, this would mean that *via* this détour the New Testament had taken up humanity's confused hopes in the virgin-mother. Such a primordial theme in human history is certainly not just meaningless.

But at the same time it is quite clear that the immediate antecedents of the New Testament accounts of Jesus' birth from the Virgin Mary lie not in the realm of the history of religions but in the Old Testament. Extra-biblical stories of this kind differ profoundly in vocabulary and imagery from the story of the birth of Jesus. The main contrast consists in the fact that in pagan texts the Godhead almost always appears as fertilizing, procreative power, thus under a more or less sexual aspect and hence in a physical sense as the "father" of the saviour-child. As we have seen, nothing of this sort appears

---

[50] Cf. W. Eichrodt, *Theologie der AT*, Vol. I, Leipzig, 1939, p. 257: ". . . These features . . . taken together point to a saviour-image well known to the people, an image in which they find their ideal unity. This is corroborated by the discovery of a series of concordant statements about the saviour-king in the whole Near Eastern world. These statements can actually be put together to form scenes from a sacred biography and show that Israel here shares widely in a common oriental heritage."

in the New Testament: the conception of Jesus is new creation,
not begetting by God. God does not become the biological
father of Jesus, and neither the New Testament nor the theology
of the Church has fundamentally ever seen in this narrative
or in the event recounted in it the ground for the real divinity
of Jesus, his "Sonship" of God. For this does not mean that
Jesus is half God, half man; it has always been a basic tenet of
the Christian faith that Jesus is *completely* God and *completely*
man. His Godhood does not imply a subtraction from his
humanity; this was the path followed by Arius and Apollinaris,
the great heretics of the ancient Church. In opposition to them
the complete intactness of Jesus' humanity was defended with
all possible emphasis and the merging of the biblical account
into the heathen myth of the god-begotten demi-god was thus
frustrated. According to the faith of the Church the Sonship
of Jesus does not rest on the fact that Jesus had no human
father; the doctrine of Jesus' divinity would not be affected if
Jesus had been the product of a normal human marriage.
For the Sonship of which faith speaks is not a biological but an
ontological fact, an event not in time but in God's eternity;
God is always Father, Son and Spirit; the conception of Jesus
does not mean that a new God-the-Son comes into being, but
that God as Son in the man Jesus draws the creature man to
himself, so that he himself "is" man.

Nothing in all this is altered by two expressions which can,
it is true, easily lead the uninformed astray. Is it not stated in
Luke's account, in connection with the promise of the
miraculous conception, that the child to be born "will be
called holy, the Son of God" (Luke 1.35)? Are Sonship and
Virgin Birth not coupled here and the path of myth thus
trodden? And so far as the theology of the Church is concerned,
does it not speak continually of the "physical" Sonship of
Jesus, and does it not thereby reveal its mythical background?
Let us take the latter point first. Indubitably the formula about
the "physical" Sonship of Jesus is extremely unfortunate and
wide open to misunderstanding; it shows that in about two
thousand years theology has not succeeded in freeing its
conceptual terminology from the shell of its Hellenistic origin.
"Physical" is meant here in the sense of the ancient concept of

"*physis*", that is, nature, or, better, "being". It signifies that which belongs to being. "Physical Sonship" therefore means that Jesus is from God in his being, not just in his conscious being; the word consequently expresses opposition to the idea of the mere adoption of Jesus by God. Obviously the being-from-God indicated by the word "physical" is meant to be taken not on the plane of biological generation but on the plane of the divine being and its eternity. The word is asserting that in Jesus human nature was assumed by him who from eternity belongs "physically" (= really, by his being) to the tri-une relationship of the divine love.

But what is one to say when such a meritorious researcher as E. Schweizer expresses himself on our question in the following terms: "Since Luke is not interested in the biological question, he does not cross the frontier to a metaphysical understanding either."[51] Pretty well everything about this statement is false. The most staggering thing about it is the quiet way in which biology and metaphysics are equated. To all appearances, the metaphysical (ontological) Sonship is misinterpreted as biological descent and its meaning thus turned completely upside down. It is in fact, as we saw, the express rejection of a biological interpretation of Jesus' divine origin. It is a little saddening to have to point out oneself that the plane of metaphysics is not that of biology. The Church's teaching about the Sonship of Jesus is based not on the story of the virgin birth but on the Abba-Son dialogue and on the relationship of Word and love which we found revealed in it. Its idea of being does not belong to the biological plane but to the "I am" of St John's gospel, which therein, as we have seen, had already unfolded the whole scope of the Son-idea — a scope which is far more comprehensive and wide-ranging than the biological God-man ideas of the myth. We have already considered all this at some length; it has only been mentioned again here because one receives the strong impression that the contemporary aversion for both the tidings of the virgin birth and the full acknowledgement of the Sonship of Jesus rests on a fundamental misunderstanding of both and on

[51] E. Schweizer, υἱός, in *Theologisches Wörterbuch zum NT*, Vol. VIII, p. 384.

the false connection between the two which seems to be widely assumed.

One question remains open: that of the Son-concept in St Luke's gospel. The process of answering it leads us at the same time to the real question that arises out of our previous reflections. If the conception of Jesus by the Virgin through God's creative power has nothing to do with his Sonship, at any rate directly, what kind of meaning does it possess? The question what the phrase "Son of God" means in the text of the Gospel can be easily answered from our earlier investigations: in contrast to the simple expression "the Son" it belongs, as we heard, to the Old Testament theology of election and hope, and marks out Jesus as the true heir to the promises, the king of Israel and of the world. The context in which the phrase is to be understood now becomes clearly visible: it is Israel's faith and hope, which, as we have said, did not remain completely unaffected by heathen hopes of miraculous births but gave them a completely new form and a totally changed meaning.

The Old Testament contains a whole series of miraculous births, always at decisive turning-points in the history of salvation: Isaac's mother, Sarah (Gen. 18), Samuel's mother (1 Sam. 1–3) and the anonymous mother of Samson (Judg. 13) are all barren and all human hope of their being blessed with children has been abandoned. With all three the birth of the child who eventually contributes to Israel's salvation comes to pass as a manifestation of the gracious mercy of God, who makes the impossible possible (Gen. 18.14; Luke 1.37), elevates the lowly (1 Sam. 2.7; 1.11; Luke 1.52; 1.48) and puts down the mighty from their thrones (Luke 1.52). With Elizabeth, John the Baptist's mother, this process is continued (Luke 1.7–25, 36), and it reaches its climax and goal with Mary. The meaning of the occurrence is always the same: the salvation of the world does not come from man and from his own power; man must let it be bestowed upon him, and he can only receive it as a pure gift. The virgin birth is not a lesson in asceticism nor does it belong directly to the doctrine of Jesus' Sonship; it is first and last theology of grace, a proclamation of how salvation comes to *us*: in the simplicity of acceptance, as the voluntary gift of the love that redeems the world. This idea of salvation through God's power alone is formulated magnificently in the Book of Isaiah in the passage which runs: "Sing, O barren one, who did not bear; break forth into singing and cry aloud, you who have not been in travail! For the children of the desolate one will be more than the children of her that is married, says the Lord" (Is. 54.1; cf. Gal. 4.27; Rom. 4.17–22). In Jesus, God has placed, in the midst of barren, despairing mankind, a new beginning which is not a product of human history but a gift from above. Even every mere human being represents something unspeakably new, something more than the sum of the chromosomes and the product of a certain environment, in fact a unique creature of God; but Jesus is the truly new, coming not from mankind's own resources but from the spirit of God. For this reason he is Adam for the second time (1 Cor. 15.47) – a new incarnation begins with him. In contrast to all those chosen before him he not only *receives* the spirit of God; in his earthly existence he *is* only through the spirit and therefore he is the fulfilment of all prophets: he is the true prophet.

It should not really be necessary to point out that all these assertions only have a meaning on the assumption that the happening whose meaning they seek to elucidate really took place. They are the interpretation of an event; if this event is removed they become empty talk which would have to be described not only as frivolous but as downright dishonest. For the rest, such attempts, however well intentioned they may sometimes be, are coloured by a contradictoriness that one feels half inclined to describe as tragic. At a moment when we have discovered the corporality of the man with every fibre of our existence and can understand his spirit only as something incarnate, something that *is* body, not *has* body, people try to save the Christian faith by completely disembodying it, by taking refuge in a region of mere "mind", of pure self-satisfying interpretation, which seems to be immune from criticism only through its lack of contact with reality. But Christian faith really means precisely the acknowledgement that God is not the prisoner of his own eternity, not limited to the solely spiritual; that he is capable of operating here and now, in the midst of my world, and that he did operate in it through Jesus, the new Adam, who was born of the Virgin Mary through the creative power of God, whose spirit hovered over the waters at the very beginning, who created being out of nothing.[52]

Another observation must be made. The meaning of the divine symbol of the virgin birth, if properly understood, indicates at the same time the proper theological place for a devotion to Mary that lets itself be guided by the faith of the New Testament. Devotion to Mary cannot be based on a Mariology that represents a sort of miniature second edition of Christology – such a duplication is neither right nor justifiable on the evidence. If one wanted to indicate a department of theology to which Mariology belonged as its concrete illustra-

---

[52] This should be compared with the speculations in which P. Schoonenberg seeks to justify the reserve of the Dutch Catechism on this matter in his contribution "De nieuwe Katechismus und die Dogmen", German translation in *Dokumentation des Holländischen Katechismus*, Freiburg, 1967, XIV–XXXIX, esp. XXXVII–XXXVIII.

What is particularly fatal about this attempt is the fundamental misunderstanding of the concept of dogma on which it rests; Schoonenberg understands "dogma" entirely from the narrow point of view of Jesuit dogmatic theology at the end of the nineteenth century, and naturally looks in vain for a dogmatic pronouncement relating to the virgin birth analogous to the dogmatization of the "immaculate conception" (=freedom from original sin) and the physical assumption of Mary into "Heaven". He thus comes to the conclusion that in the matter of the birth of Jesus from the Virgin, as opposed to the other two statements, no firm teaching by the Church is extant. In reality such an assertion turns the history of dogma upside down and attributes absoluteness to a mode of exercising the teaching function only in regular use since Vatican I. This is unacceptable not only in view of the dialogue with the Eastern Church but also from the very nature of the matter itself, and even Schoonenberg himself does not stick to it through thick and thin. In fact the proclamation of a dogma as a single principle by the Pope "*ex cathedra*" is the latest and lowest way of forming dogma. The original form in which the Church states its faith in a binding fashion is the Creed or symbolum; the profession of faith in the birth of Jesus from the Virgin, a statement quite unequivocal in meaning, belongs firmly from the start to all symbola and is thus a constituent part of the original dogma of the Church. To question the binding nature of Lateran I or Paul V's bull of 1555, as Schoonenberg does, is thus a completely pointless proceeding; and the attempt to make even the symbola capable of merely "spiritual" interpretation would be enveloping the history of dogma in a smoke-screen.

tion, it would probably be the doctrine of grace, which of course goes to form a whole with ecclesiology and anthropology. As the true "daughter of Sion", Mary is the image of the Church, the image of believing man, who can only come to salvation and to himself through the gift of love – through grace. The saying with which Bernanos ends his *Diary of a Country Priest* – "Everything is grace" – a saying in which a life which seemed to be only weakness and futility can see itself as full of riches and fulfilment – truly becomes in Mary, "full of grace" (Luke 1.28), a concrete reality. She does not contest or endanger the exclusiveness of salvation through Christ; she points to it. She represents mankind, which as a whole is expectation and which needs this image all the more when it is in danger of laying aside waiting and putting its trust in doing, which – indispensable as it is – can never fill the void which threatens man when he does not find that absolute love which gives him meaning, salvation, all that life really needs.

2. "SUFFERED UNDER PONTIUS PILATE, WAS CRUCIFIED, DEAD AND BURIED"

(a) Righteousness and grace

What position is really occupied by the cross within faith in Jesus as the Christ? That is the question with which this article of the Creed confronts us once again. We have already assembled in our previous reflections the essential components of an answer and must now try to survey them as a whole. As we have already established, the universal Christian consciousness in this matter is extensively influenced by a much-coarsened version of St Anselm's theology of atonement, the main lines of which we have considered in another context. To many Christians, and especially to those who only know the faith from a fair distance, it looks as if the cross is to be understood as part of a mechanism of injured and restored right. It is the form, so it seems, in which the infinitely offended righteousness of God was propitiated again by means of an infinite expiation. It thus appears to people as the expression of an attitude which insists on a precise balance between debit and credit; at the same time one gets the feeling that this balance is based nevertheless on a fiction. One gives first secretly with the left hand what one takes back again ceremonially with the right. The "infinite expiation" on which God seems to insist thus moves into a doubly sinister light. Many devotional texts actually force one to think that Christian faith in the cross visualizes a God whose unrelenting righteousness demanded a human sacrifice, the sacrifice of his own Son, and one turns away in horror from a righteousness whose sinister wrath makes the message of love incredible.

This picture is as false as it is widespread. In the Bible the cross does not appear as part of a mechanism of injured right; on the contrary, in the Bible the cross is quite the reverse: it is the expression of the radical nature of the love which gives itself completely, of the process in which one is what one does, and does what one is; it is the expression of a life that is completely being for others. To anyone who looks more closely, the scriptural theology of the cross represents a real revolution as compared with the notions of expiation and redemption entertained by non-Christian religions, though it certainly cannot be denied that in the later Christian consciousness this revolution was largely neutralized and its whole scope seldom recognized. In other world religions expiation usually means the restoration of the damaged relationship with God by means of expiatory actions on the part of men. Almost all religions centre round the problem of expiation; they arise out of man's knowledge of his guilt before God and signify the attempt to remove this feeling of guilt, to surmount the guilt through conciliatory actions offered up to God. The expiatory activity by which men hope to conciliate the divinity and to put him in a gracious mood stands at the heart of the history of religion.

In the New Testament the situation is almost completely reversed. It is not man who goes to God with a compensatory gift, but God who comes to man, in order to give to him. He restores disturbed right on the initiative of his own power to love, by making unjust man just again, the dead living again, through his own creative mercy. His righteousness is grace; it is active righteousness, which sets crooked man right, that is, bends him straight, makes him right. Here we stand before the twist which Christianity put into the history of religion. The

New Testament does not say that men conciliate God, as we really ought to expect, since after all it is they who have failed, not God. It says on the contrary that "God was in Christ reconciling the world to himself" (2 Cor. 5.19). This is truly something new, something unheard of – the starting-point of Christian existence and the centre of New Testament theology of the cross: God does not wait until the guilty come to be reconciled; he goes to meet them and reconciles them. Here we can see the true direction of the incarnation, of the cross.

Accordingly, in the New Testament the cross appears primarily as a movement from above to below. It does not stand there as the work of expiation which mankind offers to the wrathful God, but as the expression of that foolish love of God's which gives itself away to the point of humiliation in order thus to save man; it is *his* approach to us, not the other way about. With this twist in the idea of expiation, and thus in the whole axis of religion, worship too, man's whole existence, acquires in Christianity a new direction. Worship follows in Christianity *first of all* in thankful acceptance of the divine deed of salvation. The essential form of Christian worship is therefore rightly called "*Eucharistia*", thanksgiving. In this form of worship human achievements are not placed before God; on the contrary, it consists in man's letting himself be endowed with gifts; we do not glorify God by supposedly giving to him out of our resources – as if they were not his already! – but by letting ourselves be endowed with his own gifts and thus recognizing him as the only Lord. We worship him by dropping the fiction of a realm in which we could face him as independent business partners, whereas in truth we can only exist at all in him and from him. Christian sacrifice does not consist in a giving of what God would not have without us but in our becoming totally receptive and letting ourselves be completely taken over by him. Letting God act on us – that is Christian sacrifice.

(b) The cross as worship and sacrifice

This is not the whole story, it is true. If one reads the New Testament from beginning to end one cannot suppress the question whether it does not depict Jesus' deed of expiation as the offering of a sacrifice to the Father, and the cross as the sacrifice which Christ hands over obediently to the Father. In a whole series of texts it does appear as the upward movement of mankind to God, so that all that we have just rejected seems to rise to the surface again. In fact, the content of the New Testament cannot be harmonized with the descending line alone. How then are we to explain the relationship between the two lines? Must we perhaps exclude one in favour of the other? And if we wanted to do this, what criterion should we be justified in using? It is clear that we cannot proceed in this way: by doing so we should in the last analysis be elevating our own capricious opinion to the status of the criterion of faith.

In order to make any progress we must broaden our question and ask where the point of departure of the New Testament interpretation of the cross lies. One must first realize that to the disciples the cross of Jesus seemed at first like the end, the wreck of his enterprise. They had thought that they had found in him the king who could never more be overthrown, and had become unawares the companions of an executed criminal. The resurrection, it is true, gave them the certainty that Jesus was nevertheless king, but the point of the cross they had to learn slowly. The means of understanding was offered to them in Scripture, that is, the Old Testament, with whose images and concepts they strove to explain what had happened. So they adduced its liturgical texts and precepts too, in the conviction that everything meant there was fulfilled in Jesus; indeed that, *vice versa*, one could now understand properly for the first time from him what things in the Old Testament were really all about. In this way we find that in the New Testament the cross is explained by, among other things, ideas taken from Old Testament cult theology.

The most consistent execution of this project is to be found in the Epistle to the Hebrews, which connects the death of Jesus on the cross with the ritual and theology of the Jewish feast of reconciliation and expounds it as the true cosmic reconciliation feast. The epistle's train of thought could be briefly summarized more or less as follows: all the sacrificial activity of mankind, all attempts to conciliate God by cult and ritual, were bound to remain helpless human work, because

God does not seek bulls and goats or whatever may be ritually offered to him. One can sacrifice whole hecatombs of bulls to God all over the world; he does not need them, because they all belong to him anyway and nothing is given to the Lord of All when such things are burnt in his honour. "I will accept no bull from your house, nor he-goat from your folds. For every beast of the forest is mine, the cattle on a thousand hills. I know all the birds of the air, and all that moves in the field is mine. If I were hungry, I would not tell you; for the world and all that is in it is mine. Do I eat the flesh of bulls, or drink the blood of goats? Offer to God a sacrifice of thanksgiving. . . ." So runs a saying of God in the Old Testament (Ps. 50 [49]. 9–14). The author of the Epistle to the Hebrews places himself in the spiritual line of this and similar texts. With still more conclusive emphasis he stresses the fruitlessness of ritual effort. God does not seek bulls and goats but man; man's unqualified "yes" to God could alone form true worship. Everything belongs to God, but to man is lent the freedom to say yes or not, the freedom to love or to reject; love's free "yes" is the only thing for which God must wait – the only worship or "sacrifice" that can have any meaning. But the "yes" to God, in which man gives himself back to God, cannot be replaced or represented by the blood of bulls and goats. "For what can a man give in return for his life", it says at one point in the Gospel (Mark 8.37). The answer can only be: there is nothing with which he could outweigh himself.

But as all pre-Christian cults were based on the idea of substitution, of representation, and tried to replace the irreplaceable, they were bound to remain vain. In the light of faith in Christ, the Epistle to the Hebrews can dare to draw up this devastating balance sheet of the history of religion, although to express this view in a world seething with sacrifices must have seemed a tremendous outrage. It can dare to make this unqualified assertion that religions have run aground because it knows that in Christ the idea of the substitute, of the proxy, has acquired a new meaning. Christ, who from an ecclesiastical point of view was a layman and held no office in Israel's religious organization, was – so the text says – the one true priest in the world. His death, which from a purely historical angle represented a completely profane event – the execution of a man condemned to death as a political offender – was in reality the one and only liturgy of the world, a cosmic liturgy, in which Jesus stepped, not in the limited arena of the liturgical performance, the temple, but publicly, before the eyes of the world, into the real temple, that is, before the face of God himself, in order to offer, not things, the blood of animals or anything like that, but himself (Heb. 9.11ff.).

Let us note the fundamental reversal involved in the central idea of this epistle: what from the earthly point of view was a secular happening is the true worship for mankind, for he who performed it broke through the confines of the liturgical act and made truth: he gave himself. He took from man's hands the sacrificial offerings and put in their place his sacrificed personality, his own "I". When our text says that Jesus accomplished the expiation through his *blood* (9.12), this blood is again not to be understood as a material gift, a quantitatively measurable means of expiation; it is simply the concrete expression of a love of which it is said that it extends "to the end" (John 13.1). It is the expression of the totality of his surrender and of his service; an embodiment of the fact that he offers no more and no less than himself. The gesture of the love that gives all – this, and this alone, according to the Epistle to the Hebrews, was the real means by which the world was reconciled; therefore the hour of the cross is the cosmic day of reconciliation, the true and final feast of reconciliation. There is no other kind of worship and no other priest but he who accomplished it: Jesus Christ.

(c) The nature of Christian worship

Accordingly, the nature of Christian worship does not consist in the surrender of things, nor in any kind of destruction, an idea that has continually recurred since the sixteenth century in theories of the sacrifice of the Mass. According to these theories God's overlordship of all had to be recognized in this fashion. All these laborious efforts of thought are simply overtaken by the event of Christ and its biblical explanation. Christian worship consists in the absoluteness of love, as it could only be poured out by the one in whom God's own love had become human love; and it consists in the new form of representation included in this love, namely that he stood for us and we let ourselves be taken over by him. So it means that we can put aside our own attempts at justification, which at bottom are only excuses and range us against each other – just as Adam's attempt at justification was an excuse, a pushing of the guilt on to the other, indeed in the last analysis an attempt to accuse God himself: "The woman whom thou gavest to be with me, she gave me fruit of the tree, and I ate . . ." (Gen. 3.12). It demands that instead of indulging in the destructive rivalry of self-justification we accept the love of Jesus Christ that "stands in" for us, let ourselves be united in it, and thus become worshippers with him and in him. From this angle it will probably be possible to answer very briefly a few questions that still arise.

1. In view of the New Testament's message of love, there is more and more of a tendency today to resolve the Christian religion completely into brotherly love, "fellowship", and not to admit any direct love of God or adoration of God: only the horizontal is recognized; the vertical of immediate relationship to God is denied. It is not difficult to see, after what we have said, how this at first sight very attractive conception fails to grasp not only the substance of Christianity but also that of true humanity. Brotherly love that aimed at self-sufficiency would become for this very reason the extreme egoism of self-assertion. It refuses its last openness, tranquillity and selflessness if it does not also accept this love's need for redemption through him who alone loves sufficiently. And, for all its good will, in the last resort it does others and itself an injustice, for man cannot perfect himself in the reciprocity of human fellowship alone; he can only do this in the co-operation of that pointless love which God himself glorifies. The pointlessness of simple adoration is humanity's highest possibility; it alone forms his true and final liberation.

2. Above all, the traditional Passiontide devotions throw up again and again the question of the precise relationship between sacrifice (and thus worship) and pain. According to the conclusions which we reached above, the Christian sacrifice is nothing other than the exodus of the "For" that abandons

itself, a process perfected in the man who is all exodus, all self-surpassing love. The governing principle of Christian worship is consequently this movement of exodus with its two-in-one direction towards God and fellow man. By carrying humanity to God, Christ incorporates it in his salvation. The reason why the happening on the cross is the bread of life "for the many" (Luke 22.19) is that he who was crucified has smelted the body of humanity into the "yes" of worship. It is completely "anthropocentric", entirely related to man, because it was radical theocentricity, delivery of the "I" and therefore of the creature man to God. Now to the extent that this exodus of love is the ec-stasy of man outside himself, in which he is stretched out infinitely beyond himself, torn apart, as it were, far beyond his apparent capacity for being stretched, *to the same extent* worship (sacrifice) is always at the same time the cross, the pain of being torn apart, the dying of the grain of wheat that can only come to fruition in death. But it is thus at the same time clear that this element of pain is a secondary one, resulting only from a preceding primary one, from which alone it draws its meaning. The governing principle of the sacrifice is not destruction, but love. And even this principle only belongs to the sacrifice to the extent that love breaks down, opens up, crucifies, tears – as the form that love takes in a world characterized by death and self-seeking.

There is an important passage on this subject by Jean Daniélou. It really forms part of a different enquiry but it might well help to elucidate the idea which we are striving to understand:

Between the heathen world and the threefold God there is only one link, and that is the cross of Christ. Yet when we move into this no-man's-land and try afresh to twitch the threads that link the heathen world and the threefold God, should we still be surprised that we can only do it in the cross of Christ? We must make ourselves resemble this cross, bear it within ourselves, "always carrying in the body the death of Jesus", as St Paul says of the preacher of the faith (2 Cor. 4.10). This feeling of being torn asunder, which is a cross to us, this inability of our heart to carry within itself simultaneously love of the most holy Trinity and love of a world alienated from the Trinity, is precisely the death-agony of the only-begotten Son, an agony which he calls on us to share. He who bore this division within himself in order to abolish it within himself, and who could only abolish it because he had previously borne it within himself – he stretches from one end to the other. Without leaving the bosom of the Trinity he stretches out to the ultimate limit of human misery and fills the whole space in between. This stretching-out of Christ, symbolized by the four directions of the cross, is the mysterious expression of our own dismemberment and makes us like him.[53]

In the last analysis pain is the product and expression of Jesus Christ's being stretched out from being in God right down to the hell of "My God, why hast thou forsaken me?" Anyone who has stretched his existence so wide that he is simultaneously immersed in God and in the depths of the God-forsaken creature is bound to be torn asunder, as it were; such a one is truly "crucified". But this process of being torn apart is identical with love; it is its realization to the extreme (John 13.1) and the concrete expression of the breadth which it creates.

From this standpoint it should be possible to bring out clearly the true basis of meaningful devotion to the Passion; it should also become evident how devotion to the Passion and apostolic spirituality overlap. It should become evident that the apostolic element – service to man and in the world – is permeated with the very essence of Christian mysticism and of Christian devotion to the cross. The two do not impede each other; at the deepest level, each lives on the other. Thus it should now also be plain that with the cross it is not a matter of an accumulation of physical pain, as if its redemptive value consisted in its involving the largest possible amount of physical torture. Why should God take pleasure in the suffering of his creature, indeed his own Son, or even see in it the currency with which reconciliation has to be purchased from him? The Bible and right Christian belief are far removed from such ideas. It is not pain as such that counts, but the breadth of the love which spans existence so completely that it unites the distant and the near, bringing God-forsaken man into relation with God. It alone gives the pain an aim and a meaning. Were it otherwise, then the executioners round the cross would have

[53] J. Daniélou, *Essai sur le mystère de l'histoire*, Paris, 1953.

been the real priests; they, who had caused the pain, would have offered the sacrifice. But this was not the point; the point was that inner centre that bears and fulfils the pain, and therefore the executioners were not the priests; the priest was Jesus, who reunited the two separated ends of the world in his love (Eph. 2.13f.).

Basically this also answers the question with which we started, whether it is not an unworthy concept of God to imagine for oneself a God who demands the slaughter of his son to pacify his wrath. To such a question one can only reply, indeed God must not be thought of in this way. But in any case such a concept of God has nothing to do with the idea of God to be found in the New Testament. The New Testament is the story of the God who of his own accord wished to become, in Christ, the omega – the last letter – in the alphabet of creation. It is the story of the God who is himself the act of love, the pure "For", and who therefore necessarily put on the disguise of the smallest worm (Ps. 22 [21]. 7). It is the story of the God who identifies himself with his creature and in this *contineri a minimo*, in being grasped and overpowered by the least of his creatures, displays that "excess" which identifies him as God.

The cross is revelation. It does not reveal any particular thing, but God and man. It reveals who God is and who man is. There is a curious presentiment of this situation in Greek philosophy: Plato's image of the crucified "just man". In the *Republic* the great philosopher asks what is likely to be the position of a completely just man in this world. He comes to the conclusion that a man's righteousness is only complete and guaranteed when he takes on the appearance of unrighteousness, for only then is it clear that he does not follow the opinion of men but pursues justice only for its own sake. So according to Plato the truly just man must be misunderstood and persecuted in this world; indeed, Plato goes so far as to write: "They will say that our just man will be scourged, racked, fettered, will have his eyes burnt out, and at last, after all manner of suffering, will be crucified. . . ."[54]

[54] *Republic*, Book II, 361e–362a, in A. D. Lindsay's translation. Cf. on this theme H. U. von Balthasar, *Herrlichkeit* III/1, Einsiedeln, 1965, pp. 156–161; E. Benz, "Der gekreuzigte Gerechte bei Plato, im N T und in der alten Kirche", *Abhandlungen der Mainzer Akademie* 1950, number 12.

This passage, written four hundred years before Christ, is always bound to move a Christian deeply. Serious philosophical thinking here surmises that the completely just man in this world must be the crucified just man; something is sensed of that revelation of man which comes to pass on the cross.

The fact that when the perfectly just man appeared he was crucified, delivered up by justice to death, tells us pitilessly who man is: thou art such, man, that thou canst not bear the just man – that he who simply loves becomes a fool, a scourged criminal, an outcast. Thou art such because, unjust thyself, thou dost always need the injustice of the next man in order to feel excused, and thus canst not tolerate the just man who seems to rob thee of this excuse. Such art thou. St John summarized all this in the *"Ecce homo"* ("Look, this is [the] man!") of Pilate, which means quite fundamentally: this is how it is with man; this is man. The truth of man is his complete lack of truth. The saying in the Psalms, that every man is a liar (Ps. 116 [115]. 11) and lives in some way or other against the truth, already reveals how it really is with man. The truth about man is that he is continually assailing truth; the just man crucified is thus a mirror held up to man in which he sees himself unadorned. But the cross does not only reveal man; it also reveals God. God is such that he identifies himself with man right down into this abyss and that he judges him by saving him. In the abyss of human denial is revealed the still more inexhaustible abyss of the divine love. The cross is thus truly the centre of revelation, a revelation that does not reveal any previously unknown principles but reveals us to ourselves, by revealing us before God and God in our midst.

3. "DESCENDED INTO HELL"

Possibly no article of the Creed is so far from present-day attitudes of mind as this one. Together with the belief in the birth of Jesus from the Virgin Mary and that in the Ascension of the Lord, it seems to call most of all for "demythologization", a process which looks devoid of danger and unlikely to provoke opposition. The few places where Scripture seems to say anything about this matter (1 Pet. 3.19f.; 4.6; Eph. 4.9;

Rom. 10.7; Matt. 12.40; Acts 2.27, 31) are so difficult to understand that they can easily be expounded in many different
ways. Thus if in the end one eliminates the statement altogether one seems to have the advantage of getting rid of a
curious idea, and one difficult to harmonize with our own
modes of thought, without making oneself guilty of a particularly disloyal act. But is anything really gained by this? Or has
one simply evaded the difficulty and obscurity of reality? One
can try to deal with problems either by denying their existence
or by facing up to them. The first method is the more comfortable one, but only the second leads anywhere. Instead of pushing the question aside, then, should we not learn to see that
this article of faith, under whose aegis Holy Saturday stands
liturgically in the Church's year, is particularly close to our
day and is to a particular degree the experience of our century?
On Good Friday our gaze remains fixed on the crucified
Christ, but Holy Saturday is the day of the "death of God",
the day which expresses the unparalleled experience of our
age, anticipating the fact that God is simply absent, that the
grave hides him, that he no longer awakes, no longer speaks,
so that one no longer needs to gainsay him but can simply
overlook him. "God is dead and we have killed him." This
saying of Nietzsche's belongs linguistically to the tradition of
Christian Passiontide piety; it expresses the content of Holy
Saturday, "descended into hell".[55]

This article of the Creed always reminds me of two scenes in
the Bible. The first is that cruel story in the Old Testament in
which Elias (Elijah) challenges the priests of Baal to implore
their God to give them fire for their sacrifice. They do so, and
naturally nothing happens. He ridicules them, just as the
"enlightened rationalist" ridicules the pious person and finds
him laughable when nothing happens in response to his
prayers. Elias calls out to the priests that perhaps they had not
prayed loud enough: "Shout louder. Baal is indeed a god. But
perhaps he is deep in thought, or has gone out; or perhaps he
is asleep and will wake up!" (1 Kings 18.27). When one reads
today this mockery of the devotees of Baal, one can begin to
feel uncomfortable; one can get the feeling that *we* have now

[55] Cf. H. de Lubac, *The Tragedy of Humanism without God*, 1950, pp. 21–31.

arrived in that situation and that the mockery must now fall on us. No calling seems to be able to awaken God. The rationalist seems entitled to say to us, "Pray louder, perhaps your God will then wake up". "Descended into hell"; how true this is of our time, the descent of God into muteness, into the dark silence of the absent.

But alongside the story of Elias and its New Testament analogue, the story of the Lord sleeping in the midst of the storm on the lake (Mark 4.35-41 par.), we must put the Emmaus story (Luke 24.13-35). The disturbed disciples are talking of the death of their hope. To them, something like the death of God has happened: the point at which God finally seemed to have spoken has disappeared. God's envoy is dead, and so there is a complete void. Nothing replies any more. But while they are there speaking of the death of their hope and can no longer see God they do not notice that this very hope stands alive in their midst; that "God", or rather the image they had formed of his promise, had to die so that he could live on a bigger scale. The image which they had formed of God, and into which they sought to compress him, had to be destroyed, so that over the ruins of the demolished house, as it were, they could see the sky again and him who remains the infinitely greater. The German Romantic poet Eichendorff formulated the idea – in the comfortable, to us almost too harmless fashion of his age – like this:

> *Du bist's, der, was wir bauen,*
> *Mild über uns zerbricht,*
> *Dass wir den Himmel schauen –*
> *Darum so klag ich nicht.**

Thus the article about the Lord's descent into hell reminds us that not only God's speech but also his silence is part of the Christian revelation. God is not only the comprehensible word that comes to us; he is also the silent, inaccessible, uncomprehended and incomprehensible ground that eludes us. To be sure, in Christianity there is a primacy of the *logos*, of the word, over silence; God *has* spoken. God *is* word. But this does not

---

* "Thou art he who gently breaks about our heads what we build, so that we can see the sky – therefore I have no complaint" (Trans.).

H

entitle us to forget the truth of God's abiding concealment.
Only when we have experienced him as silence may we hope
to hear his speech too, which proceeds in silence.[56] Christology
reaches out beyond the cross, the moment when the divine love
is tangible, into the death, the silence and the eclipse of God.
Can we wonder that the Church and the life of the individual
are led again and again into this hour of silence, into the forgotten and almost discarded article, "Descended into hell"?

When one ponders on this, the question of the "scriptural
evidence" solves itself; at any rate in Jesus' death-cry, "My
God, my God, why hast thou forsaken me?" (Mark 15.34),
the mystery of Jesus' descent into hell is illuminated as if in a
glaring flash of lightning on a dark night. We must not forget
that these words of the crucified Christ are the opening lines
of one of Israel's prayers (Ps. 22 [21]. 2) which summarizes in
a shattering way the needs and hopes of this people chosen by
God and apparently at the moment so utterly abandoned by
him. This prayer that rises from the sheer misery of God's
seeming eclipse ends in praises of God's greatness. This element
too is present in Jesus' death-cry, which has been recently
described by Ernst Käsemann as a prayer from hell, as the
erection of the first commandment in the wilderness of God's
apparent absence: "The Son still holds on to faith when faith
seems to have become meaningless and the earthly reality
proclaims the absent God of whom the first thief and the mock-
ing crowd speak – not for nothing. His cry is not for life and
survival, not for himself, but for the Father. His cry stands
against the reality of the whole world." After this, do we still
need to ask what prayer in our hour of darkness must be?
Can it be anything else but the cry from the depths in company

[56] Cf. the significance of silence in the writings of Ignatius of Antioch:
Epistola ad Ephesios, 19, 1: "And to the prince of this world the virginity of
Mary and her confinement remained hidden, likewise also the death of the
Lord – these loudly-calling secrets which were accomplished in God's
peace." Quoted by J. A. Fischer, *Die Apostolischen Väter*, Darmstadt, 1956,
p. 157); cf. *Epistola ad Magnesios*, 8, 2, which speaks of the λόγος απὸ σιγῆς
προελθών (the word that comes from silence), and the meditation on speech
and silence in the *Epistola ad Ephesios*, 15, 1. On the historical background,
H. Schlier, *Religionsgeschichtliche Untersuchungen zu den Ignatiusbriefen*, Berlin,
1929.

with the Lord who "has descended into hell" and who has established the nearness of God in the midst of abandonment by God?

Let us look at another aspect of this complex mystery, which cannot be elucidated from one side alone. Let us first take account of one of the findings of exegesis. We are told that in this article of the Creed the word "hell" is only a false translation of *scheol* (in Greek, Hades), which denoted in Hebrew the state after death, which was very vaguely imagined as a kind of shadow existence, more non-being than being. Accordingly the statement meant originally, say the scholars, only that Jesus entered the *scheol*, that is, that he died. This may be perfectly correct, but the question remains whether it makes the matter any simpler or less mysterious. In my view it is only at this point that we come face to face with the problem what death really is, what happens when someone dies, that is, enters the fate of death. Confronted with this question we all have to admit our embarrassment. No one really knows the answer because we all live on this side of death and are unfamiliar with the experience of death. But perhaps we can try to get somewhere near by starting again from Jesus' cry on the cross, which we found to contain the heart of what Jesus' descent into hell, his sharing of man's mortal fate, really means. In this last prayer of Jesus, as in the scene on the Mount of Olives, what appears as the innermost heart of his passion is not any physical pain but radical loneliness, complete abandonment. But in the last analysis what comes to light here is simply the abyss of loneliness of man in general, man who is alone in his innermost being. This loneliness, which is usually thickly overlaid but is nevertheless the true situation of man, is at the same time in fundamental contradiction with the nature of man, who cannot exist alone; he needs company. That is why loneliness is the region of fear, which is rooted in the exposure of a being that must exist but is pushed out into a situation which he cannot endure.

A concrete example will help to make this clearer. When a child has to walk through a wood in the dark it feels frightened, however convincingly it has been shown that there is nothing at all to be frightened of. As soon as it is alone in the darkness, and thus has the experience of utter loneliness, fear arises, the fear peculiar to man, which is not fear of anything in particular but simply fear in itself. Fear of a particular thing is basically harmless; it can be removed by taking away the thing concerned. For example, if someone is afraid of a spiteful dog the matter can be swiftly settled by putting the dog on a chain. Here we come up against something much deeper, namely the fact that where man falls into extreme loneliness he is not afraid of anything definite that could be explained away; on the contrary, he experiences the fear of loneliness, the uneasiness and nakedness of his own nature, something that cannot be overcome by rational means. Let us take another example. If someone has to keep watch alone in a room with a dead person he will always feel his position to be somehow or other uncanny, even if he is unwilling to admit it to himself and is capable of explaining to himself rationally the groundlessness of his fear. He knows perfectly well in his own mind that the corpse can do him no harm and that his position might be more dangerous if the person concerned were still alive. What arises here is a completely different kind of fear, not fear of anything in particular, but, in being alone with death, the uncanniness of loneliness in itself, the exposed nature of existence. How then, we must ask, can such fear be overcome if proof of its groundlessness has no effect? Well, the child will lose its fear the moment that there is a hand there to take it and lead it, and a voice to talk to it; at the moment therefore at which it experiences the fellowship of a loving human being. Similarly, he who is alone with the corpse will feel the bout of fear recede when there is a human being with him, when he experiences the nearness of a "You". This conquest of fear reveals at the same time once again the nature of the fear: that it is the fear of loneliness, the anxiety of a being that can only live with a fellow being. The fear peculiar to man cannot be overcome by reason but only by the presence of someone who loves him.

We must now push our question a stage further. If there were such a thing as a loneliness which could no longer be penetrated and transformed by the word of another; if a state of abandonment were to arise which was so deep that no "You" could reach into it any more, then we should have real, total loneliness and frightfulness, what theology calls "hell". We can now define exactly what this word means: it denotes a loneliness which the word love can no longer penetrate and which therefore indicates the exposed nature of existence in itself. In this connection who can fail to remember that writers and philosophers of our time take the view that basically all encounters between human beings remain superficial, that no man has access to the real depths of another? According to this view, no one can really penetrate into the innermost being of someone else; every encounter, beautiful as it may seem, basically only dulls the incurable wound of loneliness. Thus hell, despair, would dwell at the very bottom of each of us, in the shape of that loneliness which is as inescapable as it is dreadful. As is well known, Sartre has based his anthropology on this idea. But even such an apparently conciliatory and tranquilly cheerful poet as Hermann Hesse allows the same thought to appear in his work:

> *Seltsam, im Nebel zu wandern!*
> *Leben ist Einsamsein.*
> *Kein Mensch kennt den andern,*
> *Jeder ist allein!**

In truth – one thing is certain: there exists a night into whose solitude no voice reaches; there is a door through which we can only walk alone – the door of death. In the last analysis all the fear in the world is fear of this loneliness. From this point of view it is possible to understand why the Old Testament has only one word for hell *and* death, the word *scheol*; in the last resort it regards both as identical. Death is absolute loneliness. But the loneliness into which love can no longer reach is – hell.

This brings us back to our starting-point, the article of the Creed that speaks of the descent into hell. This article thus asserts that Christ strode through the gate of our final loneliness, that in his passion he went down into the abyss of our abandonment. Where no voice can reach us any longer, there

---

* "Curious, to walk in a mist!
Life is loneliness.
No man knows his neighbour,
Everyone is alone!"

is he. Hell is thereby overcome, or, to be more accurate, death, which was previously hell, is hell no longer. Neither is the same any longer because there is life in the midst of death, because love dwells in it. Now only deliberate self-enclosure is hell or, as the Bible calls it, the second death (Rev. 20.14, for example). But death is no longer the path into icy solitude; the gates of the *scheol* have been opened. From this angle, I think, one can understand the images – which at first sight look so mythological – of the Fathers, who speak of fetching up the dead, of the opening of the gates. The apparently mythical passage in St Matthew's gospel becomes comprehensible too, the passage which says that at the death of Jesus tombs opened and the bodies of the saints were raised (Matt. 27.52). The door of death stands open since life – love – has dwelt in death. . . .

4. "ROSE AGAIN FROM THE DEAD"

To the Christian, faith in the resurrection of Jesus Christ is the expression of the certainty that the saying which seems to be only a beautiful dream is in fact true: "Love is strong as death" (Song of Sol. 8.6). In the Old Testament this sentence comes in the middle of praises of the power of *eros*. But this by no means signifies that we can simply push it aside as a hymnal exaggeration. The boundless demands of *eros*, its apparent exaggerations and extravagance, do in reality give expression to a basic problem, indeed *the* basic problem, of human existence, in so far as they reflect the nature and intrinsic paradox of love: love demands infinity, indestructibility; indeed it *is*, so so speak, a call for infinity. But it is also a fact that this cry of love's cannot be satisfied, that it demands infinity but cannot grant it; that it claims eternity but in fact is included in the world of death, in its loneliness and its power of destruction. Only from this angle can one understand what "resurrection" means. It *is* the greater strength of love in face of death.

At the same time it is proof of what only immortality can create: being in the other who still stands when I have fallen apart. Man is a being who himself does not live for ever but is necessarily delivered up to death. For him, since he has no continuance in himself, survival, from a purely human point of view, can only become possible through his continuing to exist in another. The statements of Scripture about the connection between sin and death are to be understood from this angle. For it now becomes clear that man's attempt "to be like God", his striving for autonomy, through which he wishes to stand on his own feet alone, means his death, for he just cannot stand on his own. If man – and this is the real nature of sin – nevertheless refuses to recognize his own limits and tries to be completely self-sufficient, then precisely by adopting this attitude he delivers himself up to death.

Of course man does understand that his life alone does not endure and that he must therefore strive to exist in others, so as to remain through them and in them in the land of the living. Two ways in particular have been tried. First, living on in one's own children: that is why in primitive peoples failure to marry and childlessness are regarded as the most terrible curse; they mean hopeless destruction, final death. Conversely, the biggest possible number of children offers at the same time the greatest possible chance of survival, hope of immortality, and thus the most genuine blessing that man can expect. Another way discloses itself when man discovers that in his children he only continues to exist in a very unreal way; he wants more of himself to remain. So he takes refuge in the idea of fame, which should make him really immortal if he lives on through all ages in the memory of others. But this second attempt of man's to give himself immortality by existing-in-others fails just as badly as the first: what remains is not the self but only its echo, a mere shadow. So self-made immortality is really only a Hades, a *scheol*: more non-being than being. The inadequacy of both ways lies partly in the fact that who holds my being after my death cannot carry this being itself but only its echo; and even more in the fact that even the other person to whom I have, so to speak, entrusted my continuance will not last – he too will perish.

This leads us to the next step. We have seen so far that man has no permanence in himself and consequently can only continue to exist in another, but that his existence in another is only shadowy and once again not final, because this other must

perish too. If this is so, then only *one* could truly give lasting
stability: he who *is*, who does not come into existence and pass
away again but abides in the midst of transience: the God of
the living, who does not hold just the shadow and echo of my
being, whose ideas are not just copies of reality. I myself am
his thought, which establishes me more securely, so to speak,
than I am in myself; his thought is not the posthumous shadow
but the original source and strength of my being. In him I can
stand as more than a shadow; in him I am truly closer to myself than I should be if I just tried to stay by myself.

Before we return from here to the resurrection, let us try to
see the same thing once again from a somewhat different side.
We can start again from the dictum about love and death and
say: only where someone values love more highly than life,
that is, only where someone is ready to put life second to love,
for the sake of love, can love be stronger and more than
death. If it is to be more than death it must first be more than
mere life. But if it could be this, not just in intention but in
reality, then that would mean at the same time that the power
of love had risen superior to the power of the merely biological
and taken it into its service. To use Teilhard de Chardin's
terminology, where that took place, the decisive complexity or
"complexification" would have occurred; *bios* too would be
encompassed by and incorporated in the power of love. It
would cross the boundary – death – and create unity where
death divides. If the power of love for another were so strong
anywhere that it could keep alive not just his memory, the
shadow of his "I", but that person himself, then a new stage
in life would have been reached. This would mean that the
realm of biological evolutions and mutations had been left
behind and the leap made on to a quite different plane, on
which love was no longer subject to *bios* but made use of it.
Such a final stage of "mutation" and "evolution" would itself
no longer be a biological stage; it would signify the end of the
sovereignty of *bios*, which is at the same time the sovereignty
of death; it would open up the realm which the Greek Bible
calls "*zoe*" that is, definitive life, which has left behind the rule
of death. The last stage of evolution needed by the world to
reach its goal would then no longer be achieved within the

realm of biology but by the spirit, by freedom, by love. It would no longer be evolution but decision and gift in one.

But what has all this to do, it may be asked, with faith in the resurrection of Jesus? Well, we had previously considered the question of the possible immortality of man from two sides, which now turn out to be aspects of one and the same state of affairs. We had said that as man has no permanence in himself his survival could only be brought about by his living on in another. And we had said, from the point of view of this "other", that only the love which takes up the beloved in itself, into its own being, could make possible this existence in the other. These two complementary aspects are mirrored again, so it seems to me, in the two New Testament ways of describing the resurrection of the Lord: "Jesus has risen" and "God (the Father) has awoken Jesus." Both formulas meet in the fact that Jesus' total love for men, which leads him to the cross, is perfected in total stepping-over to the Father and therein becomes stronger than death, because in this it is at the same time total "being held" by him.

From this a further step results. We can now say that love always found some kind of immortality; even in its pre-human stage it points, in the form of preservation of the species, in this direction. Indeed, this founding of immortality is not something incidental to love, not one thing that it does among others, but what really gives it its specific character. This principle can be reversed; it then signifies that immortality *always* proceeds from love, never out of the autarchy of that which is sufficient to itself. We may even be bold enough to assert that this principle, properly understood, also applies even to God as he is seen by the Christian faith. God too is absolute permanence, as opposed to everything transitory, for the reason that he is the relation of three persons to one another, their incorporation in the "for-one-another" of love, act-substance of the love that is absolute and therefore completely "relative", living only "in relation to". As we said earlier, it is not autarchy, which knows no one but itself, that is divine; what is revolutionary about the Christian view of the world and of God, we found, as opposed to those of antiquity, is that it learns to understand the "absolute" as absolute "relativity", as *relatio subsistens*.

To return to our argument, love founds immortality, and
immortality proceeds from love alone. This statement to which
we have now worked our way also means that he who has
love for all has founded immortality for all. That is precisely
the meaning of the biblical statement that *his* resurrection is
our life. The – to us – curious reasoning of St Paul in his First
Epistle to the Corinthians now becomes comprehensible: if he
has risen, then we have too, for then love is stronger than death;
if he has not risen, then we have not either, for then the situation is still that death has the last word, nothing else (cf. 1 Cor.
15.16f.). Since this is a statement of central importance let us
spell it out once again in a different way: either love is stronger
than death or it is not. If it has become so in him, then it became
so precisely as love for others. This also means, it is true, that
our own love, left to itself, is not sufficient to overcome death;
taken in itself it would have to remain an unanswered cry. It
means that only his love, coinciding with God's own power of
life and love, can found our immortality. Nevertheless, it still
remains true that the *mode* of our immortality will depend on
our mode of living. We shall have to return to this in the section on the Last Judgement.

A further point emerges from these considerations. It goes
without saying that the life of him who has risen from the dead
is not once again *bios*, the bio-logical form of our mortal life
inside history; it is *zoe*, new, different, definitive life; life which
has stepped beyond the mortal realm of *bios* and history, a
realm which has here been surpassed by a greater power. And
in fact the resurrection narratives of the New Testament allow
us to see clearly that the life of him who has risen again does
not lie within the historical *bios*, but beyond and above it. It
is also true, of course, that this new life begot itself *in* history
and had to do so, because after all it is there *for* history, and the
Christian message is basically nothing else than the transmission of the testimony that love has here broken through death
and thus transformed fundamentally the situation of all of us.
Once we have realized this, it is no longer difficult to find the
right kind of hermeneutics for the difficult business of expounding the biblical resurrection narratives, that is, to acquire a
clear understanding of the sense in which they must properly

be understood. Obviously we cannot attempt here a detailed discussion of the questions involved, which today present themselves in a more difficult form than ever before; especially as historical and — for the most part inadequately pondered — philosophical statements are becoming more and more inextricably intertwined and exegesis itself quite often produces its own philosophy, which is intended to appear to the layman as a supremely refined distillation of the biblical evidence. Many points of detail will here always remain open to discussion, but it is possible to recognize a fundamental dividing line between explanation that remains explanation and arbitrary speculation.

First of all it is quite clear that after his resurrection Christ did not go back to his previous earthly life, as we are told the young man of Naim and Lazarus did. He rose again to definitive life, which is no longer governed by the chemical and biological laws and therefore stands outside the possibility of death, in the eternity conferred by love. That is why the encounters with him are "appearances"; that is why he with whom people had sat at table two days earlier is not recognized by his best friends and, even when recognized, remains alien: only where *he* grants vision *is* he seen; only when he opens men's eyes and makes their hearts open up can the countenance of the eternal love that conquers death become recognizable in our mortal world, and in the new, different world, the world of him who is to come. That is also why it is so difficult, indeed absolutely impossible, for the gospels to describe the encounter with the risen Christ; that is why they can only stammer when they speak of these meetings and seem to provide contradictory descriptions of them. In reality they are surprisingly unanimous in the dialectic of their statements, in the simultaneity of touching and not-touching, or recognizing and not-recognizing, of complete identity between the crucified and the risen Christ and complete transformation. People recognize the Lord and yet do not recognize him again; people touch him, and yet he is untouchable; he is the same and yet quite different. As we have said, the dialectic is always the same; it is only the stylistic means by which it is expressed that changes.

For example, let us examine a little more closely from this point of view the Emmaus story, which we have already touched upon briefly. At first sight it looks as if we are confronted here with a completely earthly conception of resurrection; as if nothing remains of the mysterious and indescribable elements to be found in the Pauline accounts. It looks as if the tendency to detailed depiction, to the concreteness of legend, supported by the apologist's desire for something palpable, had completely won the upper hand and fetched the risen Lord right back into earthly history. But this impression is soon contradicted by his mysterious appearance and his no less mysterious disappearance. Still more contradictory is the fact that here too he remains unrecognizable to the accustomed eye. He cannot be firmly grasped as he could be in the time of his earthly life; he is discovered only in the realm of faith; he sets the hearts of the two wanderers aflame by his interpretation of the Scriptures and by breaking bread he opens their eyes. This is a reference to the two basic elements in early Christian worship, which consisted of the liturgy of the word (the reading and expounding of Scripture) and the eucharistic breaking of bread. In this way the evangelist makes it clear that the encounter with the risen Christ lies on a quite new plane; he tries to describe the indescribable in terms of the liturgical facts. He thereby provides both a theology of the resurrection and a theology of the liturgy: one encounters the risen Christ in the word and in the sacrament; divine service is the fashion in which he becomes touchable to us and recognizable as the living Christ. And conversely, the liturgy is based on the mystery of Easter; it is to be understood as the Lord's approach to us. In it he becomes our travelling companion, sets our dull hearts aflame and opens our sealed eyes. He still walks with us, still finds us worried and downhearted, and still has the power to make us see.

Of course, all this is only half the story; to stop at this alone would mean falsifying the evidence of the New Testament. Experience of the risen Christ is something other than a meeting with a historical man, and it must certainly not be traced back to conversations at table and recollections which would have finally crystallized in the idea that he still lived and went about his business. Such an interpretation reduces what happened to the purely human level and robs it of its specific quality. The resurrection narratives are something other and more than disguised liturgical scenes: they make visible the founding event on which all Christian liturgy rests. They testify to an approach which did not rise from the hearts of the disciples but came to them from outside, convinced them *against* their doubts and made them certain that the Lord had truly risen. He who lay in the grave is no longer there; he – really he himself – lives. He who had been transposed into the other world of God showed himself powerful enough to make it palpably clear that he himself stood opposite them again, that in him the power of love had really proved itself stronger than the power of death.

Only by taking this just as seriously as what we said first does one remain faithful to the testimony of the New Testament; only thus too is its seriousness in world history preserved. The comfortable attempt to spare oneself the belief in the mystery of God's mighty actions in this world and yet at the same time to have the satisfaction of remaining on the foundation of the biblical message leads nowhere; it measures up neither to the honesty of reason nor to the claims of faith. One cannot have both the Christian faith and "religion within the bounds of pure reason"; a choice is unavoidable. He who believes will see more and more clearly, it is true, how rational it is to have faith in the love that has conquered death.

5. "ASCENDED INTO HEAVEN, SITTETH AT THE RIGHT HAND OF GOD THE FATHER ALMIGHTY"

To our generation, whose critical faculty has been awoken by Bultmann, talk of the ascension, together with that of the descent into hell, conjures up that picture of a three-storey world which we call mythical and regard as finished with once and for all. "Above" and "below", the world is everywhere just world, governed everywhere by the same physical laws, basically susceptible everywhere of the same kind of investigation. It has no storeys and the concepts "above" and "below" are relative, depending on the standpoint of the observer.

Indeed, since there is no absolute point of reference (and the earth certainly does not represent one), basically one cannot any longer speak at all of "above" and "below" – or even of "left" and "right"; the cosmos no longer exhibits any firm directions. No one today will seriously contest these discoveries. There is no longer such a thing as a world arranged literally in three storeys. But was such a conception ever really intended in the articles of faith about the Lord's descent into hell and ascension to heaven? It certainly provided the imagery for them but it was just as certainly not the decisive factual element in them. On the contrary, the two assertions, together with faith in the historical Jesus, express the total range of human existence, which certainly spans three metaphysical dimensions if not three cosmic storeys. To that extent it is only logical that the "modern" attitude should dispense not only with the ascension and the descent into hell but also with the historical Jesus, that is, with all three dimensions of human existence; what is left *can* only be a variously draped ghost, on which – understandably – no one any longer wishes to build anything serious.

But what do our three dimensions really imply? We have already come to see that the descent into hell does not really refer to any outer depths of the cosmos; these are quite unnecessary to it. In the basic text, the prayer of the crucified Christ to the God who has abandoned him, there is no trace of any cosmic reference. On the contrary, this article of the Creed turns our gaze to the depths of human existence, which reaches down into the valley of death, into the zone of untouchable loneliness and rejected love, and thus embraces the dimension of hell, carrying it within itself as one of its own possibilities. Hell, existence in the definitive rejection of "being for", is not a cosmographical destination but a dimension of human nature, the abyss into which it reaches down at its lower end. We know today better than ever before that everyone's existence touches these depths; and since in the last analysis mankind is "*one* man" these depths affect not only the individual but also the one body of the whole human race, which must therefore bear the burden of them as a corporate whole. From this angle it can be understood once again how Christ, the "new Adam", undertook to bear the burden of these depths with us and did not wish to remain sublimely unaffected by them; conversely, of course, total rejection in all its unfathomability has only now become possible.

On the other hand, the ascension of Christ points to the opposite end of human existence, which stretches out an infinite distance above and below itself. This existence embraces, as the opposite pole to utter solitude, to the untouchability of rejected love, the possibility of contact with all other men through the medium of contact with the divine love itself, so that human existence can find its geometrical resting place, so to speak, inside God's own being. The two possibilities of man thus covered by the words heaven and hell are, it is true, completely different in nature and can be quite clearly distinguished from each other. The depths we call hell man can only give to himself. Indeed, we must put it more pointedly: hell consists in man's being unwilling to receive anything, in his desire to be self-sufficient. It is the expression of enclosure in one's own being alone. These depths accordingly consist by nature of just this: that man will not accept, will not take anything, but wants to stand entirely on his own feet, to be sufficient unto himself. If this becomes utterly radical, then man has become the untouchable, the solitary, the rejecter. Hell is wanting-only-to-be-oneself; what happens when man barricades himself up in himself. Conversely, it is the nature o fthat upper end of the scale which we have called heaven that it can only be received, just as one can only give hell to oneself. "Heaven" is by nature what one has not made oneself and cannot make oneself; in scholastic language it was said to be, as grace, a "*donum indebitum et superadditum naturae*" ("an unowed gift added on top of nature"). As fulfilled love, heaven can always only be granted to man; but hell is the loneliness of the man who will not accept it, who declines the status of beggar and withdraws into himself.

Only from this standpoint does it become clear what is really meant in the Christian view by heaven. It is not to be understood as an everlasting place above the world, nor simply as an eternal metaphysical region. On the contrary, "heaven" and "the ascension of Christ" are indivisibly connected; it is only this connection that makes clear the christological, personal, history-centred meaning of the Christian tidings of

heaven. Let us look at it from another angle: heaven is not
a place which before Christ's ascension was barred off by a
positive, primitive decree of God's, to be opened up one day
in just as positive a way. On the contrary, the reality of heaven
only comes into existence through the confluence of God and
man. Heaven is to be defined as the contact of the being "man"
with the being "God"; this confluence of God and man took
place once and for all in Christ with his stride over *bios* through
death to new life. Heaven is accordingly that future of man and
of mankind which the latter cannot give to itself, which is
therefore closed to it so long as it waits for itself, and which was
first and thoroughly opened up in the man whose field of
existence was God and through whom God entered into the
creature "man".

Therefore heaven is always more than a private, individual
destiny; it is necessarily connected with the "last Adam", with
the definitive man and accordingly necessarily with the future
of man as a whole. I think that from this point again it should
be possible to gain some important hermeneutic insights, which
in this context can only be hinted at. One of the most striking
facts in the biblical evidence, a fact by which exegesis and
theology have been profoundly exercised for the last fifty years
or so, is formed by the so-called "eschatology of imminence".
By this is meant that in the preaching of Jesus and the apostles
it looks as if the end of the world was announced as imminent.
Indeed, one can even gain the impression that news of the
approaching end was the real heart of the preaching of Jesus
and the early Church. The figure of Jesus, his death and his
resurrection are brought into connection with this idea in a
way that is as strange as it is incomprehensible. Obviously we
cannot here deal in detail with the many questions involved.
But have not our last reflections indicated the direction in which
the answer can be sought? We described resurrection and
ascension as the final merging of the being "man" with the
being "God", a process that offers man the possibility of
everlasting existence. We have tried to understand the two
happenings as love's being stronger than death and thus as the
decisive "mutation" of man and cosmos, in which the frontier
of *bios* is broken down and a new field of existence created. If

this is all correct, then it means the beginning of "eschatology", of the end of the world. With the crossing of the frontier of death the future dimension of mankind is opened up and its future has in fact already begun. It thus also becomes evident how the individual's hope of immortality and the possibility of immortality for mankind as a whole intertwine and meet in Christ, who may just as well be called the "centre" as, properly understood, the "end" of history.

Another idea must be weighed in connection with the article of the Creed that speaks of the Lord's ascension. The statement about the ascension which, as we have now seen, is decisive for the understanding of man's existence beyond the grave is just as decisive for his life here and now, or alternatively for the question how the two existences can approach each other, and therefore for the question of the possibility and meaning of human relations with God. In our consideration of the first article of the Creed we replied affirmatively to the question whether the infinite can hear the finite, the eternal the temporal, and demonstrated that the true God's greatness is to be seen precisely in the fact that to him the smallest thing is not too small and the biggest not too big; we tried to understand that, as the *logos*, he is the reason which not only speaks to all but also hears all, and from which nothing remains excluded because of its insignificance. We replied to the worried questioning of our age: "Yes, God can hear." But one question still remains open. If anyone, following our train of thought, says, "Good, he can hear", must he not go on to ask, "But can he also answer our prayers?" Or is not the prayer of petition, the call of the creature up to God, in the last analysis a pious trick to elevate man psychologically and to comfort him, because he is seldom capable of higher forms of prayer? Surely the whole thing serves solely to set man in motion somehow or other towards transcendence, although in reality nothing can happen or be changed as a result of his prayers; for what is eternal is eternal, and what is temporal is temporal – no path seems to lead from one to the other. This too we cannot consider in detail here, because a very exhaustive critical analysis of the concepts of time and eternity would be required. One would have to investigate their foundations in ancient thought and the synthesis of this thought with the biblical faith, a synthesis whose imperfection lies at the root of modern questioning. One would have to consider once again the relationship of scientific and technical thinking to the thinking of faith. These are tasks which go far beyond the scope of this book. So here again detailed answers must be replaced by a pointer to the direction in which the general answer is to be sought.

Modern thinking usually lets itself be guided by the idea that eternity is imprisoned, so to speak, in its unchangeableness; God appears as the prisoner of his eternal plan conceived "before all ages". "Being" and "becoming" do not mingle. Eternity is thus understood in a purely negative sense as timelessness, as the opposite to time, as something that cannot make its influence felt in time for the simple reason that it would thereby cease to be unchangeable and itself become temporal. Fundamentally these ideas remain the products of a pre-Christian mentality which takes no account of a concept of God that finds utterance in a belief in creation and incarnation. At bottom they take for granted the antique dualism - something that we cannot go into here – and are signs of an intellectual naïvety that looks at God in human terms. For if one thinks that God cannot alter retrospectively what he planned "before" eternity, then without noticing it one is again conceiving eternity in terms of time, with its distinction between "before" and "after".

But eternity is not the very ancient, which existed before time began, but the quite other, which is related to every passing age as its today, and is really contemporary with it; it is not itself barred off into a "before" and "after"; it is much rather the power of the present in all time. Eternity does not stand by the side of time, quite unrelated to it; it is the creatively supporting power of all time, embracing passing time in its own present and thus giving it the ability to be. It is not timelessness but control of time. As the present that is contemporary with all ages it can also make its influence felt in any age.

The incarnation of God in Jesus Christ, by virtue of which the eternal God and temporal man meet in one single person, is nothing else than the last concrete manifestation of God's control of time. At this point of Jesus' human existence God took hold of time and drew it into himself. His power over time stands embodied before us, as it were, in Christ. Christ is really, as St John's gospel says, the "door" between God and man (John 10.9), the "mediator" (1 Tim. 2.5), in whom the Eternal One has time. In Jesus we temporal beings can speak to the temporal one, our con-temporary; but in him, who with us is time, we simultaneously make contact with the Eternal One, because with us Jesus is time and with God eternity.

Hans Urs von Balthasar – speaking, it is true, in a somewhat different context – has cast a searching light on the spiritual significance of these insights. He first recalls that in his earthly life Jesus did not stand above time and space but lived from the midst of his time and in his time. The humanity of Jesus, which placed him in the midst of that age, hits us in every line of the gospels; and we have, from many points of view, a clearer and more living picture of him than was vouchsafed to earlier periods. But this "standing in time" is not just an outward cultural and historical framework, behind which could be found somewhere or other, untouched by it, the supratemporal essence of his real being; it is much rather an anthropological state of affairs, which profoundly affects the form of human existence itself. Jesus has time and does not anticipate in sinful impatience the will of the Father. "Therefore the Son, who in the world has time for God, is the original place where God has time for the world. God has no other time for the world than in the Son; but in him he has all time."[57] God is not the prisoner of his eternity: in Jesus he has time – for us, and Jesus is thus in actual fact "the throne of grace" to which at any time we can "draw near with confidence" (Heb. 4.16).

6. "FROM THENCE HE SHALL COME TO JUDGE THE LIVING AND THE DEAD"

Rudolf Bultmann reckons that the belief in an "end of the world" signalled by the return of the Lord in judgment is one

[57] H. U. von Balthasar, *Theologie der Geschichte*, Einsiedeln, 1959, p. 31; cf. G. Hasenhüttl, *Der Glaubensvollzug*, Essen, 1963, p. 327.

of those ideas, like the Lord's descent into hell and ascension into heaven, which for modern man are "disposed of". Every reasonable person, he declares, is convinced that the world will go on as it has done now for nearly two thousand years since the eschatological proclamation of the New Testament. It seems all the more important to clarify our thinking on this point since the biblical treatment of it unquestionably contains marked cosmological elements and therefore reaches into the domain which we see before us as the field of natural science. Of course, in the phrase about the end of the world, the word "world" does not mean primarily the physical structure of the cosmos but the world of man, human history; thus in the first instance this manner of speaking means that *this* kind of world – the human world – will come to an end dictated and achieved by God. But it cannot be denied that the Bible presents this essentially anthropological event in cosmological (and also partly in political) imagery. How far it is a question *only* of imagery and how close the imagery is to the reality is difficult to decide.

Certainly one can only base one's observations on this subject on the larger context of the Bible's whole view of the world. And for the Bible the cosmos and man are not two clearly separable quantities, with the cosmos forming the fortuitous scene of human existence, which in itself could be parted from the cosmos and allowed to accomplish itself without a world. On the contrary, world and human existence belong necessarily to one another, so that neither a worldless man nor even a world without man seems thinkable. The first of these two concepts can be accepted again today without argument; and after what we have learned from Teilhard the second should no longer be quite incomprehensible either. Going on from there, one might be tempted to say that the biblical message about the end of the world and the return of the Lord is not simply anthropology in cosmic imagery; that it does not even merely present a cosmological aspect alongside an anthropological one, but depicts with the inner logic of the total biblical view the coincidence of anthropology and cosmology in definitive Christology, and precisely *therein* portrays the end of the "world", which in its two-in-one construction out of cosmos and man has always pointed to this unity as its final goal. Cosmos and man, which already belong to each other even though they so often stand opposed to one another, will become one through their "complexification" in the larger entity of the love that, as we said earlier, steps beyond and encompasses *bios*. Thus it becomes evident here once again how very much end-eschatology and the breakthrough represented by Jesus' resurrection are in reality one and the same thing; it becomes clear once again that the New Testament rightly depicts this resurrection as *the* eschatological happening.

In order to make any further progress we must clarify this idea a little further. We said just now that the cosmos was not just an outward framework of human history, not a static mould – a kind of container holding all kinds of living creatures which could just as well be poured into a different container. This means, on the positive side, that the cosmos is movement; that it is not just a case of history *existing in* it, that the cosmos itself *is* history. It does not merely form the scene of human history; before human history began and later with it, it is itself "history". Finally, there is only one single all-embracing world-history, which for all the ups and downs, all the forwards and backwards that it exhibits, nevertheless has a general direction and goes "forward". Of course, to him who only sees a section of it, this piece, even though it may be relatively big, looks like a circling in the same spot. No direction is perceptible. It is only observed by him who begins to see the whole. But in this cosmic movement, as we have already seen, spirit is not just some chance by-product of development, of no importance to the whole; on the contrary, we were able to establish that, in this movement or process, matter and its evolution form the pre-history of spirit or mind.

From this position the belief in the return of Jesus Christ and in the consummation of the world could be explained as the conviction that our history is advancing to an "omega" point, at which it will become finally and unmistakably clear that the element of stability which seems to us to be the supporting ground of reality, so to speak, is not mere unconscious matter; that on the contrary the real, firm ground is mind.

Mind holds being together, gives it reality, indeed *is* reality: it is not from below but from above that being receives its capacity to subsist. That there is such a thing as this process of "complexification" of material being through spirit, and from the latter its combination into a new kind of unity, can already be seen today in a certain sense in the remodelling of the world by technology. In reality's susceptibility to manipulation the boundaries between nature and technology are already beginning to disappear; the two cannot be clearly separated from each other. To be sure, this analogy must be regarded as questionable in more than one respect. Yet such processes hint at a kind of world in which spirit and nature do not simply stand alongside each other, but spirit, in a new "complexification", draws the apparently merely natural into itself, thereby creating a new world which at the same time necessarily means the end of the old one. Now the "end of the world" in which the Christian believes is certainly something quite different from the total victory of technology. But the welding together of nature and spirit which occurs in it enables us to grasp in a new way how the reality of belief in the return of Christ is to be conceived: as faith in the final unification of reality by spirit or mind.

This opens the way to a further step. We said before that nature and mind form one single history, which advances in such a way that mind emerges more and more clearly as the all-embracing element and thus anthropology and cosmology finally in actual fact coalesce. But this assertion of the increasing "complexification" of the world through mind necessarily implies its unification round a personal centre, for mind is not just an undefined something or other; where it exists in its own specific nature it subsists as individuality, as person. It is true that there is such a thing as "objective mind", mind invested in machines, in works of the most varied kind; but in all these cases mind does not exist in its original, specific form; "objective mind" is always derived from subjective mind; it points back to person, mind's only real mode of existence. Thus the assertion that the world is moving towards a "complexification" through mind also implies that the cosmos is moving towards a unification in the personal.

This confirms once again the infinite precedence of the individual over the universal. This principle evolved earlier appears again here in all its importance. The world is in motion towards unity in the person. The whole draws its meaning from the individual, not the other way about. Perception of this also justifies once again Christology's apparent positivism, the conviction – a scandal to men of all periods – that makes one individual the centre of history and of the whole. The intrinsic necessity of this "positivism" here becomes apparent afresh: if it is true that at the end stands the triumph of spirit, that is, the triumph of truth, freedom and love, then it is not just some force or other that finally ends up victorious; what stands at the end is a countenance. The omega of the world is a "you", a person, an individual. The all-encompassing "complexifica-tion", the unification infinitely embracing all, is at the same time the final denial of all collectivism, the denial of the fanaticism of the mere idea, even the so-called "idea of Christi-anity". Man, person always takes precedence over the mere idea.

This implies a further and very important consequence. If the breakthrough to the ultra-complexity of the final phase is based on spirit and freedom, then it is by no means a neutral, cosmic drift; it includes responsibility. It does not happen of its own accord, like a physical progress, but rests on decisions. That is why the return of the Lord is not only salvation, not only the omega that sets everything right, but also judgment. Indeed at this stage we can actually define the meaning of the talk of judgment. It means precisely this, that the final stage of the world is not the result of a natural current but the result of responsibility based on freedom. This must also be regarded as the key to understanding why the New Testament clings fast, in spite of its message of grace, to the assertion that at the end men are judged "by their works" and no one can escape giving account of the way he has lived his life. There is a freedom which is not cancelled out even by grace and indeed is brought by it face to face with itself: man's final fate is not forced upon him regardless of the decisions he has made in his life. This assertion is any case also necessary as a warning sign against false dogmatism and a false Christian self-confidence.

It alone confirms the equality of men by confirming the identity of their responsibility. Since the days of the early Christian fathers it has always been an essential task of Christian preaching to make people aware of this identity of responsibility and to contrast it with the false confidence engendered by merely appealing to the Lord.

It might be useful in this context to recall certain things said by the great Jewish theologian Leo Baeck. The Christian will not entirely agree with them but he cannot disregard their seriousness. Baeck points to the fact that Israel's "life apart" turned into an awareness of serving the future of mankind. "The *special character of the call* is asserted, but *no exclusiveness of salvation* is proclaimed. Judaism was preserved from falling into the religious narrowness of the concept of a Church that alone confers salvation. Where it is not faith but the deed that leads to God, where the community offers to its children as a sign of spiritual membership the ideal and the task, a place in the covenant of faith cannot of itself guarantee the salvation of the soul." Baeck then shows how this universalism of the salvation founded on the deed crystallizes more and more firmly in the Jewish tradition and finally emerges quite clearly in the "classical" saying: "Even the pious who are not Israelites share in the eternal bliss." No one will be able to read without dismay when Baeck then goes on to say that one need only "compare with this principle Dante's picture of the place of damnation, the destination of even the best pagans, with all its cruel images corresponding to the notions entertained by the Church in the centuries before and after, to feel the sharpness of the contrast".[58]

Of course, much in this passage is inaccurate and calls for contradiction; nevertheless it contains a serious assertion. It can make clear in its fashion wherein the indispensability of the article about the universal judgment of all men "according to their works" lies. It is not part of our task to consider in detail how this assertion can co-exist with the full weight of the doctrine of grace. Perhaps in the last analysis it is impossible to escape a paradox whose logic is completely disclosed only

[58] L. Baeck, *Das Wesen des Judentums*, 6th ed., Cologne, 1960, p. 69.

to the experience of a life based on faith. Anyone who entrusts himself to faith becomes aware that both exist: the fullness of the grace that frees weak man and, no less, the abiding seriousness of the responsibility that claims man day after day. Both together mean that the Christian enjoys on the one hand the liberating, detached tranquillity of him who lives on that excess of divine justice known as Jesus Christ. There is a tranquillity that knows: in the last analysis I cannot destroy what he has built up. For in himself man lives with the dreadful knowledge that his power to destroy is infinitely greater than his power to build up. But this same man knows that in Christ the power to build up has proved itself infinitely stronger. This is the source of a profound freedom, a knowledge of God's unrepining love; he sees through all our errors and remains well disposed to us. It becomes possible to do one's own work fearlessly; it has shed its sinister aspect because it has lost its power to destroy: the issue of the world does not depend on us but lies in God's hands. At the same time the Christian knows on the other hand that he is not free to do whatever he pleases, that his activity is not a game which God allows him and does not take seriously. He knows that he must answer for his actions, that he owes an account as a steward of what has been entrusted to him. There can only be responsibility where there is someone to be responsible to, someone to put the questions. Faith in the last judgment holds this questioning of our life over our heads so that we cannot forget it for a moment. Nothing and no one empowers us to trivialize the tremendous seriousness involved in such knowledge; it shows our life to be a serious business and precisely by doing so gives it its dignity.

"To judge the living and the dead" – this also means that no one but *he* has the right to judge in the end. This implies that the unrighteousness of the world does not have the last word, not even by being wiped out indifferently in a universal act of grace; on the contrary, there is a last court of appeal which preserves justice, in order thus to be able to perfect love. A love that overthrew justice would create injustice and thus cease to be anything but a caricature of love. True love is excess of justice, excess that goes further than justice, but never destruction of justice, which must be and must remain the basic form of love.

Of course, one must guard against the opposite extreme. It cannot be denied that faith in the judgment has at times assumed in the Christian consciousness a form in which, in practice, it was bound to lead to the destruction of the full faith in the redemption and the promise of mercy. The example always adduced is the profound contrast between "*Maran atha*" and "*Dies irae*". The early Christians, with their cry "Our Lord, come" (*Maran atha*), interpreted the second coming of Jesus as an event full of hope and joy, stretching their arms out longingly towards it as the moment of the great fulfilment. To the Christians of the Middle Ages, on the other hand, that moment appeared as the terrifying "day of wrath" (*Dies irae*), which makes man feel like dying of pain and terror, and to which he looks forward with fear and dread. The return of Christ is then only judgment, the day of the great reckoning which threatens everyone. Such a view forgets a decisive aspect of Christianity, which is thus reduced for all practical purposes to moralism and robbed of that hope and joy which are the very breath of its life.

Perhaps it will have to be admitted that the tendency to such a false development, which only sees the dangers of responsibility and no longer the freedom of love, is present in the Creed, in which the idea of Christ's return is reduced, at any rate verbally, to the idea of judgment: "From thence he shall come to judge the living and the dead." Of course, in the circles which formed the spiritual home of the Creed the original Christian tradition was still very much alive; the phrase about the last judgment was taken in self-evident conjunction with the message of mercy. The statement that it is *Jesus* who judges immediately tinged the judgment with hope. I should just like to quote a passage from the so-called "Second Epistle of Clement" in which this becomes quite clear: "Brothers, we must think of Jesus as God, as him who judges the living and the dead. We must not think little of our salvation, for by thinking little of him we also think little of our hope."[59]

[59] 2 Clem. 1, 1f.; cf. Kattenbusch II, p. 660.

Here the real emphasis of this article of the Creed becomes evident: it is not simply – as one might expect – God, the Infinite, the Unknown, the Eternal, who judges. On the contrary, he has handed the judgment over to one who, as man, is our brother. It is not a stranger who judges us but he whom we know in faith. The judge will not advance to meet us as the quite other, but as one of us, who knows human existence from inside and has suffered.

Thus over the judgment glows the dawn of hope; it is not only the day of wrath but also the second coming of our Lord. One is reminded of the mighty vision of Christ with which the Book of Revelation begins (1.9–19): the seer sinks down as though dead before this being full of sinister power. But the Lord lays his hand on him and says to him as once in the days when they were crossing the Lake of Gennesaret in wind and storm: "Fear not, it is I" (1.17). The Lord of all power is that Jesus whose comrade the visionary had once been in faith. The Creed's article about the judgment transfers this very idea to our meeting with the judge of the world. On that day of fear the Christian will be allowed to see in happy wonder that he "to whom all power is given in heaven and on earth" (Matt. 28.18) was the companion in faith of his days on earth, and it is as if through the words of the Creed Jesus were already laying his hands on him and saying: Be without fear, it is I. Perhaps the problem of the intertwining of justice and mercy can be answered in no more beautiful way than it is in the idea that stands in the background of our Creed.

PART THREE

THE SPIRIT
AND THE CHURCH

Chapter I

THE INTRINSIC UNITY OF THE LAST STATEMENTS IN THE CREED

In the original Greek text the central statement in the last section of the Creed runs simply: "I believe in Holy Spirit". The definite article to which we are accustomed in our translation is thus missing. This is very important for the interpretation of the original meaning, for it means that this article was at first really understood as referring to the history of salvation, not to the Trinity. In other words, the third section of the Creed refers in the first place not to the Holy Ghost as the third person in the Godhead but to the Holy Spirit as God's gift to history in the community of those who believe in Christ.

Of course, the trinitarian interpretation, the reference to the triune God, is not excluded. After all, we saw in our introductory reflections that the whole Creed grew up out of the triple baptismal question about faith in the Father, Son and Spirit, a question which for its part rests on the baptismal formula recorded in Matthew (Matt. 28.19). To that extent the oldest form of the Creed with its tripartite arrangement is indeed one of the main roots of the trinitarian image of God. It was only the gradual expansion of the baptismal questions into a detailed creed that somewhat obscured the trinitarian structure. The whole story of Jesus from conception to second coming was now incorporated to form the central section, as we have seen. As a result, the first section too was now taken in a more historical sense; it was referred essentially to the story of creation and the pre-Christian age. This made a historical view of the whole text inevitable: the third section was bound to be understood as a prolongation of the story of Christ in the gift of the Spirit, and therefore as a reference to the "last days" between the coming of Christ and his return. Of course, this development did not simply cancel out the trinitarian view, just as conversely the baptismal questions were not concerned with an other-worldly God outside history but with the God who has turned his face to us. To this extent the interaction of "history of salvation" and trinitarian viewpoints is characteristic of the oldest stages of Christian thought. Later on this interaction was more and more forgotten, with unfortunate results, so that a split arose into theological metaphysics on the one side and theology of history on the other. Henceforth both co-exist alongside each other as two completely different things; people indulge either in ontological speculation or anti-philosophical theology of salvation, thus losing in a really tragic way the original unity of Christian thought. At the start Christian thinking is neither merely "salvationist" nor merely "metaphysical", but moulded by the unity of history and being. Here lies an important task for modern theological work, which is torn once again by this dilemma.[1]

But let us leave these general considerations and ask what in fact our text, as it stands now, really means. It speaks, as we have already seen, not of God's inner life but of "God facing outward", of the Holy Spirit as the power through which the risen Lord remains present in the history of the world as the principle of a new history and a new world. This tendency produced of its own accord a further consequence. The fact that it is a question here not of the Spirit as a person within God but as the power of God in the history that opens with the resurrection of Jesus produced the effect that in the consciousness of those praying faith in the "Spirit" and faith in the Church interfered with each other. This is in fact only a practical illustration of the interaction between trinity and history-of-salvation discussed above. Once again one must regard it as unlucky for later developments that this interaction ceased to operate; as a result, both teaching about the Church and teaching about the Holy Spirit were no longer interpreted from the angle of pneumatology and charisma, but seen exclusively – in an all too resolutely earthly way – from the standpoint of the

<hr />

[1] Cf. J. Ratzinger, "Heilsgeschichte und Eschatologie", in *Theologie im Wandel* (Tübinger Festschrift), Munich, 1967, pp. 68–89.

incarnation, and finally expounded entirely on the basis of the power-categories of worldly thinking. In this fashion the teaching about the Holy Spirit also became homeless; in so far as it did not drag out a miserable existence in the realm of mere edification it was absorbed into the general speculation about the Trinity and thus for all practical purposes had no function for the Christian consciousness. Here the text of the Creed poses a completely concrete problem: teaching about the Church must take its departure from teaching about the Holy Spirit and his gifts. But its goal lies in a doctrine of the history of God with men or, alternatively, of the function of the story of Christ for mankind as a whole. This indicates at the same time in what direction Christology must evolve. It is not to be developed as a doctrine of God's taking root in the world, a doctrine which, starting from Jesus' humanity, interprets the Church in an all too worldly fashion. Christ remains present through the Holy Spirit with all his openness and breadth and freedom, which by no means exclude the institutional form but limit its claims and do not allow it simply to make itself the same as worldly institutions.

The remaining statements in the third section of the Creed are intended to be more than developments of its basic profession, "I believe in Holy Spirit". These developments proceed in two directions. First comes the phrase about the communion of saints, which did not figure in the original text of the creed formulated in the city of Rome itself but nevertheless represents an ancient tradition of the Church. Then comes the phrase about the forgiveness of sins. Both statements are to be understood as concretizations of the words about the Holy Spirit, as descriptions of the way in which this Spirit works in history. Both have a directly sacramental meaning of which we are hardly aware today. The saying about the communion of saints refers first of all to the eucharistic community which through the body of the Lord binds the Churches scattered all over the earth into *one* Church. Thus originally the word "*sanctorum*" ("of the holy ones") does not refer to persons but means the holy gifts, the holy *thing*, granted to the Church in her eucharistic feast by God as the real bond of unity. Thus the Church is not defined as a matter of offices and organization but on the basis of her worship of God: as a community at one table round the risen Christ who gathers and unites them everywhere. Of course, very soon people began to include in this idea the persons who themselves are united among themselves and sanctified by God's one, holy gift. The Church began to be seen not just as the unity of the eucharistic table but also as the community of those who through this table are united among themselves. Then from this point a cosmic breadth very soon entered into the concept of Church: the communion of saints spoken of here extends beyond the frontier of death; it binds together all those who have received the one Spirit and his one, life-giving power.

The phrase about the forgiveness of sins, on the other hand, refers to the other fundamental sacrament of the Church, namely baptism; and from there it very soon came to include the sacrament of penance. At first, of course, baptism was the great sacrament of forgiveness, the moment when a visible transformation took place. Only gradually, through painful experience, did people come to see that even the baptized Christian needs forgiveness, with the result that the renewed remission of sins granted by the sacrament of penance advanced more and more into the foreground, especially since baptism moved to the beginning of life and thus ceased to be an expression of active conversion. Nevertheless, the fact remains even now that one cannot become a Christian by birth, but only by rebirth: Christianity only ever comes into being by man's turning his life round, turning away from the self-satisfaction of mere existence and being "converted". In this sense baptism remains, as the start of a lifelong conversion, the fundamental pattern of the Christian existence, as the phrase about the "remission of sins" is intended to remind us. But if Christianity is regarded not as a chance grouping of men but as the about-turn into real humanity, then this profession of faith goes beyond the circle of the baptized and means that man does not come to himself if he simply abandons himself to his natural centre of gravity. To become truly a man he must oppose this inclination, he must turn round: even the waters of his nature do not climb upward of their own accord.

To summarize all this, we can now say that in our Creed

the Church is understood as proceeding from the Holy Spirit, as the centre of the Spirit's activity in the world. In concrete terms, it is seen from the two angles of Baptism (Penance) and the Eucharist. This sacramental approach produces a completely theocentric understanding of the Church: the foreground is occupied not by the group of men composing it but by the gift of God which turns man round towards a new being which he cannot give to himself, to a communion which he can only receive as a gift. Yet precisely this theocentric image of the Church is entirely human, entirely real; by centring round conversion and unification, and understanding both as a process that cannot be brought to completion within history, it reveals the human connection in meaning between sacrament and Church. Thus the "objective" view (from the angle of the gift of God) brings the personal element into play of its own accord: the new being of forgiveness leads us into fellowship with those who live from forgiveness, forgiveness establishes communion, and communion with the Lord in the Eucharist leads necessarily to the communion of the converted, who all eat one and the same bread, to become in it "one body" (1 Cor. 10.17) and indeed "one single new man" (cf. Eph. 2.15).

The concluding words of the Creed too, the profession of faith in the "resurrection of the flesh" and "life everlasting", are to be understood as the unfolding of faith in the Holy Ghost and his transforming power, whose final effect they depict. For the prospect of resurrection, on which the whole section here converges, follows necessarily from faith in the transformation of history that started with the resurrection of Jesus. With this event, as we have seen, the frontier of *bios*, in other words death, was crossed and a new continuum was opened up: the biological has been overtaken by the spirit, by love, which is stronger than death. The barrier of death has been broken through and a definitive future opened up for man and world. This conviction, in which faith in Christ and acknowledgement of the power of the Holy Spirit meet, is expressly applied in the last words of the Creed to the future of all of us. The sight of the omega of world history, in which everything will be fulfilled, results by an inner necessity from faith in the God who himself wished to be, in the cross, the omega of the world, its last letter. Precisely by this he has made the omega into *his* point, so that one day love is definitively stronger than death and out of the "complexification" of *bios* by love the final complex emerges, the finality of the person and the finality of unity which comes from love. Because God himself became a mere worm, the last letter in the alphabet of creation, the last letter has become his letter and thereby turned history towards the final victory of love: the cross really is the salvation of the world.

Chapter II

TWO MAJOR QUESTIONS POSED BY THE ARTICLES ON THE SPIRIT AND THE CHURCH

In the foregoing reflections we tried to bring out the wealth and scope of the last few sentences of the Creed. The Christian notion of man, the problem of sin and redemption, are echoed in them once again, but their chief function is to affirm the sacramental idea which for its part forms the heart of the concept of the Church: Church and sacrament stand or fall together; a Church without sacraments would be an empty organization, and sacraments without a Church would be rites without meaning or inner connection. So one of the important questions thrown up by the last article of the Creed is that of the nature of the Church; the other big problem it sets us is contained in the saying about the resurrection of the body, an idea which is no less of a stumbling-block to the modern mind, if for different reasons, than it was to the "spiritualism" of the Greek world. To conclude our survey of the Creed we shall now try to explore a little further the implications of these two questions.

1. "THE HOLY, CATHOLIC CHURCH"

Obviously it cannot be our aim here to develop a complete doctrine of the Church; leaving aside the individual, specialized theological questions we shall simply make a brief attempt to discern the real nature of the stumbling-block which we encounter in pronouncing the formula about the "holy, Catholic Church" and strive to understand the answer implied in the text of the Creed itself. What we have to say presupposes our earlier reflections about the spiritual location and inner connection of these words, which on the one hand refer to the powerful operation of the Holy Spirit in history and on the other are explained in the phrases about the forgiveness of sins and the communion of saints, phrases in which Baptism, Penance and Eucharist are declared to be the framework of the Church, its real content and its true mode of existence.

Perhaps much of what disturbs us about the profession of faith in the Church is removed by the mere consideration of this double context. Nevertheless let us speak out and say plainly what worries us today at this point in the Creed. We are tempted to say, if we are honest with ourselves, that the Church is neither holy nor Catholic: the Second Vatican Council itself ventured to the point of speaking no longer merely of the holy Church but of the sinful Church, and the only reproach it incurred was that of still being far too timorous; so deeply aware are we all of the sinfulness of the Church. This may well be partly due to the Lutheran theology of sin and also to an assumption arising out of dogmatic prejudgments. But what makes these "dogmatics" so reasonable is their harmony with our own experience. The centuries of the Church's history are so filled with human failure that we can quite understand Dante's ghastly vision of the Babylonian whore sitting in the Church's chariot; and the dreadful words of William of Auvergne, Bishop of Paris in the thirteenth century, seem perfectly comprehensible. William said that the barbarism of the Church must make everyone who saw it go rigid with horror: "Bride is she no more, but a monster of frightful ugliness and ferocity . . ."[2]

The catholicity of the Church seems just as questionable as its holiness. The one rock of the Lord is torn between the disputing parties, the one Church is divided up into many Churches, every one of which claims more or less insistently to be alone in the right. And so for many people today the

[2] Cf. the great contribution by H. U. von Balthasar, "Casta meretrix", in his volume of essays *Sponsa Verbi*, Einsiedeln, 1961, pp. 203–305; the passages quoted occur on pp. 204–207; see also H. Riedlinger, *Die Makellosigkeit der Kirche in den lateinischen Hoheliedkommentaren des Mittelalters*, Münster, 1958.

Church has become the main obstacle to belief. They can no longer see in it anything but the human struggle for power, the petty spectacle of those who, with their claim to administer official Christianity, seem to stand most in the way of the true spirit of Christianity.

There is no theory in existence which could refute such ideas by mere reason, just as conversely these ideas themselves do not proceed from mere reason but from the bitterness of a heart which may perhaps have been disappointed in its high hopes and now, in the pain of wronged love, can see only the destruction of its hopes. How, then, are we to reply? In the last analysis one can only confess why one can still love this Church in faith, why one still dares to recognize in the distorted features the countenance of the holy Church. Nevertheless, let us start from the objective elements. As we have already seen, in all these statements of faith the word "holy" does not apply in the first place to the holiness of human persons but refers to the divine gift which bestows holiness in the midst of human unholiness. The Church is not called "holy" in the Creed because its members, collectively and individually, are holy, sinless men – this dream, which appears afresh in every century, has no place in the waking world of our text, however movingly it may express a human longing which man will never abandon until a new heaven and a new earth really grant him what this age will never give him. Even at this point we can say that the sharpest critics of the Church in our time secretly live on this dream and, when they find it disappointed, bang the door of the house shut again and denounce it as a deceit. But to return to our argument: the holiness of the Church consists in that power of sanctification which God exerts in it in spite of human sinfulness. We come up here against the real mark of the "New Covenant": in Christ God has bound himself to men, has let himself be bound by them. The New Covenant no longer rests on the reciprocal keeping of the agreement; it is granted by God as grace which abides even in face of man's faithlessness. It is the expression of God's love, which will not let itself be defeated by man's incapacity but always remains well-disposed towards him, welcomes him again and again precisely because he is sinful, turns to him, sanctifies him and loves him.

Because of the Lord's devotion, never more to be revoked, the Church is the institution sanctified by him for ever, an institution in which the holiness of the *Lord* becomes present among men. But it is really and truly the holiness of the *Lord* that becomes present in it and that chooses again and again as the vessel of its presence – with a paradoxical love – the dirty hands of men. It is holiness that radiates as the holiness of Christ from the midst of the Church's sin. So to the faithful the paradoxical figure of the Church, in which the divine so often presents itself in such unworthy hands, in which the divine is only ever present in the form of a "nevertheless", is the sign of the "nevertheless" of the ever greater love shown by God. The existing interplay of God's loyalty and man's disloyalty which characterizes the structure of the Church is grace in dramatic form, so to speak, through which the reality of grace as the pardoning of those who are in themselves unworthy continually becomes visibly present in history. One could actually say that precisely in its paradoxical combination of holiness and unholiness the Church is in fact the shape taken by grace in this world.

Let us go a step further. In the human dream of a perfect world, holiness is always visualized as untouchability by sin and evil, as something unmixed with the latter; there always remains in some form or other a tendency to think in terms of black and white, a tendency to cut out and reject mercilessly the current form of the negative (which can be conceived in widely varying terms). In contemporary criticism of society and in the actions in which it vents itself, this merciless side always present in human ideals is once again only too evident. That is why the aspect of Christ's holiness that upset his contemporaries was the complete absence of this condemnatory note – fire did not fall on the unworthy nor were the zealous allowed to pull up the weeds which they saw growing luxuriantly on all sides. On the contrary, this holiness expressed itself precisely as mingling with the sinners whom Jesus drew into his vicinity; as mingling to the point where he himself was made "to be sin" and bore the curse of the law in execution as a criminal – complete community of fate with the lost (cf. 2 Cor. 5.21; Gal. 3.13). He has drawn sin to himself, made it his lot and so revealed what true "holiness" is: not separation but union, not judgment but redeeming love. Is the Church not simply the continuation of God's deliberate plunge into human wretchedness; is it not simply the continuation of Jesus' habit of sitting at table with sinners, of his mingling with the misery of sin to the point where he actually seems to sink under its weight? Is there not revealed in the unholy holiness of the Church, as opposed to man's expectation of purity, God's true holiness, which is love, love which does not keep its distance in a sort of aristocratic, untouchable purity but mixes with the dirt of the world, in order thus to overcome it? Can therefore the holiness of the Church be anything else but the mutual support which comes, of course, from the fact that all of us are supported by Christ?

I must admit that to me this unholy holiness of the Church has in itself something infinitely comforting about it. Would one not be bound to despair in face of a holiness that was spotless and could only operate on us by judging us and consuming us by fire? Who would dare to assert of himself that he did not need to be borne by others, indeed borne up by them? And how can someone who lives on the forbearance of others himself renounce forbearance? Is it not the only gift he can offer in return, the only comfort remaining to him, that he endures just as he too is endured? Holiness in the Church begins with forbearance and leads to bearing up; where there is no more bearing there is no more bearing up either, and existence, lacking support, can only sink into the void. People may well say that such words express a weakly existence – but it is part of being a Christian to accept the impossibility of autonomy and the weakness of one's own resources. At bottom there is always hidden pride at work when criticism of the Church adopts that tone of rancorous bitterness which today is already beginning to become a fashionable habit. Unfortunately it is accompanied only too often by a spiritual emptiness in which the specific nature of the Church as a whole is no longer seen, in which it is only regarded as a political instrument whose organization is felt to be pitiable or brutal, as the case may be, as if the real function of the Church did not lie beyond organization, in the comfort of the Word and of the sacraments which she provides in good and bad days alike. Those who really believe do not attribute too much importance to the struggle for the reform of ecclesiastical ritual. They live on what the Church always is; and if one wants to know what the Church really is one must go to them. For the Church is most present not where organizing, reforming and governing are going on but in those who simply believe and receive from her the gift of faith that is life to them. Only he who has experienced how, regardless of changes in her ministers and forms, the Church raises men up, gives them a home and a hope, a home that is hope – the path to eternal life – only he who has experienced this knows what the Church is, both in days gone by and now.

This does not mean that everything must be left undisturbed and endured as it is. Endurance can also be a highly active process, a struggle to make the Church herself more and more that which supports and endures. After all, the Church does not live otherwise than in us; she lives from the struggle of the unholy to attain holiness, just as of course this struggle lives from the gift of God, without which it could not exist. But this effort only becomes fruitful and constructive if it is inspired by the spirit of forbearance, by real love. And here we have arrived at the criterion by which that critical struggle for better holiness must always be judged, a criterion that is not only not in contradiction with forbearance but is demanded by it. This criterion is constructiveness. A bitterness that only destroys stands self-condemned. A slammed door can, it is true, become a sign that shakes up those inside. But the idea that one can do more constructive work in isolation than in fellowship with others is just as much of an illusion as the notion of a Church of "holy people" instead of a "holy Church" that is holy because the Lord bestows holiness on her as a quite unmerited gift.[3]

This brings us to the other word applied to the Church by the Creed: it calls her "catholic". The shades of meaning acquired by this word during the course of time are numerous, but one main idea can be shown to be decisive from the start.

[3] Cf. H. de Lubac, *Die Kirche*, Einsiedeln, 1968 (3rd French ed., 1954), pp. 251–282. English trans. of original French: *The Splendour of the Church,* trans. and ed. by M. Mason, 1956.

This word refers in a double way to the unity of the Church. It refers first to local unity – only the community united with the bishop is the "Catholic Church", not the sectional groups which have broken away from it, whatever their reasons for splitting off may be. Second, the term describes the unity formed by the combination of the many local Churches, which are not entitled to encapsulate themselves in isolation; they can only remain the Church by being open to one another, by forming one Church in their common testimony to the Word and in the communion of the eucharistic table, which is open to everyone everywhere. In the old commentaries on the Creed the "Catholic" Church is contrasted with those "Churches" which only exist "from time to time in their provinces"[4] and thereby contradict the true nature of the Church.

Thus the word "catholic" expresses the episcopal structure of the Church and the necessity for the unity of all the bishops with one another; there is no allusion in the Creed to the crystallization of this unity in the bishopric of Rome. It would indubitably be a mistake to conclude from this that such a focal point was only a secondary development. In Rome, where our Creed arose, this idea was taken for granted from the start. But it is true enough that it is not to be counted as one of the primary elements in the concept of "Church" and certainly cannot be regarded as the point round which the concept was constructed. On the contrary, the basic elements of the Church appear as forgiveness, conversion, penance, eucharistic communion, and hence plurality and unity: plurality of the local Churches which yet only remain "the Church" through incorporation in the unity of the one Church. This unity is first and foremost the unity of Word and sacrament: the Church is one through the one Word and the one bread. The episcopal organization stands in the background as the *means* to this unity. It is not there for its own sake, but belongs to the category of means; its position is summed up by the

---

[4] Kattenbusch, Vol. II, p. 919. See also pp. 917–927 on the history of the reception of the word "catholic" in the Apostles' Creed and on the history of the word in general; cf. also W. Beinert, *Um das dritte Kirchenattribut*, 2 vols, Essen, 1964.

phrase "in order to": it serves to turn the unity of the local Churches in themselves and among themselves into a reality. The function of the Bishop of Rome would thus be to form the next stage in the category of means.

One thing is clear: the Church is not to be deduced from her organization; the organization is to be understood from the Church. But at the same time it is clear that for the visible Church visible unity is more than "organization". The concrete unity of the common faith testifying to itself in the word, and of the common table of Jesus Christ, is an essential part of the sign which the Church is to erect in the world. Only if she is "catholic", that is, visibly one in spite of all her variety, does she correspond to the demand of the Creed.[5] In a world torn apart she is to be the sign and means of unity, she is to bridge nations, races and classes and unite them. How often she has failed in this, we know: even in antiquity it was infinitely difficult for her to be simultaneously the Church of the barbarians and of the Romans; in modern times she was unable to prevent strife between the Christian nations; and today she is still not succeeding in so uniting rich and poor that the excess of the former becomes the satisfaction of the latter – the ideal of sitting at a common table remains largely unfulfilled. Yet even so one must not forget all the imperatives that have issued from the claim of catholicity; above all, instead of reckoning up the past, we should face the challenge of the present and try in it not only to profess catholicity in the Creed but to make it a reality in the life of our torn world.

2. "THE RESURRECTION OF THE BODY"

(a) The content of the New Testament hope of resurrection[6]

The article about the resurrection of the body puts us in a curious dilemma. We have discovered anew the indivisibility of man; we live our corporality with a new intensity and feel

[5] I have given my view on "Church and Churches", the problem that arises in connection with this, in J. Ratzinger, Das Konzil auf dem Weg, Cologne, 1964, pp. 48–71.

[6] The following arguments are closely linked to those in my article "Auferstehung" in Sacramentum Mundi, I, edited by Rahner–Darlap, Freiberg, 1967, pp. 397–402, where there is also a bibliography.

it as the indispensable mode of realization of the one being of
man. From this angle we can understand afresh the biblical
message, which promises immortality not to a separated soul
but to the whole man. Such feelings have in this century made
evangelical theology in particular turn emphatically against
the Greek doctrine of the immortality of the soul, which is
wrongly regarded as a Christian idea too. In reality, so it is
said, this idea expresses a thoroughly un-Christian dualism;
the Christian faith knows only of the waking of the dead by
God's power. But doubts arise at once here: the Greek doctrine
of immortality may well be problematical, but is not the
biblical assertion still more incapable of fulfilment for us? The
unity of man, fine, but who can imagine, on the basis of our
present-day image of the world, a resurrection of the body?
This resurrection would also imply – or so it seems, at any
rate – a new heaven and a new earth; it would require immortal
bodies needing no sustenance, and a completely different
condition of matter. But is this not all completely absurd, quite
contrary to our understanding of matter and its modes of
behaviour, and therefore hopelessly mythological? Well, I
think that in fact one can only arrive at an answer if one
enquires carefully into the real intentions of the biblical statement and at the same time considers anew the relation between
the biblical and the Greek ideas. For their encounter with each
other has modified both conceptions and thus overlaid the
original intentions of both approaches with a new combined
view which we must first remove if we want to find our way
back to the beginning. First of all, the hope of the resurrection
of the dead simply represents the basic form of the biblical
hope of immortality; it appears in the New Testament not
really as a supplement to a preceding and independent immortality of the soul but as the fundamental statement on the
fate of man. There were, it is true, in late Jewish teachings
hints of immortality on the Greek pattern, and this was
probably one of the reasons why very soon the all-embracing
scope of the idea of resurrection in the Graeco-Roman world
was no longer grasped. Instead, the Greek notion of the
immortality of the soul and the biblical message of the resurrection of the dead was each understood as half the answer to the

question of the fate of man and the two were added together. It was thought that the already existing Greek fore-knowledge about the immortality of the soul had had added to it by the Bible the revelation that at the end of the world bodies would be awoken too, to share henceforth for ever the fate of the soul – damnation or bliss.

As opposed to this, we must grasp the fact that originally it was not a question of two complementary ideas; on the contrary, we are confronted with two different total views, which cannot simply be added together: the image of man, of God and of the future, is in each case quite different, and thus at bottom each of the two views can only be understood as an attempt at a total answer to the question of human fate. The Greek conception is based on the idea that man is composed of two intrinsically alien substances, one of which (the body) perishes, while the other (the soul) is in itself imperishable and therefore goes on existing in its own right independent of any other beings. Indeed, it was only in the separation from its essentially alien body, so it was thought, that the soul came fully into its own. The biblical train of thought, on the other hand, presupposes the undivided unity of man; for example, Scripture contains no word denoting only the body (separated and distinguished from the soul), while conversely in the vast majority of cases the word soul too means the whole corporeally existing man; the few places where a different view can be discerned hover to a certain extent between Greek and Hebrew thinking and in any case by no means abandon the old view. The awakening of the dead (not of bodies!) of which Scripture speaks is thus concerned with the salvation of the *one*, undivided man, not just with the fate of one (so far as possible secondary) half of man. It now also becomes clear that the real heart of the faith in resurrection does not consist at all in the idea of the restoration of the body, to which we have reduced it in our thinking; such is the case even though this is the pictorial image used throughout the Bible. What, then, is the real content of the hope symbolically proclaimed in the Bible in the shape of the resurrection of the dead? I think that this can best be worked out by means of a comparison with the dualistic conception of ancient philosophy.

1. The idea of immortality denoted in the Bible by the word "resurrection" is an immortality of the "person", of the *one* creation "man". In Greek thought the typical man is a perishable creature which as such does not live on but goes two different ways in accordance with its heterogeneous formation out of body and soul; but according to the biblical belief it is precisely this being, man, that as such goes on existing, even if transformed.

2. It is a question of a "dialogic" immortality (=awakening!); that is, immortality results not simply from the self-evident inability-to-die of the indivisible but from the saving deed of the lover who has the necessary power: man can no longer totally perish because he is known and loved by God. All love wants eternity, and God's love not only wants it but effects it and is it. In fact the biblical idea of awakening grew directly out of this dialogal theme: he who prays knows in faith that God will restore the right (Job 19.25ff.; Ps. 73.23ff.); faith is convinced that those who have suffered in the interests of God will also receive a share in the redemption of the promise (2 Macc. 7.9ff.). Immortality as conceived by the Bible proceeds not from the personal force of what is in itself indestructible but from being drawn into the dialogue with the Creator; *that is why* it must be called awakening. Because the Creator means not just the soul but the man physically existing in the midst of history and gives *him* immortality, it must be called "awakening of the dead" = "of men". It should be noted here that even in the formula of the Creed, which speaks of the "resurrection of the body", the word "body" means in effect "the world of man" (in the sense of biblical expressions like "all flesh will see God's salvation", etc.); even here the word is not meant in the sense of a corporality isolated from the soul.

3. That the awakening is expected on the "Last Day", at the end of history, and in the community of all mankind, indicates the communal character of human immortality, which is related to the whole of mankind, from which, towards which and with which the individual has lived and hence becomes happy or unhappy. At bottom this association results automatically from the collective character of the biblical idea of immortality.

To the soul as conceived by the Greeks the body, and so history too, is completely exterior; the soul goes on existing apart from them and needs no other being in order to do do. For man understood as a unity, on the other hand, fellowship with his fellow men is constitutive; if *he* is to live on, then this dimension cannot be excluded. Thus on the biblical premise the much-discussed question whether after death there can be any fellowship between men seems to be solved; at bottom it could only arise at all through a preponderance of the Greek element in the intellectual premises: where the "communion of saints" is an article of faith, the idea of the *anima separata* (the "separated soul" of scholastic theology) has in the last analysis become obsolete.

These ideas could only attain their full scope after the New Testament had given concrete shape to the biblical hope – in the last analysis the Old Testament by itself leaves the question of the future of man in the air. Only with Christ, the man who is "one with the Father", the man through whom the being "man" has entered into God's eternity, does the future of man finally appear open. Only in him, the "second Adam", is the question of man's identity finally answered. Christ is man, completely; to that extent the question who we men are is present in him. But he is at the same time God speaking to us, the "Word of God". In him the conversation between God and man which has been going on since the beginning of history has entered a new phase: in him the Word of God became "flesh" and was really injected into our existence. But if the dialogue of God with man means life, if it is true that God's partner in the dialogue himself has life precisely through being addressed by him who lives for ever, then this means that Christ, as God's word to us, is himself "the resurrection and the life" (John 11.25). It also means that the entry into Christ known as faith becomes in a qualified sense an entry into that being known and loved by God which is immortality: "Whoever believes in the Son *has* eternal life" (John 3.15; 3.36; 5.24). Only from this angle is it possible to understand the train of thought of the fourth evangelist, who in his account of the Lazarus episode wants to make the reader understand that resurrection is not just a distant happening at the end of the world but happens now through faith. Whoever believes is in the conversation with God which is life and which outlasts death. At this point, too, the "dialogic" strand in the biblical concept of immortality, the one related directly to God, and the "human fellowship" strand meet and join. For in Christ, the man, we meet God; but in him we also meet the community of those others whose path to God runs through him and so towards one another. The orientation towards God is in him at the same time towards the community of mankind, and only the acceptance of this community is movement towards God, who does not exist apart from Christ and thus not apart either from the context of the whole history of humanity and its common task.

This also clarifies the question, much discussed in the time of the Fathers of the Church and again since Luther, of the "intermediate state" between death and resurrection: the existence-with-Christ inaugurated by faith is the start of resurrected life and therefore outlasts death (Phil. 1.23; 2 Cor. 5.8; 1 Thess. 5.10). The dialogue of faith is itself already life, which can no longer be shattered by death. The idea of the sleep of death continually discussed by Lutheran theologians and recently also brought into play by the Dutch Catechism is therefore untenable on the evidence of the New Testament and not even justifiable by the frequent occurrence in the New Testament of the word "sleep": the whole train of thought of every book in the New Testament is completely at variance with such an interpretation, which could hardly be inferred even from late Jewish thinking about the life after death.

(b) The essential immortality of man

The foregoing reflections may have made a little clearer what is involved in the biblical pronouncements about the resurrection: their essential content is not the conception of a restoration of bodies to souls after a long interval; their aim is to tell men that they, they themselves, live on; not by virtue of their own power but because they are known and loved by God in such a way that they can no longer perish. In contrast to the dualistic conception of immortality expressed in the

Greek body-soul schema, the biblical formula of immortality through awakening is trying to impart a collective and dialogic conception of immortality: the essential part of man, the person, remains; that which has ripened in the course of this earthly existence of corporeal spirituality and spiritualized corporeality goes on existing in a different fashion. It goes on existing because it lives in God's memory. And because it is the man himself who will live, not an isolated soul, the element of human fellowship is also part of the future; for this reason the future of the individual man will only then be full when the future of humanity is fulfilled.

A whole series of questions arises at this point. The first is this: Does this view not make immortality into a pure grace, although in reality it must fall to man's lot by virtue of his nature as man? In other words, does one not finish up here with an immortality only for the pious, and thus in a division of human fate which is unacceptable? To put it in theological terms, are we not here confusing the natural immortality of the being "man" with the supernatural gift of eternal love which makes man happy? Must we not hold fast, precisely for the sake of the humanity of the Christian faith, to natural immortality, for the reason that a continued existence conceived in purely christological terms would necessarily slide into the miraculous and mythological? This last question can indubitably be answered only in the affirmative. But this is by no means at variance with our original premise. It too entitled us to say decisively: The immortality which we have called, precisely because of its dialogic character, "awakening" falls to the lot of man, *every* man, as man, and is not some secondary "supernatural" addition. But we must then go on to ask: What really makes man into man? What is the final distinguishing mark of man? To that we shall have to answer: The distinguishing mark of man, seen from above, is his being addressed by God, the fact that he is God's partner in a dialogue, the being called by God. Seen from below, this means that man is the being that can think of God, the being opened on to transcendence. The point here is not whether he really does think of God, really does open himself to him, but that he is fundamentally the being who is in himself capable of doing so, even if in fact, for whatever reasons, he is perhaps never able to utilize this capacity.

Now one could say: Is it not then much simpler to see the distinguishing mark of man in the fact that he has a spiritual, immortal soul? This definition is perfectly sound; but we are in fact at this moment engaged in the process of trying to elucidate its concrete meaning. The two definitions are not in the least contradictory; they simply express the same thing in different modes of thought. For "having a spiritual soul" means precisely being willed, known and loved by God in a special way; it means being a creature called by God to an eternal dialogue and therefore capable for its own part of knowing God and of replying to him. What we call in substantialist language "having a soul" will be described in a more historical, actual language as "being God's partner in a dialogue". This does not mean that talk of the soul is false (as is sometimes asserted today by a one-sided and uncritical biblical approach); in one respect it is indeed even necessary in order to describe the whole of what is involved here. But on the other hand it also needs to be complemented if we are not to fall back into a dualistic conception which cannot do justice to the dialogic and personalistic view of the Bible.

So when we say that man's immortality is based on his dialogic relationship with God, whose love alone bestows eternity, we are not claiming a special destiny for the pious but emphasizing the essential immortality of man as man. After the foregoing reflections it is also perfectly possible to develop the idea out of the body-soul schema, whose importance, perhaps even indispensability, lies in the fact that it emphasizes this essential character of human immortality. But it must also be continually put back in the biblical perspective and corrected by it in order to remain serviceable to the view of man's future opened up by faith. For the rest, it becomes evident once again at this point that in the last analysis one cannot make a clear distinction between "natural" and "supernatural": the basic dialogue which first makes man into man moves over without a break into the dialogue of grace known as Jesus Christ. How could it be otherwise if Christ actually is the "second Adam", the real fulfilment of that infinite longing which ascends from the first Adam – from man in general?

(c) The question of the resurrected body

We have still not reached the end of our questions. If this is the position, is there really such a thing as a resurrected body or can the whole thing be reduced to a mere symbol for the immortality of the person? This is the problem that still awaits us. It is no new problem; even Paul was bombarded with questions of this sort by the Corinthians, as we can see from the fifteenth chapter of the First Epistle to the Corinthians, where the Apostle tries to provide an answer, so far as such a thing is at all possible on this point which lies beyond the limits of our imagination and those of the world accessible to us. Many of the images employed by Paul have become alien to us: but his answer as a whole is still the noblest, boldest and most convincing one ever formulated to this question.

Let us start from verse 50, which seems to me to be a sort of key to the whole: "I tell you this, brethren: flesh and blood cannot inherit the kingdom of God, nor does the perishable inherit the imperishable." It seems to me that the sentence occupies much the same position in this text as verse 63 occupies in the eucharistic chapter 6 of St John's gospel: for these two apparently widely separated texts are much more closely related than is apparent at first sight. There, in St John, it says, just after the real presence of the flesh and blood of Jesus in the Eucharist has been sharply emphasized: "It is the spirit that gives life, the flesh is of no avail." In both the Johannine and the Pauline texts it is a question of developing the Christian realism of "the flesh". In John the realism of the sacraments, that is, the realism of Jesus' resurrection and of his "flesh" that comes to us from it, is emphasized; in Paul it is a question of the realism of the resurrection of the "flesh", of the resurrection of Christians and of the salvation achieved for us in it. But both passages also contain a sharp counterpoint which emphasizes Christian realism as realism beyond the physical world, realism of the Holy Spirit, as opposed to a purely worldly, quasi-physical realism.

Here English cannot complete with the ambiguity of biblical Greek. In Greek the word "*soma*" means something like "body", but at the same time it also means "the self". And this "*soma*" can be "*sarx*", that is, "body" in the earthly, historical, and thus chemical, physical, sense; but it can also be "breath" – according to the dictionary it would then have to be translated "spirit"; in reality this means that the self, which now appears in a body that can be conceived in chemico-physical terms, can, again, appear definitively in the guise of a trans-physical reality. In Paul's language "body" and "spirit" are not opposites; the opposites are called "fleshly body" and "body in the fashion of the spirit". We do not need to try here to pursue the complicated historical and philosophical problems posed by this. One thing at any rate may be fairly clear: both John (6.53) and Paul (1 Cor. 15.50) state with all possible emphasis that the "resurrection of the flesh", the "resurrection of the body" is not a "resurrection of physical bodies". Thus, from the point of view of modern thought, the Pauline sketch is far less naïve than later theological erudition with its subtle constructions on the question how there can be eternal physical bodies. To recapitulate, Paul teaches not the resurrection of physical bodies but the resurrection of persons, and this not in the return of the "fleshly body", that is, the biological structure, an idea which he expressly describes as impossible ("the perishable cannot become imperishable"), but in the different form of the life of the resurrection, as shown in the risen Lord?

Has then the resurrection no relation at all to matter? And does this make the "Last Day" completely pointless in comparison with the life that always comes from the call of the Lord. Basically we have already answered this last question in our reflections on the return of Christ. If the cosmos is history and if matter represents a moment in the history of spirit, then there is no such thing as an eternal, neutral combination of matter and spirit but a final "complexity" in which the world finds its omega and unity. In that case there is a final connection between matter and spirit in which the destiny of man and of the world is consummated, even if it is impossible for us today to define the nature of this connection. In that case there is such a thing as a "Last Day", on which the destiny of the individual man becomes full because the destiny of mankind is fulfilled.

The goal of the Christian is not private bliss but the whole. He believes in Christ, and for that reason he believes in the future of the world, not just in his own future. He knows that this future is more than he himself can create. He knows that there is a meaning which he is quite incapable of destroying. Is he therefore to sit quietly with his hands in his lap? On the contrary; because he knows that there is such a thing as meaning he can and must cheerfully and undismayed do the work of history, even though from his little section of it he will have the feeling that it is a task like that of Sisyphus and that the stone of human destiny is rolled anew, generation after generation, up the hill only to roll down again once more and nullify all previous efforts. Whoever believes knows that things move "forward", not in a circle. Whoever believes knows that history is not like Penelope's tapestry, which was always being woven anew only to be undone again. Even the Christian may be assailed by the nightmares, induced by the fear of fruitlessness, out of which the pre-Christian world created these moving images of the anxiety that all human activity is vain. But his nightmare is pierced by the saving, transforming voice of reality: "Have courage, I have conquered the world" (John 16.33). The new world, with the description of which, in the image of the final Jerusalem, the Bible ends, is no Utopia but certainty, which we advance to meet in faith. A salvation of the world does exist – that is the confidence which supports the Christian and which still makes it rewarding even today to be a Christian.

INDEX